Zig-Zag-and-Swirl

PRACTICAL
AERONAUTICS.

ORGANIZER

FINANCIER

INVENTOR

PILOT

DESIGNER

NAVIGATOR

MANUFACTURER

PRACTICAL EXPERIENCE

ALFRED W. LAWSON
Designer and Navigator of the First Airliner

ZIG-

ALFRED W. LAWSON'S

ZAG-

QUEST FOR GREATNESS

AND-

BY LYELL D. HENRY, JR.

SWIRL

University of Iowa Press   Iowa City

University of Iowa Press, Iowa City 52242

Printed in the United States of America
First edition, 1991

Design by Richard Hendel

Printed on acid-free paper

Frontispiece from *Aerial Age Weekly*,
October 25, 1920

Library of Congress Cataloging-in-
Publication Data
Henry, Lyell D., 1935–
    Zig-zag-and-swirl: Alfred W. Lawson's quest
for greatness/by Lyell D. Henry, Jr.—1st ed.
        p.   cm.
    Includes bibliographical references and
index.
    ISBN 0-87745-312-8 (alk. paper)
    1. Lawson, Alfred W. (Alfred William),
1869–1954. 2. Aircraft industry—United
States—Biography. I. Title.
TL540.L35H46   1991
338.7′629133′34092—dc20   90-49730
    [B]   CIP

Contents

Preface

Alfred William Lawson has been much on my mind since I began the research for this book a full dozen years ago, but he has been *in* my mind far longer than that. My awareness of Lawson dates back to the 1940s and early 1950s, when I was growing up in Ames, Iowa, and Lawson was promulgating his unusual doctrine of "Lawsonomy" at the so-called Des Moines University of Lawsonomy (DMUL). So great was the uproar set off in Des Moines that word of it even reached my young ears thirty miles away in Ames.

On trips to Des Moines I also saw the mysterious "university" many times before it was razed in 1955, one year after Lawson's death. Sequestered behind high fence and locked gate, DMUL threw off dark hints of menace and nefarious goings-on— or so it seemed to my impressionable adolescent mind. To this day, DMUL remains deeply incised in my memory, the only landmark I can still recall from that remote day before the boomers and the boosters had begun to transform the face of Des Moines.

It was not nostalgia which brought me back to Lawson in the late 1970s, but rather my fascination with unorthodox science as an element of American popular culture. In his classic study, *Fads and Fallacies in the Name of Science* (1957), Martin Gardner devoted a whole chapter to Lawson, who ever since has been celebrated by aficionados as one of the great unorthodox scientists. But no sooner was I sweating over Lawson's many scientific treatises than I discovered something not generally known: Lawson was also a utopian reformer, who sought in Des Moines to create a new mode of communal living and thereby to initiate an upgrading of humanity. At this point, another of my interests—American utopianism—was engaged, and I set out to pin down what went on at the Des Moines University of Lawsonomy.

Eventually my investigation led me back through three earlier phases of Lawson's infatuation with utopia; moreover, each of these phases, I found, was linked to a respective phase of a gaudy entrepreneurial career running through professional baseball, pioneer aviation, and financial reform agitation during the Great Depression. In other words, Lawson's was an astounding life, in both its utopian and its entrepreneurial aspects—so much so, I concluded, that his story deserved to be told in full.

Although my book centers on the life of Lawson, it is not, in the strictest sense, a biography. Lawson deserves a biography, but it probably never will or can be written: too much of the information needed for a full account of his life either doesn't exist today or is likely to remain inaccessible. Lawson's first four decades are especially sparse in documentation, but there are many gaps in the record of his subsequent years, too. "The Lawson papers," if such there be, are not in hands making them accessible to the public; virtually all libraries I contacted had something on Lawson but rarely more than a few items—usually some of his books, a few clippings, or miscellaneous ephemeral items published by Lawson. If they even exist, the records from Lawson's business activities prior to 1931 and from his reform organizations after 1931 are not available to investigators today. Possibly Lawson's ideological heirs hold some valuable documentary material, but getting access to this material was a problem I was unable to solve. The same was true concerning access to information from members of Lawson's family. Lawson went to great lengths to shield his family from publicity, and their privacy and whereabouts are still protected by the Lawsonomists.

On the other hand, Lawson was sufficiently in the public eye throughout his adult life to have landed often in newspapers and other public records. From these sources, I was able to learn much about his base ball and aviation activities and about his years in Des Moines. The public record of his agitational activities in the 1930s was far less ample, but for those years I was at least able to track down all of Lawson's numerous ephemeral publications, including published transcriptions of many of his speeches. A stroke of good fortune, too, was Lawson's proclivity for publishing photographs, documents, and newspaper clippings concerning his life's activities, especially in aviation. The books containing these valuable materials—and indeed, all of Lawson's major writings—are still kept in print today by the Humanity Benefactor Foundation, the financial and publishing arm of Lawson's enterprises since 1931.

Thus, after putting in several frustrating years pursuing many leads which didn't pan out or yielded only fragments of evidence, I found that I had nonetheless assembled much material from every adult phase of Lawson's life. If distressing gaps in my information remained, and if some very basic questions still were unanswered (for example, what books did Lawson read?), still I had enough information to discern the major episodes and activities in Lawson's life. Above all, I could see beyond any doubt that his life had had a dominant theme—the pursuit of greatness. Lawson's quest for greatness not only was unprecedented in intensity but took him into a lifetime of activities notable for their variety and into realms of thought unequaled in novelty. This book is organized around that theme and those activities and gives extensive consideration to Lawson's ideas. My goals have been to describe Lawson's unique quest and its diverse products, account for that quest so far as I could, and relate the life which resulted from that quest to the context of his time and place. The outcome of my efforts, as I have said, is not fully a biography, yet I hope it may still hold up as a contribution to American studies and, in any event, as an enjoyable tale of a remarkable life and mind.

Early in my investigation, I succeeded in making contact with several of Lawson's followers, who kindly invited my wife and me to the Lawsonomists' annual reunions in 1979 and 1980. Although we were received very cordially, I found considerable wariness about what kind of book I planned to write. Even so, I managed to get some useful information there, especially from interviews with persons who once lived at the Des Moines University of Lawsonomy. By the end of the second reunion, my relations with the Lawsonomists had even warmed up enough, I thought, to kindle hope that I might soon get access to whatever documentary materials they had in their custody. Alas, my hope was not to be realized. Taking offense at a short article (actually, a quite sympathetic one) which I published on Lawson's baseball career, a high-ranking Lawsonomist wrote to say that he was washing his hands of me. Unfortunately, his place among the Lawsonomists was such that his severing of ties sent crashing my dreams of future breakthroughs in data collection. His action also made it impossible for me to attend further reunions and difficult even to cultivate continuing contacts with Lawsonomists singly.

This episode exposed an inherent source of tension in my relations with the Lawsonomists: virtually anything I wrote about Lawson, no matter how sympathetic, was bound to collide at many points with their exalted estimation of the man, and certainly I suffer no delusion that they will agree with the account offered here. Clearly my Lawson is not the Lawson of the true believers. Where they are ready always to take at face value Lawson's claims and self-assessments, I have often found grounds for skepticism. Throughout, I have also worked on a premise apparently not accepted by the Lawsonomists—namely, that Lawson, like any other human being, had his shortcomings and was capable of erring. Yielding to no compunctions in addressing Lawson's flaws and foibles realistically, I have not hesitated to criticize him at many places.

Yet if I fail to see Lawson as the saint or demigod revered by the Lawsonomists, neither do I find him to be merely the bamboozler or buffoon often depicted in the newspapers of his day. What emerges from my inquiry is a more complex and appealing figure than is described by any of these labels. The picture I end with is of an extraordinary human being, for whom I have great affection and considerable admiration—feelings which I assume shine through in these pages. In fact, here I actually go a long way in the direction of the Lawsonomists: although my reasons for doing so differ from theirs, I readily join them in hailing their leader and in saluting his life as a great one. And even as the Lawsonomists reject the picture of Lawson which I draw, I trust that they will recognize it as a more sympathetic and measured one than has ever been rendered before by anyone not a Lawsonomist. In any event, it is the product of a sincere effort to write as accurate, well-grounded, and judicious an account as possible within the constraints of the limited information available to me.

Keenly aware that more testimony and help from Lawsonomists would doubtless have made this a better book, I greatly regret that circumstances arose making it impossible to pursue more information from this source. To those Lawsonomists who did talk with me, especially several who were unafraid to have an outsider take a scholarly look at Lawson and who went to very great lengths to be helpful, I offer my most sincere thanks. Only because it might not do them any good in Lawsonomy circles to have their names linked to mine do I refrain from identifying them here or in my text.

Also providing information were many non-Lawsonomists, whose names and contributions I have identified in my "Notes and Sources" section. However, from two fellow students of Lawson I received so much information and help and benefited so much from discussions that I want to identify and thank them here; they are Jerrold Kuntz and George Hardie, Jr. For reading portions of the final manuscript and giving me the benefit of their respective expertises, I wish to thank Mr. Hardie and also Michael Altimore, Michael Chibnik, Wayne Franklin, Ellis Hawley, Drake Hokanson, Lyman Tower Sargent, Peter Snow, Albert Stone, and my editor, Holly Carver. For giving me counsel, encouragement, and critical readings in the early stages of my struggle to organize my thoughts on Lawson and to get something down on paper, I am indebted to Lane Davis, Lawrence Gelfand, Keith Huntress, Russel B. Nye, Mulford Q. Sibley, and, again, Wayne Franklin and Albert Stone. My thanks, too, go to two excellent typists, Melody Scherubel and Lorna Olson, for their skillful conversion of my penciled scrawls on yellow legal pads into typed, readable copy.

Finally, I want to record my gratitude here to University House, a University of Iowa research center, for awarding me a 1987 summer fellowship to support the writing of chapters 6 through 9; to the University of Iowa Graduate College for travel grants helping to defray the costs of two trips made in the course of my research; and to

Mount Mercy College, for two January interim leaves and a 1988 sab-
batical leave, which gave me much needed time to bear down on the
completion of this book by freeing me from the usual teaching duties.

I dedicate this book to my mother and the memory of my father
and also to Gretchen, who lovingly bears with my weakness for sciosophy.

Prologue

"YES,

ALFRED

WILLIAM

LAWSON

IS

GOD'S

GREAT

ETERNAL

GIFT TO

MAN"

Wartime jitters, the growing Soviet menace, and the commie-whooping of Senator Joe McCarthy were not the only things roiling the calm of Des Moines, Iowa, during the 1940s and early 1950s. A vexation closer to home was the Des Moines University of Lawsonomy. Coming into being without warning in 1943 on the campus of the former Des Moines University, this mysterious institution with the odd name soon retreated from neighborliness behind a high fence and a locked gate. A thick file of clippings from newspapers of that time attests to the great hullabaloo attending this so-called university during its eleven-year sojourn in Des Moines.

Probably what most enraged Des Moines residents about the Des Moines University of Lawsonomy (DMUL) was their inability to figure out what it was and what went on there. An exchange of letters in February, 1952, suggested as much. An alumna of Des Moines University, rebuffed by DMUL's fence on a visit to her defunct alma mater, wrote to the Greater Des Moines Chamber of Commerce seeking information. In reply, the chamber's general secretary identified both Lawsonomy and DMUL as the creations of "Alfred Lawson of Detroit." However, he confessed, "Lawsonomy is almost as much a mystery to us as it is to you," and as for DMUL, "we are not able to find anything they do." "About all we know," he concluded, "is that [DMUL] is not operated as a college or university as we know them."

Although the general secretary was right about this last point, his surmise that "the whole project is a semireligious sect" was not fully on target. The practice of a novel religion did figure prominently there but certainly could not account for all of DMUL's activities and purposes.

The University of Lawsonomy was, in fact, a utopian or intentional community, whose members, led by Alfred Lawson (1869–1954), sought to perfect all aspects of their individual lives and their life in common. These first few steps toward perfection, Lawson believed, would also initiate a transformation in the human condition, issuing someday in the universal reign of the values and pattern of living espoused at DMUL. At least in these respects Lawson's community was like many other American utopian communities—a fact usually missed by observers, however, because little solid information about DMUL ever got over the fence to the outer world. Too, Lawson's touting of his community as a university sowed confusion, misleading even those who recognized that DMUL wasn't a real university. Finally, so clearly was Lawson the star of the show that the attention of puzzled and angry neighbors drifted inexorably from the community to its leader.

Doubtless most in Des Moines at that time saw Lawson as a megalomaniacal leader of a personal cult. In this view, Lawson unceasingly tapped followers for fawning praise, donations, and unpaid labor, including their peddling of his many publications. Hardly the whole, accurate story, this account did seem to have some facts in its favor.

Shortly after the University of Lawsonomy was established, for instance, its residents had fanned out through the city hawking Lawson's books and his newspaper, *Benefactor*. Anyone listening to their sales pitches heard some outsized claims made about Lawson—but in Lawson's publications the author himself made claims to greatness no less extreme. All at DMUL, including the founder, agreed: Alfred Lawson was the wisest, noblest, and greatest man ever to walk the earth; he had, in fact, been sent by God to lead humanity to glorious new heights. A line from a song sung at the university said it best: "Yes, Alfred William Lawson is / God's great eternal gift to man."

The greatness of Lawson hymned at DMUL included a mighty intellect, unrivaled in puissance; the evidence was Lawsonomy, which its discoverer defined as "the knowledge of life and everything pertaining thereto." In this doctrine embracing the physical and life sciences as well as economics, philosophy, and theology, Lawson reformulated much of existing knowledge and jettisoned the remainder. Leader and followers alike believed that the large shelf of Lawsonomy books was "an oasis of truth in a desert of lies."

But Lawson's genius was also a practical one, reflected in an amazing succession of activities. He had honed his entrepreneurial skills during twenty-one years (1887–1908) spent in minor league baseball (with a brief stint in the major leagues as well). Beginning as a pitcher, he soon moved up to manager and ended as an organizer and owner of teams and leagues. But his gifts, including a talent for self-promotion, were brought up to even greater amperage during two decades (1908–1929) invested in aviation. He was probably the first of that field's "early birds" to perceive clearly aviation's great promise and certainly pursued the opportunities with panache and gusto. Among his achievements as an aviation pioneer were the construction and flight of the first airliner.

When Lawson's ambitious schemes in aviation didn't pan out, however, he turned his hand full-time to economic reform. Identifying conspiratorial manipulations by "the financiers" as the cause of the Great Depression of the 1930s (and of his failures in aviation, as well), he went after the malefactors. Throughout that decade, Lawson built up and led the Direct Credits Society, a uniformed army of thousands which aimed at achieving a capitalist utopia through financial reform. From this crusade evolved his community in Des Moines, reflecting his final conviction that more than institutional reform was needed; although now in his mid-seventies, he was ready to undertake nothing less than the reform of human nature itself.

In their leader Lawson's followers perceived a selfless soul dedicated to liberating his fellows from squalid thinking and shameful conduct. In 1931 Lawson had sworn to go the rest of his life as a "penniless, propertyless man" devoted to advancing the improvement of humanity, and from then on, his disciples believed, everything he did was done exclusively for others. Lawson wholeheartedly concurred, often claiming that the Direct Credits campaign turned him away from the likelihood of his earning billions in aviation.

But a division of Lawson's life into a pre-1931 entrepreneurial xviPROLOGUE

phase and a post-1931 utopian phase won't hold up. Lawson was always a utopian reformer with a deep-seated itch to perfect humanity's existence already finding clear expression in his baseball and aviation years. And Lawson was always an entrepreneur. The reform activities of the last twenty-four years of his life, though they flew under the colors of disinterested service to humanity, were transparent exercises in self-aggrandizement worthy of the baseball promoter and the aircraft industrialist. Clearly, strong competing impulses toward both the conventional American success ethic and a loftier service ethic were complexly intertwined within Lawson throughout his life.

Lawson's claim to have foregone earning billions thus should not be taken as an indication that money had ever been his main goal, for from early adulthood, amassing great wealth had only a low priority for Lawson. Because he always lived on a modest scale, he was able to get by without a large income (even though he never was quite as impoverished after 1931 as he let on). Often short of the large sums needed to finance his various projects, he well knew that money, or at least access to money, was indispensable for them. But carrying out projects primarily for the purpose of making money seemed to be utterly foreign to him, and some projects he pursued even when he knew there was little chance that they would be remunerative.

In truth, it was the pursuit of greatness, not wealth, that reached to the springs of Lawson's conduct and accounted for all that he did. His competing impulses toward both self-advancement and altruistic service were reconciled neatly in his striving for greatness.

For Lawson, greatness meant tackling tasks of immense size, novelty, and difficulty. He always thought big and in every phase of his life strove to do remarkable new things on a heroic scale. And he never left unstated the necessary condition for his accomplishment of stupendous feats: he must be put in absolute control, his orders accepted unquestioningly. A strong yen to run things was evident in every activity in his life.

At least as important to Lawson as the immediate gratifications coming from giving orders, mastering difficulties, and creating prodigies was the acclaim which would flow from performing mighty deeds in the service of humanity. When an ungrateful public—corrupted by

"the financiers" or otherwise far gone in degradation or obtuseness—
usually didn't oblige, Lawson turned to his personal following to keep
him well supplied with lavish praise. He also used barrels of ink and
carloads of paper to post his own vaunted claims for his greatness. In
any other person, this might be put down as insufferable vanity or
megalomaniacal delusion, but both Lawson and his minions saw it
simply as giving praise where praise was due.

Boiled down to essences, Lawson's quest for greatness was a quest
for both *power* and *fame*. He sought an imperishable recognition built
upon achievements so earthshaking that humanity would forever acknowledge the unique wonderworking of Alfred Lawson. The older
he became, the more ardently he thirsted for this kind of fame and
the more daunting were the tasks he set for himself. The more extreme, too, grew his claims for his achievements and his entitlement to
lead humanity to a higher destiny.

Always aiding Lawson's celebration of his greatness was his remarkable talent for capturing that greatness in catchy phrases and
monikers. Over a long and eventful life, the self-bestowed honorifics
piled up. Indeed, so numerous and increasingly grandiloquent were
they by the time he reached Des Moines that even the most be-
spangled Supreme Worthy Potentate of a fraternal lodge might have
blushed. Not Alfred Lawson, however, who knew that his ringing
titles fairly reflected his multifaceted greatness.

The first of Lawson's heroic titles appeared in his days as a baseball
promoter, when he identified himself in press releases as the "Magic
Man of Baseball" in recognition of his success in building teams and
leagues for small-town America. Then came Lawsonian prodigies in
other fields, always accompanied by newly minted titles and accolades,
until at last Lawson believed he had reached the very pinnacle of
greatness. To give fitting recognition to his final exalted standing, he
concocted a new title having a rich Lawsonian ring: the "First Knowledgian." This magnificent title captured perfectly Lawson's unique
standing as the master student, discoverer, and practitioner of God's
laws, the possessor of complete moral and scientific truth in Lawsonomy. It also conveyed his credentials, and hinted at the obligation
laid upon him, to lead the most important undertaking in history—

the development of a "new species" of humanity, spiritually, intellectually, and physically improved by Lawsonomy.

It was for this last purpose that the First Knowledgian had founded his community in Des Moines. Through his efforts at the Des Moines University of Lawsonomy, he confidently expected to achieve what Nietzsche had called a "revaluation of all values"—a complete reordering of the terms on which humanity thinks and acts. DMUL was also to be the means by which Lawson would make his ultimate thrust for power and fame. On the basis of DMUL's success, the First Knowledgian would be celebrated forever as one of Hegel's "world-historical persons"—heroes so attuned to major historical transformations that they give defining expression to new epochs. No greater power or fame could be imagined. But no aspirations were also more ambitious, fraught with difficulties, or likely to stir up opposition. The people of Des Moines can surely be excused for never having the least idea what Lawson was up to.

Undergirding Lawson's progression from sixth-grade dropout to self-proclaimed greatest teacher and benefactor of humanity were some unusual endowments—most notably, his astounding conviction of omnicompetence, his incredibly high energy level, and his great imaginative powers. The siren call beckoning him to greatness during twenty-year stints in fields as disparate as baseball and aviation just as handily carried him through four distinct phases of utopian reform. Simultaneously an entrepreneur and a reformer, so was Lawson at once a thinker, writer, and doer, a man of both reflection and action. And from his mind and hands came an immense outpouring of novel ideas, inventions, PR gambits, business enterprises, reform organizations, schemes for human uplift, speeches to admiring throngs, ephemeral publications, and treatises of unorthodox science, economics, and theology. Also strewing his life's path were not a few instances of failure, bad judgment, and muffed opportunities. The characteristic effect of these, however, was to send Lawson off along new lines of endeavor with intensified resolve in his assault on greatness.

What stands out in Lawson's life, then, is not simply his impassioned quest for greatness but also the manner in which he chased greatness down so many corridors. As it happens, one of Lawsonomy's most important scientific concepts depicts well the unusual course of its founder's life. Maintaining that the motion of any body is not as simple as it appears, Lawson described its path as a "zig-zag-and-swirl," though its complete analysis, he acknowledged, awaited a "superlative mathematics" yet to be invented. His life, too, was a zig-zag-and-swirl, and in the absence of a mathematical formula which might summarize and account for all its twists and turns, many words must be called in for the job.

During the years spanning the end of the Civil War and the mid-twentieth century, Lawson was one of many colorful Americans essaying to do great things never seen or heard of before. Yet in that age of unleashed ambitions and bold undertakings, probably no one else reached quite so far or maneuvered so imaginatively or on so wide a front as did Lawson. Certainly he brought to the boards one of the most stunning and original shows ever performed in the theater of American life, whether in his age or any other. The pages ahead attempt to re-stage the major acts and scenes which comprised the amazing zig-zag-and-swirl of Alfred Lawson's quest for greatness.

Part One

SEEDTIME

OF A

SELF-MADE

MAN

Alfred William Lawson was born in London, England, on March 24, 1869, the sixth of nine surviving children of Mary Anderson Lawson and Robert Henry Lawson. Three weeks later the Lawson family set sail for Windsor, Ontario, Canada. Within another three years the family had crossed the Detroit River to take up residence on the outskirts of Detroit and to become American citizens. And then—but here, at this very early point, the chronicler of Lawson's life meets up with a hairpulling problem: further facts of equal definiteness about Lawson's early years are very hard to come by today. Indeed, the dearth of information extends all the way to his thirty-ninth year, when he began his aviation career.

Never one to trifle with the possibility that his greatness might go unnoticed, Lawson wrote about himself frequently. However, not until very late in his life did even he have much to say about his first four decades—and this in spite of the fact that on no fewer than three occasions he issued books of an autobiographical character. Of their total of nearly six hundred pages, these books devoted only a few to his childhood and baseball career. Apparently Lawson viewed those years—nearly the first half of his life—as of small account in buttressing the case for the greatness he claimed for his work in aviation and on behalf of Direct Credits.

When Lawson had at last become the First Knowledgian, however, he showed a greater interest in those years of his childhood, adolescence, and young adulthood. Now an old man and doubtless aware that he was nearing the end of his allotted time, he reached back occasionally to recall and record memories from his earliest days. In this last phase of his life, he published no new autobiographical books, relying instead on his Direct Credits newspaper, *Benefactor*, and on the back pages of his many treatises as the vehicles for his lavish claims to greatness. His childhood and baseball years were subjects of *Benefactor* articles. An addendum to his book, *Children* (1938), presented an account in words and drawings of his childhood. Lawson even wrote a play entitled *Childhood Days of Alfred Lawson* (1943), intended for presentation as part of the instruction offered at Des Moines University of Lawsonomy.

In these later writings, Lawson described his youth, like every phase of his adulthood, as of a piece with the grand meaning of his entire life. Because this life was an inexorable unfolding of greatness, he found that the First Knowledgian was clearly prefigured in the young Lawson. The child was father of the man; all the traits eventually justifying his claim to be history's greatest figure were evident from the start.

The record of Lawson's twenty years in baseball remains spotty, but at least other sources of information do exist which make it possible to verify some of Lawson's claims and add to his meager account. For all else concerning Lawson's first four decades, however, his writings late in life are the only available sources. Although they probably provide accurate information concerning such matters as Lawson's family, residences, and schooling, these writings, too, are very skimpy and, of course, are colored by Lawson's urgent need to depict a springtime befitting the man who was destined to become the First Knowledgian.

Even so, Lawson's pages provide enough information to permit the limning of a plausible likeness of his childhood and early adult years. The picture which takes shape in the mind of the observer is quite different from the one which Lawson painted. Far from being the First Knowledgian in posse in his earliest days, or even the model youth described by Horatio Alger, Lawson seems instead to have been a boy embroiled in more than the usual allotment of the emotional turmoil of childhood and adolescence. A more tranquil period came in Lawson's third decade, when he was far from home, on his own, and supporting himself as a wandering baseball player. But during these baseball-playing days, as one would expect, Lawson certainly showed no hint of having any interest in selfless service to humanity or any aspiration to spiritual or moral leadership. Even Lawson acknowledged that these were days of drift and self-indulgence, during which he fell victim to "vices."

A major turning point in Lawson's early life came in his late twenties, however, when he underwent an episode of intense self-examination. As a consequence of this unusual soul-searching experience, he carried out a thorough reform of his life. Another notable product of this transformational moment was a novel, in which Lawson not only explored issues of right conduct and the true ends of life but also laid out his first vision of a perfected social order. Published in 1904, Lawson's youthful utopian fantasy was fittingly entitled *Born Again*.

Many years later, when Lawson made his most extreme assertion of self in his bid for power and fame, he would reach back for inspiration and guidance to his original utopian vision revealed in *Born Again*. At the time, however, his personal reforms and the newfound convictions heralded in his novel did not put him on the direct road to his eventual calling as the First Knowledgian. On the contrary: his "rebirth" occasioned instead the takeoff of a highly charged and focused entrepreneurship, which found expression immediately in baseball promotional work and later, in aviation. Because the teachings of *Born Again* actually called into question the moral validity of the self-seeking entrepreneurial pursuits which Lawson was about to undertake, his words and his conduct were hard to square with one another. Nonetheless, as his fourth decade opened, Lawson had at last gotten on the track of the quest for power and fame which would consume him for the rest of his life.

1

CHILDHOOD

DAYS

"Well, this is getting back to Nature. Now I have to depend upon a horse to work with instead of the electrical engine, which I invented in England."

With this ponderous and improbable utterance, Lawson's father, Robert Henry Lawson, begins a brief soliloquy presented immediately after the curtain rises on Lawson's play, *Childhood Days of Alfred Lawson.* The setting for the scene is the small farm outside of Detroit to which the Lawson family has moved from Windsor, Ontario. Resting his pitchfork against the barn, Lawson senior continues his musings about life down on the farm, letting the audience know that farming is neither his occupational preference nor the principal calling which brought him and his family from Canada to the United States: "I wonder what that devil of a Bishop meant when he told me that this would be a nice easy Diocese for me to build up. He must have thought that I was a gorilla." Then comes the peroration, redolent of the anguish felt by many a man whose life has not met the expectations of his younger years: "What would my aristocratic associates at Oxford think of me now, with nine children and a horse, cow and a goat to feed?"

Into these infelicitous lines Lawson squeezed the principal claims which he made in many other places about his father's background: that the elder Lawson had studied at Oxford, was at first a mechanical engineer, had subsequently become a minister of the gospel, and throughout, was an inventor, who had an early "electrical engine" to his credit. In a speech made very late in life, Lawson made another entry in his father's résumé, now averring that the father had also been a successful Shakespearean actor. As a condition for marriage, however, Mary Anderson demanded that Robert Henry Lawson give up acting and put his theatrical talents to better use as a preacher. It was then, if Lawson's account is accepted, that Lawson senior, in order to meet this condition, prepared for a new career. He "studied at Oxford University," from which institution he "received a diploma." However, alumni records today reveal no one named Robert Henry Lawson having ever been a student at Oxford University.

If the educational and professional background of Lawson's father remains quite uncertain today, at least Lawson's claim that his father broke new career ground when he became a farmer in the United States seems plausible. It also is likely that farming really did not suit his taste, because a year later, according to Lawson, the family moved into Detroit, where the father—again, by Lawson's account—opened a one-man factory for the weaving of rag carpets. Lawson always added "in order to earn an honest living," as if to imply that the elder Lawson still remained far from the occupation and style of life to which his attainments entitled him. Lawson recorded that his father also preached occasionally as an assistant minister in a Disciples of Christ church in Detroit. Doubtless, however, those former "aristocratic associates at Oxford" would have continued to arch their eyebrows in contemplation of Robert Henry Lawson's final station in the New World.

But for young Alf, as he was then called, there was much in his childhood circumstances which he later recalled as having been a blessing. In particular, he thought, the necessity to play his part from the age of four in his large family's struggle for existence gave him good work habits, a wide practical experience, and a well-grounded understanding that all honest work is honorable. Lawson frequently ticked off with pride the varied jobs of his childhood and adolescence; included were newsboy, bootblack, "chief mechanic" in his father's carpet factory, painter in a furniture factory, stave-maker, farm hand, hotel bellhop, blacksmith's assistant, and door-to-door sewing machine salesman. This work also helped to build up Lawson's body. "So at the age of fifteen he was like a young race horse and more powerful in muscular development than most men," he later wrote.

Even more important in formative effect, however, was the clean living which the circumstances of his youth supplied. Although Lawson lived in a city which eventually became huge, he always stressed that in his days there, Detroit was only a small city of 79,000. He therefore felt no qualms about claiming to have had a childhood close to nature and characterized by all the advantages which Americans have frequently attributed to rural and small-town upbringing. Describing himself in the third person (a frequent Lawson mode), he rhapsodized as follows: "He lived upon nature's best products—fresh air, raw foods and pure water. He ate no meat, drank no booze and smoked no dope. He lived a clean natural life in every way. Thus he developed a powerful body of marvelous dexterity." And of course, in this bucolic life, which permitted no idleness and was free from vicious influences, he was enabled to grow in moral uprightness.

Although Lawson's purpose is celebration of the virtuous beginnings of the First Knowledgian, thus far his description of his childhood reads precisely like the standard account given by many a self-made man who traced his later success to an identical wholesomeness of his start in life. But beyond this initial coincidence, little else which Lawson recalled about his earliest days matched the specifications for an ideal childhood found in advice manuals for ambitious youths. This would not be surprising if one could accept Lawson's claim that, as a child, he was already a unique moral personage, the First Knowledgian inchoate. In young manhood and early middle age, however, Lawson proved to be as ardent a practitioner of the entrepreneurial ethic as any other American of his generation. When seen against the background of Lawson's later entrepreneurial pursuits, his childhood deviations from the standard prescriptions for success take on considerable interest and are worth exploring further.

Lawson's recollections of his relations with his mother, for instance, certainly did not jibe with the specifications found in the literature of the gospel of success. Irwin Wyllie, in his study of the self-made man doctrine, wrote as follows about the key role of mother in the life of the successful man, as described in this literature:

> When the boy ventured into the world his memories of home and mother were supposed to be a source of powerful influence on his future. Poverty and rural surroundings might school him in virtue, but the schooling was often harsh. Not so with the lessons learned at mother's knee. Of all the external influences leading young men into the byways of success, none had greater honor in the cult of self-help than that of mother. . . .[1]

Lawson, however, never pontificated about priceless lessons learned at mother's knee. Instead, his recollections of his mother centered on the occasions in his very early youth when his mother had "lied" to him. They weren't very big lies—in fact, one "lie" was the Santa Claus story—but Lawson claimed that never afterward did he feel he could trust his mother (or his father, either, for that matter). He also recalled that his "mother had a fault; she accepted gossip without substantiation, as many women do." When he got into trouble at school, which was frequently, his mother was readier to accept the teacher's or the principal's account than his. Finally, on several occasions Lawson let slip in passing his belief that his mother favored both his younger and his older brothers over him. Withal, Lawson assured his readers, he still loved his mother, but this filial protestation could not cover over the feelings of resentment and grievance which were obviously there.

Wyllie also noted that "according to most self-help advocates a young man who moved away from his parental home was not doomed thereby to lose forever the blessings of female comfort and counsel, for they assumed that a young man with ambition would marry."[2] Lawson vigorously disagreed. What he dissented from was not the logic of the argument that one must marry in order to have "the blessings of female comfort and counsel." Rather, he apparently believed that those blessings were nonexistent in marriage. In an amazing scene in his play, *Childhood Days*, Lawson has his married brothers and sisters bicker about which partner gets the worse deal in marriage! All agree that marriage is a horrible trap for one or both partners. Lawson indicated his views directly in an impromptu speech given near the end of his life: "Oh, God, it's awful when these women get hold of you and you have to come to time." Significantly, he recalled how his father had "come to time" by succumbing to the prenuptial demands of his mother: "So the poor devil had to become a preacher in order to marry her." Lawson then added, "But you know, Alfred Lawson made up his mind that he was going to go as a bachelor all his life. He went, I think, seventy years as a bachelor, and God, how he enjoyed life." Very late in life Lawson did finally marry but only "to do some good for humanity"—that is, to let his genes pass on to children. Lawson had one son and one daughter, both born when he was in his seventies.

On the surface, the basic facts about Lawson's schooling would appear to square perfectly with the specifications found in the doctrine of the self-made man. According to Wyllie, proponents of this doctrine recommended a basic grade school education, some specialized technical training, and lots of experience in the "school of hard knocks." In form, at least, Lawson followed the prescription to the letter. He attended public schools in Detroit through the primary grades, completed an industrial training course in coat making between the ages of fourteen and seventeen, and throughout and later, acquired practical experience by working at numerous jobs, as he was so fond of pointing out. Lawson's views on education also seemed to be—again, on the surface—the correct ones for the self-made man. Always contemptuous of the usual college education as not only worthless but harmful, Lawson preferred as alternatives experience and the untrammeled exercise of his own mind. Throughout his life he ranted about the unwise substitution of "theory" for "provable facts," a common prejudice among self-made men of his day.

Yet a closer look shows that Lawson's schooling and views on education did not fully match those of the self-help model, after all. Unlike proponents of the model, Lawson was contemptuous not only of higher education but of formal education at all levels. Reading and writing were the only valuable things he got in grade school, he recalled; even arithmetic was worthless, because it was nothing but a skill employed by "the financiers" in their gigantic con game. His teachers, like teachers at all levels of education, taught nonsense or worse, he believed, expecting students to swallow their lies with no questions asked.

Because Lawson constantly challenged the authority of his teachers, he was frequently in trouble in school. In act 3 of *Childhood Days*, the school principal, having come to the Lawson home to complain to Alfred's mother about her son's conduct, says, "Alfred, the teachers all say that you are the most unruly pupil that has ever attended the Tappan School, either now or during the past." The principal's first charge against Alfred runs as follows: "From the teachers' reports you apparently assume that you are there to instruct the teachers, instead of the teachers being there to instruct you. Yes, it is reported that you frequently question the teachers' statements as though they were falsehoods." Relations with schoolmates were no better, either. Lawson confessed in other writings that school for him was "just one fist fight after another."

Thus, Lawson did not exhibit as a schoolboy any of the traits called for by advocates of the self-made man philosophy. He lacked completely the disciplined application, the dutiful acceptance of adult tutelage, and the focus on preparation for the future which were essential parts of that philosophy's educational prescriptions. Not even his suspicion of the value of book learning and "theory" remained within the considerable latitude permitted or recommended in the self-help model.

If the schoolboy Lawson had been so fortunate as to live in this present age of great enlightenment, he would undoubtedly have been labeled a behaviorally disordered student, and at that point specialized staff skills and services costing thousands of dollars of public money would have been brought to bear on his case. In Lawson's day, however, no refined apparatus for bringing unruly students to heel was available. This meant that those on all sides simply had to sweat out the great unpleasantness. Both Lawson and the school authorities doubtless felt that a great trial by ordeal had ended when Lawson left school forever at the age of twelve.

In the same year, Lawson ran away from home. This, too, was not in keeping with the prescriptions for the self-made man. According to

the model identified by Wyllie, leave-taking was to occur at the pro-
pitious moment when the aspiring lad was fully prepared to make his
way in the world. It is hard to see Lawson as that lad at the age of
twelve. He certainly had acquired the ability and willingness to work
at low-level jobs but, on the threshold of adolescence, he lacked the
intellectual preparation, self-discipline, and clear focus on the future
which were parts of the specification for success. Moreover, Lawson's
reasons for leaving were purely negative: to escape the authority of
adults. It is not surprising to find that he identified as the precipitating event an action taken by his mother: "But when his mother punished him for something he did not do because she accepted a gossip-
ing woman's tale against his word then he decided that he would leave
home and travel."

When in later years Lawson pursued his career in New York, Philadelphia, Milwaukee, and Detroit, he was acting in conformance with
the self-made man philosophy, which recommended that boys leave
their small town or rural settings for the greater opportunities offered
in cities. At the time of his initial leave-taking, however, Lawson had
no specific geographical or career destination and cannot be cited as
one who escaped from small-town confinement and humble obscurity
by the prescribed route.

Within two years of his running away, Lawson returned to his parents' home and submitted to their insistence that he enroll in an industrial training course. Attendance in this course was apparently no
more to his liking than attendance in grade school had been. At least
once, he ran away again. His parents' constant pleas to return and
complete the program of training eventually prevailed, however, and
at the age of seventeen he finished an industrial course in clothing design and coat making. Because Lawson listed coat making among the
jobs of his youth, possibly he actually secured employment in this line
of work after leaving the training program. If so, he could not have
stayed with it long, because in his late teens, he claimed, he also was
following other lines of work and soon entered full-time into baseball.
In sum, it seems unlikely that he ever saw industrial training as crucial
preparation or practical grounding for a successful start in life; probably it was never more to him than something done to placate parents.

ALFRED LAWSON STUDYING ATMOSPHERIC RESISTANCE TO MOVING BODIES

At age twelve, Lawson was a runaway and already a peripatetic philosopher, usually moving by freight train. From Lawson, *Children.*

So much, then, for one more specification by the authorities on success which Lawson failed to take to heart.

Because his parents were godly people, Lawson recalled attending religious services regularly and often in his youth at the Disciples of Christ church where he claimed his father was a sometime preacher. He also attended Sunday school classes at a nearby Episcopal church. (Although Lawson told of his baptism at the former church, in a biographical sketch prepared later in life, he identified himself as an Episcopalian.)

Regular church attendance and youthful piety were de rigueur, of course, in the accounts which successful men of the rags-to-riches school gave of their childhoods. Lawson's account of his religious experiences in his youth was of a totally different character, however. Lawson never even hinted at having a shred of conventional piety as a boy; religion was one more area of life subject to his across-the-board challenge to all authority and to his determination to reach his own conclusions in all matters.

Lawson may have dutifully attended church and Sunday school, but many of the lessons taught there apparently didn't take. In his play, for instance, the principal upbraids him for challenging a teacher on the truthfulness of the biblical account of the three men who remained unscorched in the fiery furnace; Lawson responds by suggesting that the principal walk into a nearby blast furnace and see what happens. Lawson's account of his childhood baptism also lacked the spiritual flavor which a true proponent of the conventional success philosophy would have given it. Lawson told how his mother tried to bribe him with a penny to undergo total immersion. When she had upped the bribe to a nickel, he consented. About whether the experience produced any spiritual effects, Lawson said not a word. Instead, he commented, the dunking in cold water gave him such a bracing feeling that he resolved ever afterward to take only cold baths!

The foregoing material and conclusions are drawn from Lawson's writings in his old age. As a young man, however, Lawson had already tipped his hand on religious matters. The first edition of *Born Again* contained a chapter (omitted in later editions) denouncing many passages in the Old Testament as barbarous, absurd, or unjust and denying the divinity and miracle working of Jesus.

None of this is to say, however, that Lawson wanted to portray himself as having ever been hostile to true religion or indifferent to God's purposes for Lawson's life. Hardly so, because in his last days, Lawson even founded a new church and creed, Lawsonian Religion, and became a religious prophet, the First Knowledgian. His accounts of his childhood thus contained other material meant to show that in his youth Lawson already had a well-developed spiritual sense and a complete knowledge of God's moral laws.

Illustrative of his spiritual sense is the second scene of act 4 of *Childhood Days*. In this scene, Lawson demonstrates to a chum who has run away with him that an apparition seen in a graveyard is not a ghost but a goat. When the chum reveals that his dead grandfather had hated goats and once killed one (and also used to tell his grandson lies about "Santa Claus and Ghosts, and Spirits and Spooks and everything"), Lawson explains that in retribution for these offenses, the grandfather's soul now inhabited the body of the goat seen in the graveyard; this was in accordance with God's great "Law of Maneuverability," which dictates that "as you give, so you receive." As the two boys prepare to bed down in a haystack, the chum casually asks, "Alf, what is the soul?" and follows with, "Where will my soul go when I die?" This gives Lawson the opportunity to discourse at greater length on the Law of Maneuverability and the transmigration of souls. All in all, an amazing demonstration of religious precociousness by a lad of only twelve years.

In rejecting conventional religious views and expressions of piety, Lawson necessarily was rejecting an integral part of the myth of the self-made man. But at the same time, in attributing to himself as a boy a superior religious and moral insight, Lawson was intent on constructing an alternative myth about his childhood. In fact, almost everything he wrote about his childhood contributed something to the construction of that myth. By means of this myth, he was able to assign positive value to every one of his departures from the reigning success myth of his younger years. Even the strife and tensions so apparent in his childhood could be readily accommodated and explained away by this means. Most of all, the myth would show, somewhat in the manner of the biblical stories about the youth of Jesus, that Lawson's claims to a unique status as the First Knowledgian were authentic, because the qualities on which he based the claims were already evident in childhood.

Lawson as boy prophet of a new moral and religious dispensation was only one component of Lawson's myth. At least three other components can be discerned in Lawson's discussions of his younger days.

First in importance surely was the young Lawson as enemy of cant, zealous devotee of truth, and brilliant discoverer of advanced knowledge. Herein, of course, lay the source of his problems in school: he knew so much more than his teachers, and his commitment to truth compelled him to correct his teachers' many errors. He claimed, for instance, to have discovered at the age of four that suction and pressure, not energy, account for the movement of matter and, by the age of twelve, to have codified this discovery in the "Law of Penetrability." Thus, in act 2 of *Childhood Days*, when a sister asks, "Where's Alfred?," a brother replies: "He is in the bedroom working on his pet hobby, PENETRABILITY." And in the third act, when the school principal brings up the old chestnut of energy being the cause of movement, Lawson overwhelms him with a lengthy counterargument laying down the main outlines of Lawson's alternative account of the universe.

When Lawson's mother unjustly accepted and acted on false gossip about him, he could claim once again to have suffered for truth, at the hands of untruth. Under the circumstances, his decisions to leave school and to run away at a young age made perfect sense. In Lawson's account, these were not actions taken by a troubled adolescent but by a persecuted champion of truth. Lawson as a youthful martyr is, in fact, another major component of the myth of Lawson's childhood, and an important aspect of this martyrdom was his alleged willingness to accept the injustices imposed on him without feelings of ill will or rancor. Thus, in spite of her wrongful actions toward him, he claimed still to love his mother. His teachers were excused on grounds that they could not help their ignorance and were under the thumb of "the financiers." Although Lawson believed that two of his older brothers always conspired to shift some of their share of the household chores on to Lawson's back, he bore up, like Cinderella, without murmur.

This willingness to accept stoically the outsized and unfair burdens heaped on him by others is illustrated particularly well in act 2 of

At age fourteen, Lawson returned to his home in Detroit to begin an industrial course in coat making. From Lawson, *100 Great Speeches.*

Childhood Days. The occasion is Lawson's twelfth birthday, and all the family members have arrived for a party. Two of his younger brothers give him gifts suitable for a young boy—a Jew's harp and a harmonica. Then his parents and older siblings proceed to give him their gifts—a bag for carrying newspapers, a bootblack's box, a steel ax, a garden spade, a hoe, a broom, and a buck saw. The presentation speeches which Lawson puts into the mouths of his family members make plain that Lawson believed he already was paying his way in full and doing the lion's share of the work connected with each gift. In reply to each presentation, however, Lawson thanks the giver for his or her thoughtfulness in making it possible for Lawson to work even more productively and efficiently and to carry an even larger portion of responsibility for the family's support.

At the birthday party his youngest brother, Collie, gives Lawson an unusual gift—a poem which Collie has written:

> To my big brother Alf
> Who don't think of himself
> But fights for his sisters and brothers.
> Who works all of the day
> And works most of the night
> Because he wants to help others.

This poem points to the close relationship between Lawson, the uncomplaining martyr and hard-working servant of others, and the remaining component of Lawson's myth about his childhood—Lawson as defender of the weak and enemy of injustice.

The most obvious utility of this mythic element was the ennobling of Lawson's fist fights in his youth. In his many statements about them, Lawson always claimed his fighting was done to protect himself and others "against oppression." His fights were numerous, because there were many "bullies who were always ready to smash the weak" or who "took offense at his methods of getting at the truth"—that is, resented his readiness to match his fists against their attempts to promulgate falsehoods with their fists. It is an important feature of this moral drama, too, that Lawson never lost a fight. As Lawson explained, "by adopting a self made axiom, BE SURE YOU ARE RIGHT OR DON'T

FIGHT, he learned that by adding moral courage to his physical strength . . . he always came out victorious."

Lawson served justice not only by fighting but also by arbitrating disputes among his school mates, which he reported he often was called upon to do. In his recollection, "he was so thoroughly loved and respected by the members of all classes that his decisions were invariably accepted without argument."

At a tender age, Lawson claimed, he also had begun to arrive at a clear understanding of the many injustices existing in the greater world beyond the schoolyard. As a bootblack, not yet ten years old, he already had noticed that "those people who did the least work toward the production of wealth wore the best boots and those who did the hardest work . . . wore the worst boots." When a few years later he worked as an itinerant farm hand, he saw, to his regret, "that the hands that feed Civilization are the hands that are bitten by it." In school, he often was impelled "to show up the lies" which teachers and books taught at the behest of "the financiers."

Doubtless the psychohistorian would gleefully shove the foregoing self-revelations and mythic claims about Lawson's childhood through the juice squeezer two or three times, in order to extract every drop of latent meaning in them. It is enough here, however, simply to observe that the myth which Lawson created about his childhood sinks by its utter implausibility. Lawson's conflicts with teachers, his many fights in the schoolyard, his grudges against his mother, his conviction of being unfairly used by his older brothers, his early-formed antipathy to marriage, his dropping out of school and running away, his intense compulsion to challenge all authority—these are the solid features of Lawson's childhood which defy Lawson's efforts to cover them over or explain them away by myth making. Moreover, these are features pointing not to the serenity of a matured greatness of soul but rather to the storm and stress of a painful adolescence.

A reader swallowing Lawson's myth about the meaning of his childhood would soon run into another problem, already noted: how to account for Lawson's activities and conduct for the forty years of his life falling between his late teens, when he began his baseball career, and his late fifties, when he ended his aviation work. During these

four decades, the advanced moral and spiritual thinking at which
Lawson allegedly arrived in his childhood had no obvious bearing on
Lawson's conduct. As Lawson himself confessed, his life during his
first ten years in baseball was dissolute and lacking in serious purpose;
thereafter, for the next thirty years, the dominant theme of his life
was the quest for power and fame in baseball promotions and aviation—a quest for greatness which steadily grew in intensity.

Yet if Lawson's childhood days lacked convincing evidence of his
final exalted standing as the First Knowledgian, there was nothing
about them, either, that suggested he would become a single-minded,
energetic, creative entrepreneur. As this review has shown, very little
in his childhood fit the ideal pattern specified by the apostles of the
creed of the self-made man. What seemed especially to be missing was
an ambition steadily focused on the future; Lawson appeared to be a
youth adrift, lacking any sense of direction or clear purpose for his
life, even in the near term. It is easy to imagine him as doomed to
obscurity forever, endlessly shifting among low-level jobs.

Luckily enough for Lawson, however, he was a baseball pitcher of
some ability. His talent in this field proved to be his one-way ticket not
only out of his childhood environs but also into an activity in which his
ambition could eventually develop and acquire direction.

2

THE

MAGIC

MAN OF

BASEBALL

In the final scene of *Childhood Days* Lawson gives a dramatic account of "how he secured his first professional engagement" in baseball. As the scene opens, several citizens of an unspecified town talk excitedly about a baseball game in progress. It happens that the local nine have miraculously held a professional "league team" to a no-run standoff through eight innings. A young farmer asks, "Who's pitching for the home team?" A businessman replies, "A new fellow that we never saw before. They say he came to town this morning on a freight train. He's got great speed, good curves and good control. . . . I believe they called him Lawson. He's just a young fellow about seventeen years old but he can put the twisters to that ball."

Lawson goes on to win the game in a 2–0 shutout. Accompanying the young hero onto the stage, the grateful manager says, "Lawson, that was the greatest pitching that the people of this town have ever seen." Lawson quickly accepts the manager's offer of a pitching job for the summer at forty dollars a month. When the proprietor of the local hotel also throws in an offer of free board for the season, Lawson requests a meal at once, explaining that "I haven't eaten anything yet today."

Information which Lawson supplied elsewhere makes it nearly certain that the unnamed town in which this charming scene took place was Frankfort, Indiana, and the year, 1887. The veracity of the scene's action cannot be certified, of course, and at least one of the details is wrong: Lawson was eighteen, not seventeen, when he broke into professional baseball. Certain other details, however, have a great ring of plausibility. It is very easy to believe that Lawson did arrive at the debut of his baseball career precisely as he indicated—by chance, unheralded, via a freight train, and with an empty stomach.

If Lawson's entrance into baseball was a fluke, he nonetheless made the most of the opportunity which suddenly opened to him in central Indiana. He pitched the next season for the Goshen team in northern Indiana and, in 1889, for no fewer than three teams—Bloomington and Sterling, both in Illinois, and Appleton, Wisconsin. Team hopping by footloose players was hardly uncommon in that freewheeling day when team folding was common, too, and handshakes sometimes took the place of written contracts, at least in the outlaw or independent leagues in which Lawson spent his first three years. In Lawson's case, however, frequent movement was the result of a succession of clubs eagerly buying his release, in order to cash in on his impressive pitching ability: according to an article appearing in 1890 in the Boston *Daily Globe*, his record for 1889 was an astounding thirty-three wins out of thirty-five games pitched. In the baseball parlance of that day, he was a "phenomenon." No wonder, then, that he soon came to the notice of a higher class of team in the minor leagues. For the 1890 season, his services were secured by the Wilmington, Delaware, club in the Atlantic Association.

Wilmington boosters were certainly looking forward to a great 1890 season. Not only was a new ballpark under construction, but the club's owners were going all out to get topnotch playing talent. In early February, the Wilmington *Every Evening* reported almost daily on negotiations underway which, if successful, would permit "surplus material" of the Philadelphia Phillies to play for the Wilmington club. But even if the deal fell through (which it did), the newspaper was still brimming with optimism about the upcoming season: "It is not an exaggeration to say that the Wilmington club of 1890 will surpass the famous team of 1884 in playing strength."

A key factor in the *Every Evening*'s anticipation of great things ahead was Wilmington's new pitcher, Alfred Lawson. The newspaper had high expectations for him, and for good reason. Spending the winter playing for a club in Saint Augustine, Florida, Lawson was regularly turning in performances which added to the luster of his reputation as a rising star of baseball. Reports of the ongoing great success of Wilmington's "phenomenon" piled up in the pages of the *Every Evening* throughout February and March of 1890.

In its February 15, 1890, edition, the *Every Evening* excitedly recounted Lawson's outstanding play on the previous day against one of the most celebrated and respected teams of that era—the Chicago White Stockings, captained by the legendary Adrian "Cap" Anson. Starting in center field, Lawson was called to the box after "Anson's colts" had posted eleven runs in the first four innings. From that moment, however, Chicago's scoring ended; in fact, Lawson held Anson's team hitless for the next four innings, after which darkness forced the game's end. In a story headed "Lawson's Successful Game," the *Every Evening* exulted: "Chicago won the game [11−5] but all of its runs were scored when Lawson was playing in the field. Besides whitewashing the Chicago club in the four innings in which he pitched, Lawson played an errorless game and made two hits and had two put-outs. The friends of the local twirler are pleased at his good showing and feel confident that he will pitch great ball in the Atlantic Association for the Wilmington club."

Five days later, on February 20, the newspaper brought more glad tidings about Lawson: in another game between Saint Augustine and Chicago, Lawson scored one run, made "three difficult put-outs" while playing in center field, and held Chicago to one hit during several innings of pitching. Anson was now so impressed by Lawson, the story continued, that he was making efforts to hire the twenty-year-old wonder for his Chicago team.

Although the scuttlebutt about Anson's desire to buy Lawson's release continued for several more days in the pages of the *Every Evening*, no deal was ever firmed up. As the newspaper reported on February 21, "The Wilmington club's management has no intention of releasing Lawson unless Chicago should offer an unusually liberal amount for him." The star prospect for propelling the local club to a winning season in 1890, Lawson was too valuable to be let go of cheaply.

In mid-March, Lawson tried out with the National League's Brooklyn team in a game against Anson's Chicago club. Although Brooklyn lost, 8–4, Lawson was again adjudged to have acquitted himself well. Attributing Brooklyn's loss to "poor team work," a March 19 story in the *Every Evening* noted that Lawson had actually pitched better than the Chicago pitcher, who gave up eleven hits to Lawson's seven. Also, "of Brooklyn's four runs, Lawson scored two and [he also] struck out four of Anson's men."

If Lawson's hope had been to draw further attention to himself within major league circles, he succeeded. On March 25, the *Every Evening* reported that "as many as five [National] League and [American] Association clubs are after Lawson." But his prospects for moving up remained unchanged; the *Every Evening* was pleased to confirm that "the Wilmington management will retain him." The next day the newspaper announced that "Lawson arrived here from Saint Augustine, Florida, last night."

The opening game of the season on April 3 proved to be a blowout occasion in Wilmington. Over 2,500 fans turned out to inspect the new field and grandstand and to root for the home team against the Philadelphia Athletics in a non-Association contest. Many magnificoes were on hand, too, including the governor, secretary of state, mayor, and city council members. Once the mayor and the governor had finished their inevitable speeches, "cheer after cheer rang out for Governor Briggs, Mayor Harrington, and the Wilmington baseball club," and the governor finally tossed out the ball. But the festive mood continued even after the game had begun. In a detailed account running to twenty-four column-inches published the next day, the *Every Evening* reported: "As Lawson first went to bat he was presented with a beautiful bouquet by a lady admirer, and the crowd helped him acknowledge the gift by vociferous cheering. Lawson doffed his cap, and did not ignominiously strike out, as is generally the case under the circumstances, but managed to hit the ball. He retired at first."

Although Wilmington lost the game, 6–2, the *Every Evening* was able to look beyond the loss to find great promise in Lawson's performance that day:

> Lawson pitched an excellent game after the first inning. His delivery is graceful and easy and exceedingly speedy. He is not what

may be termed a "strike-out" pitcher, but on the contrary endeavors to put the ball over the corner of the plate so it can be hit to the infield. His work yesterday substantiates what had previously been said regarding him and Manager Stevenson predicts him to do good work in the Atlantic Association. His playing suited the crowd, and but for the first inning's wildness the score would have been closer.

Perhaps the hoopla of opening day and all the adulation coming his way had had a stimulating effect on Lawson's initial performance with the Wilmington team. In any case, his good start was not anywhere close to being matched by his next appearance on the mound on April 12. Going up against Syracuse in another non-Association game, Lawson lost, 11 – 1. On April 14, the *Every Evening* lamented that "Lawson did not pitch his game. His work was indifferent and the supposition that he would do good work against the Syracuse was soon shaken. Lawson's delivery was ineffective and his showing did not compare to the game he pitched against the Athletics . . . in the opening game."

Well, anyone could have an off day, and the first game of the Association season was still a week away. Surely by then Lawson would be back in form. But when that day arrived (April 19), Lawson pitched in a 15 – 5 loss against Worcester. In its April 21 issue, the *Every Evening* did not mince words about the cause of the team's loss: "Lawson's poor exhibition of pitching in the third and fourth innings, when the visitors scored eleven runs, is responsible for the team's defeat." Nor was this the newspaper's judgment only, for "the directors of the Wilmington club have suspended Lawson for two weeks without pay for his poor playing on Saturday," deciding on this stern measure in order "to enforce discipline and also to set an example."

Clearly Lawson had lost his biggest booster in Wilmington; in the space of only two weeks, the *Every Evening*'s assessment of Lawson had undergone an astonishing turnabout. Inexplicably, however, in far less time than that, Lawson was back in good standing with the club's management. On April 24, five days after he had been suspended for two weeks, the *Every Evening* ran the following item: "Pitcher Lawson, who was suspended last Saturday for alleged indifferent playing, has been reinstated."

If the Wilmington management had renewed hopes that Lawson

would at last live up to his pre-season promise, his 13–6 loss to Hartford on April 29 could not have been reassuring. Describing Lawson's pitching only as "fair," the *Every Evening* headlined its story "Wilmington Gets a Better Grip on Last Place." Following the Hartford game, Wilmington stood 0–5 in Association play—and then lost to Hartford again the next day.

At last, on April 30, came Wilmington's first Association win, against New Haven. Now 1–6 in Association standings, perhaps Wilmington could begin to work up out of the cellar, starting with another win against New Haven the next day. The pitching rotation threw to Lawson on May 1 the challenge of extending Wilmington's winning streak to two games. Would Lawson finally deliver the goods?

The next morning the Wilmington *Morning News* disclosed the sad answer: New Haven 11, Wilmington 1. Lawson's meager performance inspired eloquent derision from that newspaper's reporter: "Mr. Lawson was put in the box for the Wilmingtons; he was hit hard; it was awful; singles, two- and three-baggers were as numerous as the rain drops that patted against the roof of the grandstand. Lawson apparently did his best, but what is that?" In a more succinct account entitled "Back in the Old Rut," the *Every Evening* reported simply that "Lawson started to pitch for Wilmington but did so poorly that he retired at the end of the fourth inning." And then, in the "Diamond Gossip" section of the same issue of the paper, also appeared this brief notice: "Lawson was released today."

No wins, three lopsided losses in Association games, and a suspension for indifferent play—the circumstances of Lawson's release hardly seemed favorable for the advance of his baseball career. Yet within forty-eight hours of his release by Wilmington, Lawson had signed with the Boston club of the National League! Scooting faster than the dark cloud which had formed over his reputation in Wilmington, Lawson had actually moved up, not down. Doubtless he was cashing in on contacts made and reputation acquired during the winter months in Florida. On May 6, 1890, the Boston *Daily Globe* broke the exciting news: fast work by the Boston manager had secured the "bright looking young fellow, smooth-faced and manly in his bearing" who "will no doubt prove a valuable acquisition." Accompanied by a wood-engraved portrait of Lawson, the *Daily Globe* article appeared under the headline "Pitcher Lawson / It was Not Anson's Fault that Boston Got Him."

As for Lawson's unfortunate experience in Wilmington, the *Daily Globe* story said only this: "Lawson became dissatisfied at his treatment in Wilmington . . . and gladly welcomed this opportunity to sign with a league club." Welcomed this opportunity, indeed! The succession of events in Lawson's life between late February and early May strongly suggested that this was what he had been angling for all along. Probably, too, this was what the *Every Evening* was driving at when (April 21, 1890) that newspaper had attributed a demoralizing effect to Lawson's presence on the team and had concluded that "it would be better to give Lawson his release," on the evidence that he "either cannot *or will not play good ball* for the Wilmington club" (emphasis added).

But now, presumably, all was well. Lawson had made it to the big time, and Bostonians congratulated themselves about having been the fortunate ones to snare him—under the nose of Chicago's Anson, no less. However, the good cheer did not outlast Lawson's first—and only—game for Boston: a May 13 outing, in which he matched pitches with the celebrated Mickey Welch of New York and lost 7–2. The account which appeared in next morning's *Daily Globe* was cruel:

BOSTON LEAGUERS CAN GET NO LOWER
LAWSON'S A NICE YOUNG MAN, BUT HE COULDN'T
PITCH BALL

. . . The star of Alfred Lawson's destiny faded into the twilight that hovered over Harlem as the last Boston man crept into his hole.

The Wilmington phenomenon—save the mark!—was given a trial, and after the evidence in the shape of 12 base hits was in, he was proven guilty of possessing a slow drop ball with no speed.

Let go by Boston, Lawson secured one more chance in the majors, but in two games which he pitched for Pittsburgh, the results were even unhappier than those of his Boston debut. Following a 12–10 loss to Philadelphia on May 28, Lawson pitched on June 2 to the Chicago team led by Cap Anson, the man who had tried to hire him only several months earlier. Posting a humiliating 14–1 loss, Lawson committed three errors to boot.

No sooner was this publicity portrait made than Lawson's career with the National League's Boston team was over, after one game. From Lawson, *100 Great Speeches.*

In sum, within a three-week span in 1890, Lawson's major league career began and ended. In nineteen innings of play, he had lost all three of his games, compiled an earned run average of 6.63, allowed twenty-seven hits, and batted .000. Contrasting so vividly with his stunning displays in the 1890 pre-season, this grievously poor record in major league play must have left the experts, who had expected so much from him, scratching their heads in wonderment.

One possibility, of course, was that Lawson's paltry performances for Boston and Pittsburgh (and for Wilmington, too) were a true indication of his ability and that his brilliant winter record in Florida was a fluke—or perhaps even (along with his sensational 1889 minor league record) a fabrication. To be sure, Lawson's swift move from Wilmington to Boston revealed a gift for self-promoting effrontery, and possibly the press-agentry which became so apparent in Lawson's ventures later in his life was already at work from the start of his baseball career. It is more than a little difficult to believe, however, that he could have gone as far as he did in baseball solely on the basis of chutzpah and false claims.

Another explanation of Lawson's flop in the big leagues might be that he had genuine big-league potential but rose too fast and therefore lacked proper seasoning. On this view, encouraged to believe that he had the stuff needed to go right to the top, he promptly—and disastrously—made that his consuming goal. If he had been left alone and permitted to concentrate on playing a season or two of good ball for Wilmington, possibly the story of his transition from the minor to the major leagues would have been quite different. The main problem with this line of explanation, however, is this: if Lawson truly did have major league potential, surely it would have matured and been recognized during his subsequent eight or so years as a minor league player.

Perhaps the likeliest explanation of Lawson's failure falls somewhere between these two positions. As it happened, 1890 was not a usual year in professional baseball. During the preceding fall, the Brotherhood of Professional Baseball Players had tried, on threat of otherwise forming a rival major league, to get the National League to accept a model contract which was more favorable to the interests of the players. When the contract negotiations failed, the so-called Brotherhood Revolt led to the organization of the Players' League and the decimation of the playing ranks of the National League in 1890. Because clubs were now under extraordinary pressure to find replacement talent, it became much easier for hopefuls to get a major league tryout, and club managers had little choice but to take chances on prospects who might otherwise have been passed over. Thus, in the unusual circumstances of the season of 1890, not only may Lawson's prospects for major league success have been overrated but an opportunity may also have opened to him which even his talent for self-promotion could not have generated in a typical year.

If Lawson's rise and fall in his early years as a player remain perplexing, however, two things are certain: in baseball, he had not only aspired to the highest ranks but had actually obtained an opportunity unavailable to most players, and when his big chance in baseball came, and the payoff for his earlier achievements seemed to lie within his reach, he faltered. Together, these facts constituted the first clear instance of a recurring pattern in Lawson's life.

His brief fling in the major leagues wrapped up, Lawson returned to the minor leagues, spending the remainder of the 1890 season as manager of the Wellsville, New York, team in the Western New York League. As insignificant as Wellsville was in the history of American baseball, Lawson's one-year assignment there nonetheless secured for him a footnote in that history. It was, moreover, a favorable footnote, unlike his major league playing statistics, which have been carried forever after in the baseball encyclopedias.

What Lawson did to gain the recognition of historians was recruit for the Wellsville team the legendary John J. McGraw, then a seventeen-year-old boy playing—not very well—for Olean, New York. At Wellsville, strong hints of McGraw's later greatness as a major league player began to appear, and in future years McGraw always claimed that his season at Wellsville was the true start of his professional career. For his part, late in life Lawson was willing to take the credit not only for "bringing out" McGraw but also for teaching him the fine points of playing and managing on which McGraw's fabulous career was based.

When the playing season of 1890 was over, Lawson went to work on arrangements for an ambitious scheme he had cooked up for the winter of 1890–1891. As the new year opened, implementation was afoot: Lawson and a collection of ball players he had pieced together, mostly from Pennsylvania and New York (and including McGraw), headed south. Rendezvousing in Ocala, Lawson's team first played several games against other teams wintering in Florida. Then, in mid-January, metamorphosed as Al Lawson's American All-Stars, the motley group sailed from Tampa for Havana. At that time, baseball was in its infancy in Cuba, which was still under the control of Spain. However, enthusiasm for the sport was growing rapidly on the island, and Lawson was able to line up a half-dozen games against some home-grown Cuban clubs.

Losing all but one of these games, the American All-Stars surely were misnamed. Gate receipts were disappointing, too, yielding only enough money to cover the visitors' expenses in Cuba and return passage no farther than Key West. What a great adventure it must have been, however, for the young McGraw and the others under Lawson's tutelage! And if only a modest number of Cubans had turned out for the games, at least they were well satisfied. Partially making up for any deficiencies of prowess, the Americans had served up several sensations to the spectators. In one way, in fact, the American All-Stars definitely had dazzled: Lawson had decked them out resplendently in bright *yellow* uniforms! But what really stirred up the budding aficionados of baseball in Cuba was the play of the scrambling, pintsized McGraw, who quickly became celebrated among the locals as El Mono Amarillo—the Yellow Monkey.

Although Lawson's venture can't go into the record book as the first exhibition trip to Cuba, it was certainly one of the earliest. Of greater significance, in any event, was what the trip revealed about Lawson. It was the first manifestation on record of the "big thinking" which later came to characterize his life. Only twenty-one years old, he had conceived and pulled off, more or less successfully, a novel project having difficult staffing, financial, and logistical requirements.

When finally back from Cuba, the American All-Stars played some more games to earn their passage from Key West to Tampa. Upon

their arrival in Tampa in late February, the team then disbanded—
but not before Lawson had been called upon to defend the conduct of
his charges in Cuba. A Tampa newspaperman had gotten wind of
some nasty rumors about the American All-Stars. Was it true, he
asked Lawson, that they were frequently drunk and had thrown most
of the games which they lost? An indignant Lawson replied: "No, sir!
I want to say for my boys that they behaved themselves at all times and
any talk you may have heard about them betting on the games and
losing three of them on purpose is rot!"

Although half of his weary entourage now were determined to
depart for home, Lawson successfully appealed to the remainder
(McGraw among them) to sign on with his newest scheme, which was
to fill the team's vacancies and continue playing out of Gainesville.
There was little prospect of money in it—the contract Lawson drew
up obligated him to pay only "board, shaving and washing expenses,
also a cigar once a week"—but at least the players could delay their
return to the wintry north. Lawson then proceeded to scrounge up
engagements for the team at various places throughout central Florida.

In the interview given to the Tampa reporter, Lawson had put in a
strong plug for McGraw and made a prescient observation: "The best
player on my team is Johnny McGraw. He is a hard, left-handed
batsman, a fine short stop, a good base runner and, last but not least, a
gentleman. He is one of the coming stars of the profession." But the
decisive moment for McGraw's career came on March 26, 1891, when
the team which Lawson now heralded as "the champions of Florida"
took on the Cleveland Indians in Gainesville. Putting himself on the
mound for this very special occasion, Lawson tossed a 9–6 loss, in
which the "champions" made eleven errors. McGraw, however, was a
standout, getting four hits in five times at bat and scoring three runs.
Offers immediately flooded in from minor league managers eager to
secure his services. Only weeks later, McGraw was on his way to
Cedar Rapids, Iowa, and, a season later, to Baltimore and baseball
immortality.

From the start of the 1891 season through the end of the century,
Lawson continued his connection with baseball as a minor league
player or manager. Because he was constantly wandering, however, it

is not always possible to pin down his whereabouts or to confirm the claims which he later made. In 1891, for instance, he claimed to have been on the west coast, pitching for Oakland of the California League, Spokane, and "other clubs," but no verification from other sources has yet been dug up. And while it is definite that in the winter of 1891–1892 Lawson attempted another expedition to Cuba, it is uncertain whether the new version of the American All-Stars ever got there. (If they did, McGraw was not on the roster. The fast-rising young star had agreed to go, but when Lawson, having problems finding funding for the expedition, left him and several other players stranded in the New Orleans hotel where they had agreed to rendezvous, McGraw forever swore off involvement in Lawson's schemes.)

In 1892, Lawson pitched for Atlanta in the Southern League. But this last position he resigned, he later said, in order to manage a team on tour to England; unfortunately, he offered no further information about this undertaking. From England, Lawson reported, he then left on a "world tour," which took him in 1892–1893 to South Africa, "Australia, New Zealand, [and] Honolulu." He claimed to have started some amateur baseball clubs in Australia and other, unnamed places and, when finally out of money, to have worked his way back to the United States as a "common sailor" on a freighter.

In 1894, Lawson definitely was center-fielder and captain on the Albany team in the outlaw New York State League; however, the club disbanded on July 6, even though it was in first place. In 1895, Lawson apparently again went to England, this time, according to his report, as manager of a team of college players, the Boston Amateurs, on a playing tour. Then, he is on record as being the manager of the Pottsville team in the Pennsylvania State League in 1896. But in the final years of the century, there are only his reports to indicate his locations and activities—in 1896–1897, manager of "an independent club at North Adams [Massachusetts?]" and in 1898–1899, manager of the Anderson, Indiana, club in the outlaw Indiana State League.

As the new century opened, Lawson's baseball activities took on a decidedly different character. From 1900 on, although he still managed clubs, his most strenuous efforts went into organizing new teams and leagues. It was then that he emerged as the "Magic Man of Baseball" or, as a *Sporting News* article also dubbed him (probably with Lawson's help), the "King of League Promoters," who "really makes dead territory come alive."

No independent verification has come in yet to back up Lawson's claim to have organized in 1900 the Central League, in which league he said he also managed the Peoria club. However, he is definitely known to have reorganized the Pennsylvania State League in 1901 and to have managed the Easton club in that league until resigning on July 4, 1901. In 1902 he managed the Scranton team, also in the Pennsylvania State League, until the league fell apart in mid-season. Lawson claimed, incidentally, to have rigged up in 1901 portable lighting equipment, which he moved by flatcar among the cities of the Pennsylvania State League. Although this has not yet been verified, it is certain that in 1902 Lawson's Scranton team played exhibition games under the lights on Wednesday nights. Lawson's later claim to have invented night baseball doesn't hold up, yet it is clear that he was an early experimenter with the lighting of night games.

Patient digging has also established that in 1903–1904, Lawson was active in organizing the Tri-State League and, in 1904 the Interstate League. In 1905 he managed the Olean, New York, club and in 1906, the Oil City, Pennsylvania, club, both in the latter league. Then, in 1907 Lawson was manager first at Butler and next at Connellsville, Pennsylvania, both teams in the Western Pennsylvania League. Finally, in 1906 and 1907, he organized the outlaw Atlantic League, in which he owned the Reading club and managed it to the league title in 1907.

Aspiring to grander things as an organizer, Lawson attempted in 1907 and 1908 to form the Union League, which he brazenly billed as a competitor of the American and the National leagues. Although most baseball historians have remained unaware of Lawson's effort, he definitely did get something going. A surviving letterhead for "The Union League of Professional Base Ball Clubs of America" identifies Lawson as president, gives a Philadelphia office address and phone number for the new league, and lists as cities in the league Brooklyn, Paterson, Elizabeth, Reading, Philadelphia, Wilmington, Baltimore, and Washington.

But the odds against successfully launching a new major league in 1908 (or any other year) were enormous. For one thing, getting a high caliber of players was crucial. One investigator's preliminary study of the Union League, however, could find no involvement by former or future major leaguers! So, who were the Union League's players? The same investigator also reported that attendance generally was poor at Union League games; Baltimore, for example, averaged about one thousand spectators.[1]

On the letterhead specimen mentioned above is a typed note, unquestionably written by Lawson, which indicates an insurmountable problem finally forcing Lawson to throw in the towel: "However, after making a successful start in the spring of 1908, 'Old Jupiter Pluvious' [*sic*] caused it to rain for forty days and forty nights, and, as the managers could not stand the financial strain and quit, therefore, the Union League did not complete the season's schedule." Before the Union League expired, however, the member teams had each played between thirty and thirty-five games over a period of about a month and a half. Many double-headers had had to be played in order to meet the chronic problem of rain-outs.

Elsewhere, Lawson claimed to have aided "to a considerable degree financially" the managers of the teams in the new league, in order to help them meet expenses during the maddening six weeks of rain. If he did indeed invest heavily in the new league, it might seem perplexing that he would not have pursued the organizing effort at least for one more season. In the spring of 1908, however, Lawson was already preparing to move away from baseball into a new line of work. Because he owned the Reading team which was to have figured in the new league, he had a lingering financial interest in baseball. Also, he made a brief (and inexplicable) return to an active baseball role in 1915 as the organizer and president of the short-lived Buckeye League in Ohio, following up with a short stint in 1916 as manager of his Reading team, which now was in the Class D Atlantic League. With these exceptions, however, Lawson abandoned baseball in 1908. From that point onward, his consuming interest lay in pursuing the opportunities beckoning him to the bright new field of aviation.

Any sober assessment has to conclude that Lawson was only a minor

AL LAWSON, MAGIC MAN OF BASEBALL, MAKES "DEAD" TERRITORY COME TO LIFE—HAS ORGANIZED SIXTEEN LIVE LEAGUES DURING CAREER AS A MAGNATE

AL W. LAWSON.

When Lawson made a brief return to baseball promotions in 1915, he brought with him a fully matured gift for press agentry. From a 1915 newspaper clipping; name and location of paper not known.

figure in the history of American baseball. Certainly as a player he made no lasting impression. He was of greater consequence as a manager, yet his teams were all in the bush leagues, mostly existing beyond the domain of organized baseball. True, he "brought out" John McGraw, but it is hard to believe that Lawson gave McGraw coaching which was critical to the latter's career or that McGraw wouldn't have made it to the top quickly if he had never been connected with Lawson. Lawson always claimed to have assisted and developed many other top players, too, but the claim can't be evaluated, because Lawson never gave specifics.

Even Lawson's work as a promoter of new teams and leagues doesn't seem to have had a major impact on baseball. Lawson was one of many colorful characters hustling the opportunities in baseball promotions at the time. He had a definite talent for this line of work and also some achievements, but his claim to have organized sixteen leagues may be a stretcher. Some of those leagues—for instance, his so-called third major league—probably had greater substance in PR hype than in the organizational features and resources needed for viability. Most of his leagues were outlaw leagues, and many were short-lived. Lawson also seemed more intent on moving on to new opportunities in league promotion than on sticking with any of his creations long enough to build them up and assure their survival.

If Lawson's contribution to baseball was small, baseball was nonetheless a happy career choice for him, proving to have great significance for his life. Certainly Lawson's timing was perfect; when he came to professional baseball in the 1880s, baseball was just taking off as a growth industry. Baseball historian David Voigt has called that decade "Baseball's Golden Era." As Voigt argues persuasively, growing urbanization and rising incomes in the industrializing America of the post–Civil War years had created a new potential market for leisure activities, and professional baseball was one of the earliest and most successful efforts made to cash in on the "leisure revolution" underway. In the 1880s ticket sales swelled, baseball teams proliferated, and the demand steadily increased for skilled practitioners in a wholly new occupational category: the professional baseball player. Among baseball's other social consequences, Voigt observes, was its opening of an important new route of advancement for many second-generation Americans, and poor boys generally, into a glamorous and relatively well-paying line of work.[2]

Baseball's growth was not confined only to the decade of the 1880s or to the ranks of the major league teams. As the foremost student of minor league baseball, Robert Obojski, has written, "The number of minor leagues continued to increase throughout the 1880s and 1890s as professional baseball became the nation's number one spectator sport."[3] Indeed, Obojski notes, minor league baseball maintained its expansion until it was finally ended in the second decade of the twentieth century by World War I and competition from alternative leisure activities. Thus, Lawson's twenty years in baseball coincided with boom times in that field of endeavor, and in result, both as player and manager and as a promoter of minor leagues and teams, he had access to abundant opportunities.

Baseball provided something else of obvious importance to Lawson. Voigt entitles one of the chapters in his history of nineteenth-century baseball "America's New Heroes," which indicates an important fact about baseball: it soon provided a wholly new kind of popular idol in America. Moreover, the adulation and prestige heaped on baseball players were not reserved for the stars of the major league teams alone. In those early days, playing on or managing the local nine could lift one suddenly to the pinnacle of celebrity among the crowd hanging around the pool hall, barbershop, or cigar store in any small city. Lawson became that small-time, small-town celebrity, which was a heady jump up the status scale for a lad who only a short while before had seemed destined for a lifetime of menial jobs.

The baseball years also provided other benefits for Lawson's life. For instance, as a seasonal activity, baseball left Lawson with much spare time for the pursuit of other interests. An unusual example which Lawson gave was a "college of phonography" which he claimed to have founded and operated "at the corner of Pearl and Court Streets, Buffalo, N.Y." Lawson also purported to be "one of the professors" in this institution. The system of shorthand taught there, he alleged, was one which his father developed and Lawson perfected. Unfortunately, Lawson reported little else about this enterprise, nor has a search of Buffalo city directories and other sources yet produced corroboration or a date for this venture. Nonetheless, both its offbeat character and Lawson's specificity about the location give a certain feel of plausibility to Lawson's claims.

According to Lawson, the largest proportion of his spare time was given to study. Lawson was no doubt a rarity at the time—a baseball player and manager who had pronounced intellectual interests. True enough, his primary education gave him scant grounding for conducting independent study, but he was inclined, anyway, to reject all existing authorities and proceed along his own lines of thought. Even during his first decade in baseball, while still in his twenties, he was thinking through the "big questions" in physics, economics, ethics, and theology and arriving at his own answers. Eventually, of course, the ruminations begun during the baseball days took final shape in the many books of Lawsonomy.

Lawson always claimed another great benefit derived from baseball: the opportunity to travel and see the world. For a small-town boy, life on the road was surely a great adventure—so much so, apparently, that Lawson remained on the road forever after. In fact, travel may not simply have been a taste acquired by Lawson during those halcyon days as much as a peculiar compulsion. For the rest of his life, his work always involved much travel, and he seldom stayed put in any place for more than a year or two. Even after Lawson married late in life, he remained on the road, stopping off to see wife and children in Columbus, Ohio, only several days each month. When death came to Lawson at the age of nearly eighty-six, he was still on the road—in a hotel room in San Antonio, far from family and home.

But clearly the most important thing Lawson got from his baseball years was a well-developed sense of himself as a builder and manager of big undertakings. In the grand scheme of things, his entrepreneurial work in baseball might not have been very important or impressive. It is even possible that Lawson's success, as measured by earnings, was only modest; absolutely nothing is known for sure about Lawson's income from baseball, although later in life he claimed to have made a "fortune" in baseball, and a 1915 newspaper article (almost certainly based on a Lawson press release) identified Lawson as a baseball "magnate." In the end, however, none of these reservations about his baseball promotional work matters nearly as much as the fact that he entered baseball as an aimless youth but left baseball apparently convinced that he could do anything and ready to aspire to grand projects. He probably always had a considerable self-confidence (fortified by an enormous ego), but baseball was the first field of action in which he could bring that self-confidence to bear on a succession of concrete entrepreneurial projects. Whether or not he got rich in baseball, therefore, he certainly acquired two things determinative of the rest of his life—a "can-do" attitude and a greatly heightened and focused ambition. Both carried him out of his easy-going life in baseball in 1908.

In that year, Lawson was thirty-nine years old and had devoted two decades of his life to baseball. However, his change of careers at that time should definitely not be attributed to some simple-minded notion of a mid-life crisis. The crisis in Lawson's life had actually occurred about a decade earlier, in the closing years of the nineteenth century, commencing when Lawson was only twenty-eight years old. It was at this time that he gave sharp scrutiny to his life and concluded that not all was well. Accompanying the many changes he made in his manner of living was an apparent summoning of a previously missing sense of ambition; this was revealed quite clearly by his new focus on baseball promotions after 1899. The importance of this crisis in Lawson's life makes necessary a return to this midpoint in Lawson's baseball years for a closer look at what happened then and also at that most curious product of Lawson's soul-searching—his novel, *Born Again*.

3

BORN

AGAIN

Although Lawson found many good things in his life in baseball—camaraderie, travel, the joy of playing a game he loved—there were, alas, some things on the debit side, too. His baseball cronies proved to be a seedy and dissipated lot. Earning more money than he had ever earned before, the eighteen-year-old Lawson began to discover, with the help of his associates, many new ways to spend his money. He acquired vices; the specific ones cited by Lawson were smoking tobacco in a pipe, drinking booze, and eating rich foods, especially beefsteaks. By Lawson's report, the consequences were dreadful: "So that masterful physique of his began to deteriorate and peculiar ailments began to attack him. His teeth began to decay and his legs started to wobble. He was getting rheumatism, both in his bones and in his brain."

Eventually coming to realize that "the more he got of [these vices] the unhappier he became," Lawson thought back to the days of his childhood, "before money had eaten its way into his pockets and [when] he knew nothing about vices and ailments." He lamented not being able to turn back the clock. "But then a great idea came to him. He said: 'The clock will not turn back for me but I can add many useful years to my life by turning back the vices.'"

When, in his twenty-eighth year, after ten years of sinking indulgence, he shook off all the vile habits, he found, "like magic, all of his physical and mental ailments left him." Then followed the systematic rebuilding of his life according to elaborate schemes of a vegetarian diet, hygiene, exercise, and right-thinking. Clearly Lawson's was not a rebirth in the conventional religious sense, nor did there appear to be any specific event or low point of despair in his life which precipitated a crisis causing him to see the light and mend his ways. Whether or not he had become as dissolute and decrepit as he claimed, certainly he had arrived in his late twenties at some general philosophical conclusions likely to foment feelings of great dissatisfaction with the whole drift of his life. These settled conclusions of his "studies" had implications for his conduct which reached far beyond merely ending the consumption of tobacco, meat, and alcohol and adopting new rules for healthier living.

Lying behind Lawson's new thinking on the requirements of good health was a much broader philosophy of life and the universe. Fortunately, because he set his views down in *Born Again*, it is possible today to know quite a bit about his philosophical conclusions and to examine their connection with the changes occurring in his life at that time.

Lawson supplied little information about the writing of *Born Again*—about such matters, for instance, as where he was at the time, under what conditions he wrote, and why he chose the form of a novel (all his other books were treatises). The only things known for certain are that it was published in 1904 in New York by Wox, Conrad Company and was written during the preceding four years. A printing made in 1907 has "Ninth Edition" stamped on the cover, which suggests that the book had good sales. Speaking against that conclusion, however, is the fact that, except for a brief notice in *Arena*, the book does not appear to have been reviewed in any literary or popular journals. The "Ninth Edition" also includes this statement: "Translated and published in the United States, Great Britain, Germany, France, Switzerland, Italy, and Japan." A German edition was, in fact, published in Germany, but whether editions appeared in the other countries claimed is not known.

Born Again is a utopian fantasy with a complicated plot woven from all the possibilities implicit in having several pairs of characters—some of them good and some of them bad—who look alike and happen to have the same names. Because it is also a "novel of ideas," its action is often punctuated by philosophical depositions, and the dialogue of the characters is weighted down with a leaden rhetoric not found in ordinary speech. Although one recent critic has judged *Born Again* to be "one of the worst works of fiction ever printed,"[1] Lawson maintained that "many people" considered it "the greatest novel ever written."

The novel is narrated in the voice of its hero, John Convert, who in many of his characteristics and biographical details is suggestive of Lawson. As *Born Again* opens, Convert is twenty-two and working his way from Australia to England "as a common sailor." His lack of "diplomacy" and "hypocrisy" immediately puts him at odds with the rest of the crew, with the result that "within two weeks I was thoroughly detested by every man aboard from the captain to the cook." After two weeks crowded with fist fights, his shipmates can stand it no more and throw him overboard. When his strength finally gives out, Convert sinks—only to find, however, that he is in shallow water and able to stand. With the dawn's arrival, he sees that he is within two hundred yards of the shore of an uncharted land, lying somewhere to the southeast of the Cape of Good Hope.

Thus Convert stumbles upon the ruins of Sageland, home of an ancient civilization of superior Sagemen. There he discovers Arletta, the last survivor of Sageland, who has been in a state of suspended animation for 4,230 years. Enraptured by her beauty, Convert yields to an impulse to kiss her, which brings her out of her deep sleep. Arletta's beauty proves to be of a very advanced kind: she is seven feet tall and has prehensile toes and no teeth. Nevertheless, Convert soon falls madly in love with her—only to be dashed by the discovery that she finds him repulsive and contemptible. She explains that he and all his fellows are merely Apemen, who have failed to complete the evolutionary passage from ape to human which Sagemen made many millennia ago. However, Arletta recognizes that the machinations of "Natural Law" have brought Convert to her and that he is, in fact, a reincarnation of her lover, the noblest man of Sageland; hence, Convert's kiss releasing her from her slumber was no accidental event. She therefore undertakes to instruct Convert in Natural Law, knowing that his task will then be to return to his fellow Apemen and proclaim what they must do to upgrade themselves.

When Convert protests that the present civilization of which he is a member has already risen to a very high level, Arletta takes him on a tour of that civilization by means of "mind-sight," an advanced technique of out-of-body travel perfected by Sagemen. Because this puts him under the influence of Arletta's perception, for the first time he sees familiar institutions accurately—and is appalled.

Among his eye-opening discoveries about the civilization of which he is so proud are these: those who toil to produce something get virtually nothing, while idlers who do nothing get virtually everything. While half of the world's population is overfed, the other half starves. Placing a higher value on gold than on all other resources, as Apemen do, is absurd idolatry. Iniquities and crimes are the everyday essence of business and finance and reveal the perniciousness of the institution of money on which they are based. The killing of animals is cowardly and cruel. Eating the flesh of animals is no better than eating human flesh, and a religion which justifies it has a cannibal for a god.

When Convert's mind-tour brings him to the United States, he sadly sees that the foregoing observations apply there, too, as well as a few others: equality in the United States is a fiction, behind which the strong trample down the weak. The legal system protects the strong in their depredations. Fraud is both the slogan and the practice of government officials, and money is the real "power behind the curtain." The revered leaders of business and finance are predators, who cover over their plunderous deeds with hollow philanthropies, the support of kept preachers and churches, and the outrageous motto, "God helps those who help themselves."

About all that he sees, Convert concludes: "I had seen these same things many times before without giving them any consideration, but now for the first time, I felt that there was something wrong with the people of the world. It seemed to me now that the entire system of human endeavor had been started wrong and was running along upside down. But what was the cause of this curious state of affairs? One word alone explained it all—*Selfishness*." At that same moment, the central teaching of Natural Law spontaneously takes hold of his mind:

"*Selfishness is the root of all evil; eradicate selfishness from all human beings and the earth will be heaven.*" (Emphasis in original.)

Having won her point about the moral backwardness of Apeman's civilization, Arletta goes on to enlighten Convert about the glories of Sageland. "The history of Sageland . . . ," she says, "was simply a record of heaven on earth, in which the inhabitants lived for and loved one another. The abolition of the pernicious system of individual accumulation was the direct cause for the existence of this beautiful state of affairs."

In place of "the pernicious system" Sagemen put "the scientific and mutually beneficial plan of united labor and equal distribution as decreed by Natural Law." This was a plan by which the state owned all the means and resources of production and required each citizen to work at "the employment for which it was demonstrated he was best fitted." In return, the state distributed to each citizen everything needed for well-being. Arletta observes that the reasonableness of this scheme is "so simple and easy of comprehension that any living thing above the intellectual line of the Ape should be able to understand it."

No longer able to hoard wealth for personal advantage and required instead to contribute to production in order to live, Sagemen "lost all evil desires and endeavored to secure the highest esteem of their fellow beings by perfecting themselves mentally, morally, and physically for the good of the community." In the rare instances when citizens shirked their share of work, they were declared insane and sent to asylums, which "within two generations became obsolete for want of inmates."

In many other ways, Sageman's system produced great social blessings and plugged the leakage of wasted labor. Because each citizen was economically secure and able to devote time to "higher and purer thoughts and purposes," all crime was eliminated, thus eliminating also the need for "police, detectives, judges, lawyers, juries, etc." Because the state owned all resources, no taxes were necessary and also no "tax collectors, lawyers, treasurers, auditors, clerks, book-keepers, etc." Because everything needed by citizens was free and money was valueless, the "evils of the financial system" were done away with, as also were "such occupations as money making, money lending, banking, broking, speculating, gambling, etc." Because all products went "straight from the storehouses to the consumers" in the most direct and efficient way, no use remained for "merchants, traders, jobbers, agents, salesmen, clerks, peddlers, etc." This rational system also left "no room for such parasites as tramps, beggars, and society loafers."

If any social problem remained in Sageland, it was that Sagemen "would gladly have worked themselves to death for the public good had not the State restricted the working hours and required each person to give proper care and attention to himself as well as the public." The average workday was held down to four hours. On grounds that the mental and physical condition of citizens has public consequences, Sagemen took a very strong interest in fostering healthful living among themselves; in fact, bad health, a violation of Natural Law, was declared to be also a criminal offense. Citizens were encouraged to divide the twenty hours when they weren't working as follows: study (four hours), physical exercise (two hours), "music, painting, and other intellectual amusements" (three hours), nourishment (three hours), and sleep (eight hours).

Although Sagemen believed that "men belong to the community, and not the community to man," this did not imply a smothering, totalitarian role for public authority, or the state. After all, what was the state in Sageland? Arletta answers: "Simply the people—all of the people—working harmoniously together as a unit." In this classless society, the state, considered as coercive power, had withered away. Little was left for the public authority but, in Friedrich Engel's phrase, the mere "administration of things."

Arletta relentlessly piles much further palaver about Natural Law on the head of poor Convert. He learns, for instance, that there are two great movers in nature—centrifugal and centripetal forces—which account for the eternal building up and tearing down of formations. The bodies of the animate beings are instances of these ever-changing combinations. In contrast, the souls which inhabit these bodies are immutable and fixed in number. Souls transmigrate, departing from beings who have died and entering newborn bodies. Because all animate beings possess souls, killing any of them—human or beast—is an affront to Natural Law. Because souls move back and forth across the line separating humans and animals, eating the flesh of any animal is tantamount to cannibalism.

Within each being who has a mind, the soul is the good element, possessing knowledge of what is right and striving to direct the being to act accordingly. The soul is that which links—potentially, at least—the being to the universal intelligence of nature. However, the mind doesn't necessarily take its guidance from the soul. Possessing no thoughts inherently, and also incapable of originating thoughts, the mind is nothing but a receptor of pre-existent thoughts. "Nature created both the mountains and the thoughts," Arletta observes, and she means bad thoughts no less than good thoughts. It is within the power of each individual to reject bad thoughts and admit only good ones—that is, to follow the counsel of the soul—but this is easier said than done. Typically, then, a furious struggle takes place within each individual between soul and mind—the soul for good, the mind for evil. The history of humanity shows that the mind has been the usual winner.

Yet there is "an evolutionary tendency of all living particles toward a final state of complete intelligence," Arletta reveals. Sagemen were a clear indication of what nature is striving to accomplish. Occasionally, too, persons of the caliber of Sagemen have appeared among Apemen, preaching the Natural Law doctrines of love, right-living, and rejection of selfishness. Usually they have been burned at the stake, crucified, or forced to drink hemlock. Eventually, however, their teachings will win the adherence of increasing numbers of Apemen and finally be accepted universally. As this happens, something else very unusual will also happen: the birthrate of the lower animals will fall, accompanied by a corresponding rise in the birthrate of humans. This is inevitable, because human bodies will increasingly be needed to house the fixed number of souls in the universe. Eventually all the lower animals will have disappeared, and there will be "nothing left on earth but the very best type of human beings for all souls to inhabit."

When nature has run its evolutionary course and humanity is made an integral part of nature's "final state of complete intelligence," the life of humanity will be the heaven on earth described above. Able at last to work together cooperatively "as a unit," humans not only will be virtuous but will also acquire tremendous new powers. In passing, Arletta discloses several wondrous things, in addition to mind-sight, deriving from Sageman's enhanced mental capacities. Sagemen communicated by telepathy, for instance, and were able to read each other's minds (an excellent method, Arletta notes, for encouraging all citizens to allow none but good thoughts into their minds). Through expanded mental power, Sagemen also learned to fly without mechanical assistance. In words remindful of those announced at the start of the old *Superman* radio program, Arletta adds that Sagemen "could jump over the highest building there is in the world today [and] run faster than any of your steam locomotives."

Great technological feats lie in humanity's future, too. Again, some of the marvels of life in Sageland are illustrative. Sagemen ate their food in gaseous form, which was made only from the nutrients contained in the solid food. This fostered moderation of intake (and also explained why Arletta and other Sagemen had no teeth). They lived under roofed cities and lighted their houses by coating walls and ceilings with substances impregnated with sunlight. They listened to music sent through the air without the use of wires from transmitting stations (that is, by radio, not yet invented when Lawson wrote). Finally harnessing centripetal and centrifugal forces, they sought to free the earth from its orbit and navigate it through the heavens. Their "ultimate plans were to visit, inhabit, and control the movements of all the great bodies of the universe." The project was premature, precipitating, four millenia ago, the destruction of Sageland and a worldwide cataclysm (recorded in the Bible as the Great Flood). However, when all of humanity have finally advanced and been organized as a unit, the attempt can be made again, and there is no reason why it should not succeed next time.

Winding up her disquisition on Natural Law (which contains much more detail and philosophical gloss than can be laid out here), Arletta explains that her death is imminent. Atmospheric changes occurring over a four thousand–year period make it impossible for her to survive any longer breathing today's air. She warns Convert that in the days ahead his moral courage will be severely tested. If he would remain ever true to Natural Law, he must heed this mandate: "Always consult your soul for advice. Do no act your conscience will not sanction." The heartsick Convert then takes leave of his beloved Arletta, "born again" and ready to keep his pledge to bring the glad tidings of Natural Law to his fellow Apemen.

The remainder of the book is made very complicated by the presence of Edward Convert, an evil cousin who looks like John Convert, Arletta Wright, who looks like Arletta of Sageland and is her reincarnation, and Arletta Fogg, a sin-drenched woman who is physically a carbon copy of Arletta Wright. (Surely, however, the Arletta look-alikes have teeth and lack her prehensile toes and great height!) Because no additional philosophical ideas are presented, there is no need to recount the melodramatic events arising out of the inevitable mistaken identities. Suffice to say that Convert dies a martyr to Natural Law, but his work is carried on by Arletta Wright and a faithful band of followers whom Convert has assembled through his street-corner preaching. On the last page, in her tribute to the meaning of John Convert's life, Arletta proclaims that "through his teachings a new dispensation has sprung into existence, and . . . Sagemanism is *born again.*"

Lawson's across-the-board condemnation of contemporary civilization was not an unprecedented stance for a young man to take, but his couching of his denunciations within a whole system of ideas about human life and the universe definitely was unusual. Although some of the specific ideas at which he arrived were familiar (for instance, vegetarianism, the transmigration of souls, the egalitarian reordering of life in utopia), others were certainly unique. As is also true for every later phase of Lawson's life and thought, there is absolutely no record today of what sources may have especially influenced the development of his ideas.

It should be noted, however, that Lawson's first venture into utopianism followed closely on the heels of a spate of utopian writing, mostly novels, published by Americans in the last dozen years of the nineteenth century. Those years are now recognized as the golden age of utopian writing in the United States; a study by Kenneth Roemer has identified one hundred and sixty utopian works pub-

"THEY WERE FACING AND POINTING IN OPPOSITE DIRECTIONS."—*Page 240.*

In the frontispiece of the first edition of *Born Again,* two of the three Arlettas confront John Convert with a choice between high and low roads of life. Photo courtesy of the Widener Library, Harvard University.

lished between 1888 and 1900, far more than had appeared in all earlier years of American history combined or in any equivalent time period in the twentieth century.[2] Inasmuch as *Born Again* has numerous
features—novelistic conventions as well as utopian content—found in
many of the utopian novels of the 1890s, it is not far-fetched to believe that Lawson was aware of and stimulated by the vogue for utopian books following in the wake of the 1888 publication of Edward
Bellamy's *Looking Backward.*

In calling for an economic system built along cooperative lines
requiring collective ownership and centralized management of all
means of production and providing for an equitable distribution of
the economic product, Lawson joined many other American utopians,
but any overlap of their views with those of Marx and Engels was coincidental or apparent only. Usually the utopians (and this included
Lawson) drew back from thinking in terms of class struggle, or from
hymning the necessity of violent revolution, or even from labeling
their schemes as "socialist." Their analyses of the crisis of late nineteenth-century capitalist civilization were typically couched more in
moral than in economic terms. Moreover, as Roemer observes, "The
utopian authors not only painted the evils of the present in moralistic
tones, they also envisioned the ultimate goals of the future as being
religious"—that is, they looked forward to "the creation of a moral
civilization where true Christianity could be practiced by every person
every day."[3] Roemer also notes the ample garnishing of many of their
books with Christian terms and images; a frequently invoked symbol
was the Resurrection. Perfectly aligned with this feature of the utopian books were, of course, Lawson's recounting of John Convert's
conversion and "rebirth," his Christlike preaching mission, and his
martyrdom.

The Christianity practiced by most professed Christians or preached
in most Christian churches was not, however, what the utopian authors meant by "true Christianity." They frequently denounced (as
did Lawson) what they believed had become a corrupt, perverted, or
irrelevant institutionalized Christianity in their day. The purified religious doctrines which they heralded for the utopian future typically
proposed to go back to the ethical teachings of Jesus. However, be-

cause they also often had much humanist and other content mixed in (for instance, the rejection of the doctrine of original sin), the new creeds were not strictly or exclusively Christian in character. Certainly this was true of *Born Again*'s religious teachings, which specified familiar Judeo-Christian values and norms of conduct but claimed to derive them from an austere Natural Law accessible to reason. Lawson's Natural Law also contained much non-Christian content, including the moral imperative of vegetarian diet, the doctrine of transmigration of souls, and a karma-like scheme of punishment or reward after death through the soul's movement up or down the scale of animate creatures. Some of these teachings strongly suggest the influence of theosophical thought on Lawson—and so, too, do his general conviction that God works in both the physical and spiritual realms not by miracles or direct intervention but only through the operation of Natural Law, and his acceptance of organic evolution as one element of the lawful processes ordained by God. If the influence of theosophy and Darwinism were there, however, they were hardly unique to Lawson; Roemer cites both theosophy and Darwinism as important sources for other of the American utopian authors at the turn of the century.

In *Born Again*, Lawson emphatically rejected the possibility of moving to a perfected social organization through a process of piecemeal reform. "You cannot make right by patching up wrong," Arletta tells Convert and then elaborates: "A new and effective system cannot be created by changing the features of an old and putrid one. An entirely new foundation must be constructed in order to insure solidity and strength."

But how are the uprooting of the old system and its replacement by a new one to be accomplished? No more acceptable to Lawson than piecemeal institutional reform was revolution, which would never work so long as selfishness remained in human hearts. For this reason, Lawson put his main emphasis in *Born Again* on the need for individual reform. "The surest way to make the world better is to begin with yourself," Arletta explains to Convert. From the religions of redemption, Lawson borrowed not only this strategic principle but also the techniques needed to advance it: preaching done by the faithful and the witness of their purified lives. As Arletta observes, humanity "must be taught differently and the teachers must set the examples, not merely offer advice."

In pinpointing human nature as the main source of the social problem and in giving priority to the upgrading of humanity's moral conduct, Lawson probably was out of step with most of the American utopian writers of his time. The latter more often viewed as "the Villain," according to Roemer, not human nature but "a bad environment that encouraged people to develop the wrong habits."[4] In her recent study of utopian fiction published in the United States between 1886 and 1896, Jean Pfaelzer reaches much the same conclusion. Among the more than one hundred utopian novels she examined, Pfaelzer finds a dominant view that "society, rather than original sin, determined a person's capacity for good and evil." Working from this view, she notes, her authors arrived at another important common position: "In utopian fiction the forces of good or evil need not battle for possession of the soul or social consciousness. For the elimination of evil, the society rather than the citizen must change."[5]

This difference between Lawson and other utopians was not absolute, of course, but rather one of degree. Although he accepted as the inescapable paramount fact that the forces of good and evil were indeed locked in furious battle for the possession of the soul, Lawson also shared the more general utopian concern for direct alteration of a bad environment as a means of fostering improved human conduct. And for their part, the other utopians generally agreed that the final securing of utopia also required that its citizens undergo a change of heart, an experience which might often have all the characteristics of a religious conversion. The difference of degree remained a significant one, however, which can be seen when considering the road to utopia specified in a more representative utopian work, Edward Bellamy's *Looking Backward*.

In this most famous of the American utopian novels, Bellamy has utopia follow almost inexorably upon the full evolution of certain organizational and technological trends already occurring in late nineteenth-century American society. The dénouement of these trends is the peaceful enactment by democratic processes of Bellamy's Nationalist program. In other words, for Bellamy, human nature is certainly not the recalcitrant thing or central problem that it is for Lawson; for the most part, a citizenry suitably adapted to the new Nationalist nirvana simply follows, in Bellamy's view, in the train of fortuitous environmental changes. Nor was Bellamy's optimism about the transformation of human life and conduct in this relatively effortless manner exceptional; typically, "late nineteenth-century utopian novels . . . announced to a concerned readership that the conditions for an egalitarian future were immanent in American capitalism," according to Pfaelzer.[6]

Yet Lawson did not stand completely alone in rejecting this view and giving precedence in his utopian strategy to an all-out campaign for the redemption of human souls. Charles M. Sheldon's In His Steps (1896), for example, adopted much the same position. This novel tells the tale of a revivalist movement initiated in a small Kansas city among members of a Protestant congregation, who agree to govern all their actions by their answers to the question, "What would Jesus do?" The movement catches on elsewhere, and as the novel closes, the resulting utopian transformation of America is well underway. Among American utopian novels, Sheldon's book was exceeded at the time (and subsequently, too) in popularity and sensational splash only by Looking Backward. Because In His Steps appeared in print only one year before the occurrence of the unusual "born again" experience which subsequently led Lawson to begin writing his novel in 1900, one can at least wonder whether it had some influence on the author of Born Again.

Lawson's doctrinal differences with Sheldon and other utopians influenced directly by Christianity remained numerous and substantial. Certainly no one would ever find Lawson's views compatible with orthodox Christian teachings; his doctrine of transmigration of souls would alone rule out that possibility. There is nonetheless a familiar kind of religious aura in Born Again, generated by its never-ending talk about the requirements of the moral law, by the novel's call to degenerate humanity to undergo a cleansing of conduct, and even by the novel's title. These features of Born Again are highly misleading, however, not because they aren't real features of Lawson's position but because they don't reach his ultimate teaching, which was profoundly heretical. Far from merely calling humanity back to subordination to the sovereignty of God and God's laws, in *Born Again* Lawson taught that, by observing God's laws, humanity could eventually share in God's power through technology. In effect, humans could become gods. When finally in complete control of their own evolution and destiny, they could not only create heaven on earth but reshape and manage the heavens. In spite of all the conventional moral and religious larding found in *Born Again*, it would be hard to imagine a book smacking more of that dreaded heresy of today, the human-centered philosophy of secular humanism.

Even as Lawson published *Born Again* in 1904, he had already begun to elude the force of its most important ethical teaching in his own life, and not long after he had entered the field of aviation, his utopian views began to change dramatically. By the late 1930s, however, Lawson returned to the utopian position he had outlined in *Born Again*. The Des Moines University of Lawsonomy, Lawson's most ambitious utopian enterprise, was the result; at DMUL Lawson sought to initiate not only the upgrading of human nature called for in *Born Again*, but also humanity's journey to Sageland. Thus this novel by the neophyte author and bush league baseball manager has a standing of the utmost importance in the life and canon of Alfred Lawson.

Lawson's earliest book is significant for other reasons, too. Lawson's easy assumption that technological advance is an unqualified good and his propensity for dreaming wild dreams of humanity's future technological prowess were lifelong attributes first clearly revealed in *Born Again*. Some characteristic features of Lawson's later writings also were first seen there—for instance, his extreme moralism, his proclivity for loosing furious philippics against contemporary civilization, and the pronounced Manichaeist and authoritarian character of his thought. In *Born Again*, too, can be found the first expression of many other ideas which later went into Lawsonomy, either unchanged or in slightly altered form; Lawsonomy was, in fact, simply another name for what Lawson called Natural Law in his novel.

Shortly after publishing *Born Again*, Lawson's urge to hasten the advance of Sagemanism apparently induced him to sign on with a "radical party" in New York City. Many decades later Lawson described this exotic episode as follows: "The newspapers of those days stated my book [*Born Again*] was radical. I didn't know I was radical until the newspapers told me so. Then I looked up a radical clan who had a back room in a tumble-down building on the Bowery in New York and spent a year talking for them from soap boxes."

But the flirtation with radical politics didn't last long. When the leadership tried to recruit him to help break up a meeting of a rival radical group, the disgusted Lawson pulled out altogether. Even while it lasted, however, the experience couldn't have been very satisfactory. Speaking from soap boxes was probably congenial to Lawson's mind, and also good practice for his later campaigns to move crowds and recruit followers. But the party's doctrine—whether one of revolution or of piecemeal institutional change—could not possibly have coincided with Lawson's pitch in *Born Again* for the transformation of souls.

What was called for, quite obviously, was not a radical political haranguing from soap boxes but rather the nobler kind of testimony of words and personal example found in the life of Jesus or Socrates. But Lawson eschewed entirely any undertaking along this latter line. Having disclosed the New Dispensation in *Born Again*, perhaps he thought there was no major leadership task left for him. If so, his conclusion certainly differed from that of John Convert, who took every opportunity to preach in the streets, who organized his growing band of converts into the Natural Law Society, and who ultimately went to his death as a martyr to the new truths which he proclaimed.

Many years later Lawson did put on Convert's leadership mantle, which Lawson probably believed all along was intended for himself. When this happened, Lawson renounced moneymaking and devoted his whole effort to promoting the spread of Natural Law (a.k.a. Lawsonomy). Perhaps, however, it would have been too much to expect a young baseball player to make such sacrifices and to take on the burdens of so arduous and unique a mission. Instead, Lawson contented himself with adopting many personal reforms and abandoning his aimless life as a baseball player. But his acquisition of a new set of standards and expectations for his life appears also to have generated in him a powerful new drive, which found an immediate outlet in baseball promotional work but by 1908 had sent him on his way toward even higher levels of enterprise in an entirely different field. Having come late to the entrepreneurial life and even professing to find it a violation of Natural Law, during the next twenty years Lawson nonetheless compiled a remarkable record in aviation as he pursued the main chance, toward the end of acquiring power and fame.

Part Two

FANNING

THE

AERONAUTICAL

BLAZE

Vincent J. Burnelli's career as an aviation designer was long and distinguished; included among the more than eighty aircraft patents which he had to his credit were the flying wing concept and the retractable landing gear. Born in 1895, Burnelli had started in aviation in 1914, when both he and aviation were very young. As he looked back in retirement, many gratifying recollections came to mind, especially of his experiences during those romantic earlier years of aviation. But among the colorful experiences crowding his memory, one stood out above the rest: while Burnelli was still in his mid-twenties, Fate had caused his path and Alfred Lawson's to cross. The subsequent passage of nearly half a century, far from dimming his recollections of Lawson, instead helped to highlight in Burnelli's mind the singular character of the man. Burnelli put it this way in recollections published in *True* magazine in 1962: "Alfred W. Lawson was perhaps the craziest man I ever knew."

When Lawson asked him to join the Lawson Aircraft Corporation during World War I, Burnelli recalled in his article, "I knew he was a visionary, but I liked him," and so Burnelli signed on for a couple of years. He soon learned that the teetotaling Lawson was "a wiry megalomaniac filled with nervous energy," who "didn't need alcohol to get high: his ego kept him floating in the clouds." His boss, he concluded, was "a cross between a crackpot and a genius."

Yet in his article Burnelli also hailed

Lawson as "one of the dynamic figures of the pioneer days of aviation." Moreover, Burnelli's brief stint under the leadership of the
vainglorious visionary had given the young aircraft designer an incomparable opportunity to share in an accomplishment of a very high
order: together, Lawson, Burnelli, and several other talented associates brought into being in 1919 the first airliner ever built. When
Burnelli then went on the plane's first flight, he also had probably the
most hair-raising and madcap adventure of his life.

Burnelli judged Lawson's most striking gift to be a "positive genius"
for "latching onto a new trend." Certainly the evidence backing this
assessment was ample in every phase of Lawson's life. But his precision timing and keen sense of opportunities were never more im-
pressively showcased than in 1908, when he plunged into the realm of
aviation. Flight in heavier-than-air machines was no more than five
years old and only three Americans had ever gone up; in fact, the
Wright brothers had made their first public demonstrations of their
airplanes only a few months earlier. Not many persons could even
have discerned a new trend to latch onto. Lawson, however, had already been obsessed for at least a year by dreams of aviation's golden
promise. He later explained in *Lawson: Aircraft Industry Builder* how
this had come about:

> During a visit to London, England [in 1907] I saw a cigar-
> shaped balloon with two men in it pass over the city at a speed of
> about five miles an hour. It was equipped with a motor, pro-
> pellers and was steered in different directions.
>
> That was the spark that set me afire and forever afterward
> I was unable to extinguish the aeronautical blaze that burned
> within me. So I began to feed the flame by reading whatever
> literature I could get hold of on what had been done up to that
> time in aeronautics.

Most of the literature which Lawson found treated only kites, glid-
ers, and balloons. What really fueled the "aeronautical blaze" burning
within him, however, were dreams of flying machines yet to be—high-
powered, fast, and huge. The blaze was made to burn all the more
intensely by Lawson's convictions that the future he envisioned was
really not very far off and that he was the man to make the vision real.

It would be wrong to conclude, however, that Lawson's new obsession was called forth only by a scent of fabulous opportunity for personal wealth or greatness in aviation. As the above quotation hints, the
cigar-shaped balloon which he saw over London in 1907 was for him
truly a burning bush. For the next twenty years the cause of aviation
was to be Lawson's religion. As historian Joseph Corn has observed,
Lawson was among the most fervent proponents of what Corn calls
"the winged gospel"—that is, the view that humanity's acquisition
of the ability to leave the surface of the earth marked a crucial turning point in human evolution, after which the development of aeronautics would produce a transformation of human life and an increasing beneficence in human relations. From the start, then, Lawson's
intense pursuit of power and fame in this new field was hallowed in
his mind by a conviction of having a calling or vocation in the fullest
religious sense.

Lawson's activities in aviation fell into two roughly equal phases.
During the first phase (1908–1918) he was primarily a propagandist
for the cause of aviation, using two popular aircraft journals as vehicles for promoting both the infant aircraft industry and his unusual
vision of a world brought to perfection through aeronautical progress. Never intending to remain merely a publicist, however, Lawson
made his move in 1917 into the aircraft industry for which he had
beat the drums so long. This was the prelude to the second phase
of his aviation career (1919–1929), during which all of his entrepreneurial energies were harnessed to the effort to create ever larger
airliners and a nationwide air passenger service.

4

AIRCRAFT

INDUSTRY

BUILDER

The year 1908 was an auspicious one in the infancy of American aviation. On July 4 Glenn Curtiss was awarded the Scientific American trophy for achieving a one-mile flight in his plane "June Bug" at Hammondsport, New York. Down at Fort Myer, Virginia, on September 9 Orville Wright made the first public demonstrations of flight in one of the Wrights' airplanes, remaining in the air a little under one hour in the morning and a little over one hour in the afternoon. Less than two weeks later, on September 21, his brother Wilbur stayed in the air for slightly more than ninety minutes at Le Mans, France. And in November of that same year the first issue of *Fly, the National Aeronautic Magazine* hit the newsstands of the United States.

In a lifetime studded with bold and chancy undertakings, Lawson's founding of *Fly* stands out as one of his most audacious. It appears all the more so, too, when one recalls that less than six months earlier, Lawson was knee-deep in the promotion of a third major baseball league. However, these two astoundingly disparate projects had at least one thing in common: when the Union League of Professional Base Ball Clubs of America folded, Lawson merely adapted its headquarters in the Betz Building in Philadelphia for use as *Fly*'s editorial offices.

Fly was not absolutely the first American aviation journal, but it probably was the earliest to be aimed at a general audience and to make heavier-than-air flight its main focus. Inasmuch as only three Americans had yet flown in airplanes, however, the market prospects for such a journal must have appeared dim to almost everyone but Lawson and his partner John F. Kelley. Presumably the two partners had to supply their own initial funding, for who else would have put money into so questionable a venture? If this line of thought is correct, then it suggests that Lawson must indeed have made good earnings in his baseball activities. Nothing is known about Kelley, but this can be said about his partner, who also was editor of the new magazine: Lawson had no firsthand knowledge of aviation, was not a pilot, engineer, or mechanic, had only a rather unpromising novel to his credit as a writer, and knew nothing about publishing or editing.

The inevitable didn't happen, however. An announcement in the second issue of *Fly* that the partnership of Lawson and Kelley had been succeeded by a corporation, the Aero Publishing Company, was followed in subsequent issues by sales pitches to the general public to buy shares in the new corporation (capitalized at $50,000). Whether many, or any, did so is not known, but that *Fly* stayed in business is certain. At the end of nearly one year of publication, Lawson reported a monthly circulation of 6,000 copies, not a very large base for a magazine selling at only ten cents a copy. However, over that same time, the number of display advertisers steadily increased, as did the proportion of advertisements in the magazine purchased by national firms.

After editing *Fly* for a little more than a year, Lawson sold his interest in the magazine. Moving to New York City, he proceeded to bring out another magazine, *Aircraft*, whose first issue appeared in March, 1910. Why he did this is not known, but possibly one reason was an eagerness to exploit the word "aircraft," which Lawson always claimed to have coined. (Rare, earlier instances of the word are, in fact, on record, but Lawson can legitimately take the credit for making it a commonplace term.) Under Lawson's editorship for the next five years, *Aircraft* became not only a commercial success but an authoritative voice for early American aviation. Even before the end of his first year, Lawson reported, the monthly circulation of *Aircraft* had reached 14,000 copies.

Even a quick thumb-through of those early issues of *Fly* and *Aircraft* yields strong hints as to why the magazines succeeded: aimed at both

The cover of the first issue of Lawson's first aviation magazine.

the general reader and the flying enthusiast, Lawson's magazines were interesting, informative, well written, and well illustrated. Their pages contained controversy, such as rival claims by early contenders to priority in aircraft invention and an ongoing debate of the comparative merits of balloons and airplanes. Interspersed among many useful statistical tabulations and survey articles (for instance, articles on aerial photography, types of airplanes, and the state of aviation in various countries) were articles of advocacy (for instance, "Why Ladies Are and Should be Interested in Ballooning") and occasional articles of advice (for instance, "How to Build a Gliding Machine"). Publication of signed articles from such luminaries as Glenn Curtiss and Count Zeppelin doubtless enhanced the appeal of the magazines. Because he also filled his pages with reports on air meets, the activities of flying clubs, and the latest events and developments in aviation, Lawson succeeded in making his magazines major vehicles of communication among the devotees of flying in the United States.

But any reader today will be especially struck by Lawson's skill in conveying the romance, excitement, and promise of aviation. Instantly noticeable in this respect were the dramatic multicolored covers adorning early issues of *Aircraft*; these depicted Lawson's conceptions of huge and exotic flying machines of the future, including some without wings. But even more noteworthy were Lawson's editorials. The occasional stylistic defects discernible in these editorials were more than compensated by their remarkable vigor and arresting content. The neophyte editor proved to be a master of the "booster" school of communication beloved of George F. Babbitt. Absolutely sold on the merits of his wares, he achieved considerable force in hyping them.

Many of Lawson's favorite editorial subjects were matters of immediate moment—such things as the baleful effect of stunt flying on the cause of aviation, the desirability of organizing aero clubs, the need to resist restrictive state laws against flying, the dangerous lag of the United States behind other countries in the development of aviation, and the need to educate members of Congress and newspaper editors about aeronautics. In the February, 1912, issue of *Aircraft*, he specified how airbags could be designed for the protection of pilots in crashes. Lawson also devoted many words to whooping up the splen-

AIRCRAFT

June, 1910   Edited by ALFRED W. LAWSON   15 Cents a Copy

The cover of an early issue of Lawson's second aviation magazine depicts an unusual vision of aviation's future.

did investment opportunities in aviation, urging go-getting youths to enter the field, and encouraging all men, ages twenty to fifty, to take up flying. But much of his editorial writing went far beyond such prosaic matters to treat the greater significance of aviation for human life and to project the glorious events in aviation lying ahead. Here Lawson disclosed some astounding views, but here also was a major source of the liveliness found in Lawson's magazines.

In Lawson's judgment, humanity's acquisition of the power to fly was simply the most momentous event in history. In one way or another he expressed this view often in his editorials—for instance, in the May, 1909, issue of *Fly*: "A grand new era has just dawned upon the human race in which there are no insurmountable walls to stop man's everlasting march forward. Flying has absolutely no limitations, and progress along this line once begun will never end. It will go on and on forever."

Continuing in the same place, Lawson explained how the capacity to fly had at last brought humanity into accord with a basic characteristic of nature: "For the first law of nature is Fly—or to use another term—motion. Take your microscope and look down to the minutest thing possible for the human eye to discover, or your telescope and look up at the greatest bodies that it is possible for man to bring within range of his vision, and you will find everything FLYING." And in the February, 1911, issue of *Aircraft*, he identified another respect in which humanity's improved facility for movement through flight harmonized with nature's pattern: "TRANSPORTATION is the most essential thing in life. The ability to shift substance from one place to another is apparently nature's foremost purpose; in fact, judging from the workings of the electrons and on up to the greater bodies in space, moving things about appears to be nature's only aim."

Lawson found nearly as much grand meaning in the struggle leading to humanity's breakthrough to flight as in the event itself. Surmounting the physical problems had not been the only, or even the main, difficulty facing the pioneers of flight. In the very first number of *Fly* (November, 1908), Lawson identified "a deficiency which retards progress": "Ninety-nine per cent (roughly estimated) of the human race lack imagination." Elaborating on this problem in the next

month's issue, Lawson introduced "Ordinary Mortal," a figure who
was to appear often in his pages:

> In creating ORDINARY MORTAL nature apparently made a se-
> rious blunder. It should have put his eyes into the back of his
> head instead of in front. This would save him the trouble of twist-
> ing his neck to see what is taking place in the rear which he
> spends all of his time doing. . . .
> To ORDINARY MORTAL the future has no meaning whatso-
> ever. As far as he is concerned it is a total blank. To study the
> future is a ridiculous undertaking. There is nothing there that he
> has not already seen. How could there be? Will the people of the
> future fly? Silly! Too foolish to answer. How can they when they
> have never done it before?

Appearing in his pages as often as the backward-looking, progress-
inhibiting Ordinary Mortal was Lawson's hero, "the individual who is
capable of expanding his mind to the point where he 'sees things' not
yet observed by others"—that is, the dreamer, who "if he dreams
above a whisper" is also called the crank. "There have been many
dreamers and some cranks on the subject of flying machines during
the past few years who have been held up to all sorts of public ridicule," Lawson observed. "It appears now, however, that some of them
are about to receive the reward successful dreamers usually get—
after they are dead—public applause."

Sometimes, however, Lawson was not so optimistic about the public
vindication of the dreamers of flight. Only slowly absorbing the fact
that humans can indeed fly, Ordinary Mortal was not ready to see the
tremendous importance of the fact or to accord the airplane any
higher status than a novelty or toy. Too, Ordinary Mortal was aided
and abetted in obtuseness by a third character in this drama—the scientist, who came in for much vilification and ridicule in Lawson's
pages.

Lawson first addressed the problem of the scientist in an editorial,
"The Scientist and His Rule," published in the December, 1908, issue
of *Fly*: "In this incomprehensible state called nature, scientists are
necessary JUST AS EVERYTHING ELSE THAT IS, is necessary. But

as all things excepting time and space have limitations, so have the scientists. They are NOT infallible. In fact, they are more often wrong than right." The problem, Lawson concluded, was that most scientists "are very narrow in their views of things they do not understand. They will make no allowance for anything that will not work according to rule—they are sticklers for rule—and if a problem cannot be solved according to their methods, then it cannot be solved at all." Virtually all scientists who have ever lived have therefore "added a little to human knowledge and upon reaching the end of their rules were most dogmatic in their belief that progress was to stop right then and there."

In these circumstances, it was obviously only the dreamer who could recognize that humanity's "greatest achievements are yet to be accomplished and . . . this is to happen OFF OF THE EARTH, NOT ON IT." In fact, in the very next issue of *Fly* (January, 1909), resuming the subject of "The Dreamer," Lawson made explicit that the scientist, not Ordinary Mortal, was the true antagonist of the dreamer: "Some people think that a scientist is a dreamer. Such an impression is erroneous. A good scientist will turn black in the face at the mere suggestion of such a thing. A dreamer cannot become a scientist until he can prove his dream. It requires a thousand years for a good dreamer to become a scientist. A bad dreamer can become one in less time."

Lawson recognized himself as a dreamer, of course, thus rendering beside the point and beyond cavil his deficiencies in scientific training. Besides dreaming of things not countenanced by the scientists' rules, he was charged to counteract the nay-saying of the scientists and to rally the tiny minority capable of sharing his capacity to dream. Flattering his readers with assurances that they were not Ordinary Mortals, he urged them to ignore the scientists' predictions of a limited future for aviation and to seize the abundant opportunities presented by the greatest field of endeavor of all time.

Also contributing greatly to the tone of feverish excitement found in Lawson's editorials and articles were his numerous predictions of wonders lying ahead in aviation. His short-term predictions were doubtless the ones of greatest interest to any of his readers who may have heeded his call to commit their lives and fortunes to aeronautics.

The predictions assumed a very rapid development of the physical capabilities of aircraft—something which only a dreamer and not a scientist or Ordinary Mortal would have assumed during aviation's first decade. Consider, for instance, the following predictions, made in the March, 1911, *Aircraft*, "as to what I believe will come to pass within the next ten years":

> The flying machine will be able to ascend to a distance [i.e., altitude] of over ten miles; the flying machine will be able to stay in the air for more than five days at a stretch; the flying machine will be constructed to carry more than fifty people; the flying machine will be made capable of crossing either the Atlantic or Pacific Ocean; the flying machine will have acquired a speed of more than 200 miles per hour.

A few years later, Lawson lengthened the time period over which some of these wonders would occur. In an article entitled "Natural Prophecies," published in the October, 1916, issue of *Aircraft*, he now hedged a bit about the advent of planes carrying fifty passengers and moving at two hundred miles per hour, predicting their appearance only sometime "prior to 1970." By that year, also, the plane will have completely replaced the horse (!) for military scouting and the leading nations will be acting on the realization that the nation which controls the air also will control the earth. In a remarkable bit of prescience, Lawson foretold, too, that by 1970 so many planes would be in the air that an air traffic control system would be imperative. As for the first nonstop flight across the Atlantic Ocean, Lawson adjusted his prediction only slightly, now maintaining that it would occur "prior to 1930." By that same date, also, air passenger service would have begun, using planes capable of moving at one hundred and eighty miles per hour.

Here were heady ideas for readers to absorb in 1911 and 1916. When Lawson erred in his projections for the near future, however, it was more often than not a matter of his being too cautious. For instance, in "Natural Prophecies" he proclaimed accurately enough that future planes carrying several hundred passengers and moving at five hundred miles per hour would cross the Atlantic Ocean in six-hour flights, but he missed this as an event of the relatively near future, claiming only that it would occur sometime "prior to the year 2500." Apparently even Lawson was capable of drastic underestimation of aviation's wonderful potential for rapid development.

But Lawson took pride in being not merely a dreamer but a "good dreamer," which meant that the predictions about which he was most enthusiastic concerned the remote future and therefore lay well beyond the probability of proof or disproof in the short term. As he wrote in *Fly* (May, 1909), "Just now the best tonic for IMAGINATION is to consider the possibilities and probabilities of aerial navigation during the next hundred or thousand years." This Lawson did often and his pages were filled with his findings from his wanderings in the distant future.

Readers of the November, 1909, issue of *Fly*, for example, learned in one editorial that flying machines of the future "will not have wings or planes of any kind, but will be manipulated by certain natural forces, which are as yet unknown to [humans]" and in a second editorial were told that these wondrous machines "will carry [humans] from planet to planet." Drawing on his unique vision first disclosed in *Born Again*, Lawson added that the human of the future "should eventually be able to guide his earth or any other celestial body through space with as much precision and certainty as he now guides his palatial steamship across an ocean." However, Lawson admitted that this capability was still quite a ways off—"perhaps a few million years from now," at which point the human type itself might be unrecognizable, perhaps having evolved "into a bunch of intelligence without eyes, nose, ears, mouth, legs, or body."

In "Natural Prophecies" Lawson hailed many more technological marvels of the future. By the year 2500, for instance, a gas eight hundred times lighter than air will be discovered, he claimed, which will lead to the merging of airplanes and dirigibles into aircraft capable of carrying immense loads. Prior to the year 3000, aircraft will have power plants drawing their energy from sunlight, and vacation options will include long yachting voyages at the higher altitudes of the sky. Also by that same date, "It will be discovered that the air at different heights contains various therapeutic qualities and that cures for almost any human ailment can be effected by residing at certain altitudes for certain lengths of time. Thus great ships of the air will be utilized as floating aerial hospitals."

These and many other technological wonders which Lawson perceived in the future rested, of course, on an advanced and almost inconceivable knowledge, which raised the questions of how, when, and whether such knowledge could ever be acquired. In one of the earliest issues of *Fly* (December, 1908), Lawson addressed these questions: "When man gets out of the economic rut he is in at present and becomes more unselfish and thinks less of his own stomach than he does now, he will devote much time to the study of universal laws, and to do this successfully he will have TO GET OFF THE EARTH."

The most important point to note here is the argument that scientific and technological progress on the scale found in Lawson's vision awaited humanity's moral progress. Because this had been the principal teaching of *Born Again*, it was hardly surprising that he should bring it into his magazine only four years later. Having been trotted out once, however, this message was never heard again in the pages of *Fly* and *Aircraft*. Instead, the teaching of his subsequent editorials rested on an inverted cause-and-effect sequence: now that humans had the capacity TO GET OFF THE EARTH, a great and never-ending burst of new knowledge and fabulous technological achievements would ensue, followed inexorably (at least in the long run) by an upgrading of humanity and a beneficent reordering of collective life. In other words, so profoundly excited and enthralled was Lawson by the advent of human flight that he reversed his position and became a "technological utopian"—one who saw in technology the key to great breakthroughs in solving the knottiest problems of human relations.

One major assumption on which Lawson's new view rested was that "getting off the earth" was the necessary and sufficient step to humanity's acquisition of fantastic new knowledge lying beyond the comprehension of rule-bound scientists. Lawson found several reasons to believe this. In the first place, flying was the greatest stimulus of all time to the dreamers on whom humanity's intellectual progress depended. Flying also meant liberation from the mental torpor induced by the strong gravitational tug and high atmospheric pressure felt at the surface of the earth. Finally, especially as it would certainly lead to interplanetary exploration, flying opened up new realms of inquiry previously beyond human access. As Lawson excitedly informed his readers in the June, 1909, issue of *Fly*, "A grand new avenue for human endeavor has presented itself for the greatest intellects to traverse."

This new knowledge of "universal law" would be applied to new technology, which in turn would be used to gather further new knowledge, and so on. Lawson's second major assumption was that this upwardly spiraling interaction between knowledge and technology would redound to the benefit of humanity; about this he never expressed a doubt. Nor did he have any uncertainty about how the benefits of this process would be effected; as Lawson informed readers of the May, 1909, issue of *Fly*, "There are some great men yet to come—who will become great through achievements off of the earth not on it." To these "great men" Lawson looked for the exploitation of new knowledge for human benefit. In fact, so frequently did Lawson refer to "great men" or "the great man" that the latter should be included with Ordinary Mortal, the scientist, and the dreamer in the cast of principal characters in Lawson's scenario of human progress. And that Lawson had in mind "great men" of a bold entrepreneurial stripe was quite clear: "The men who control the aeronautical industry of the future will be the greatest men of their time and in proportion to our present 'captains of industry' will look . . . as giants to pygmies."

The final major assumption in Lawson's new vision of the future was that all of the activities associated with "getting off the earth" were the key to the redemption of humanity and the perfection of collective life. In the February, 1909, issue of *Fly*, for example, Lawson made this forecast: "The time will come . . . when all national lines are wiped out as completely as the old tribal boundaries have been swept away, when there is but one people left in the world—the human race. Aerial Flight will be a big factor in breaking down these foolish national barriers, which cause men to fight each other like wild beasts, and [will] help to unite them in one big family with the earth as its home."

How "aerial flight" would have this effect Lawson did not say, but the answer can be inferred from some statements found in other editorials. In *Fly* of June, 1909, he wrote as follows: "The basis of economic law is combination, and humanity must eventually combine its efforts as a whole instead of antagonistic parts." Although the statement is grammatically flawed and awkward, the ideas presented are clear enough. The logic of economic activity in the modern world seemed to point toward the development of large-scale, coordinated enterprises, as evidenced by the giant trusts created and directed by the "captains of industry" of Lawson's age. Fully approving the trend toward combination and coordination, Lawson expected flying— "the greatest task [humanity] has ever undertaken" (*Aircraft*, March, 1910)— to provide the incentive for the greatest feats of organization yet seen. Responding to the unprecedented challenges and opportunities provided by aeronautics, the "great men" will create enterprises which cut across national boundaries, much like the multinational corporations of the present age.

In fact, in the March, 1910, issue of *Aircraft* Lawson predicted that "the time will come when one human brain will direct the whole aeronautical machinery in all parts of the world." Nor was this all; the organizational pattern in aeronautics would be adopted more widely, with this result: "And this human brain [directing the "aeronautical machinery"] will merely be a lieutenant working in conjunction with other lieutenants acting as directors of various other branches of human industry, and all directed by one supreme mind at the head of the whole human race." At this point, national lines will have been completely obliterated, war eliminated, and humanity at last organized as a unit—rather surprising yet ineluctable outcomes of a process of aeronautical development initiated on those wind-swept dunes at Kitty Hawk in 1903.

Yet there was even more to Lawson's vision of the effects of aeronautics on human life. Besides yielding a new-modeled organization capable of channeling human conduct in socially harmonious ways, future developments in aeronautics will also stimulate an evolutionary transformation of humanity. Buried in an article (*Aircraft*, September, 1913) on "Learning to Fly" was Lawson's earliest indication that flying will "develop a superior quality of mankind as far in advance of the

present man as the present man is in advance of the ape." Returning
to this startling contention in "Natural Prophecies" he presented some
of the astounding details of what he foresaw.

By the year 3000, Lawson wrote, so many great projects will be
under way in the sky that "the evolution of a superior type of man will
have begun—the alti-man—a superhuman who will live in the upper
stratas of the atmosphere and never come down to earth at all." Having worked for long periods in the upper atmosphere, "the alti-man
of the future will have become so reconstructed physically and ana-
tomically . . . that he will not require artificial oxygen for respiration."
But he will also have "so adjusted himself to that particular altitude
that it will be impossible for him to go below a certain depth of the
aerial ocean of which he will become a permanent inhabitant." Here
was the start, then, of a line of human evolution which by the year
10,000 will have a remarkable outcome: "two distinctive types of human beings will inhabit this earthly sphere—the alti-man and the
ground-man." According to Lawson, "The alti-man will be born and
live his whole life at the very top of the atmosphere and will never go
below a certain depth while the ground-man will live upon the crust
of the earth at the bottom of the atmospheric sea like a crab or an
oyster, and will never go above a certain height."

Possibly some of Lawson's readers not gifted with a great capacity
for dreaming might have viewed alti-man as a tragic figure, caught in
a trap of his own making and in any event, exiled from his true home
upon the earth's surface. Given a choice, many readers might also
have elected to remain among the crabs and oysters at the bottom of
the atmospheric sea. These were not Lawson's sentiments, however.
In his view, not only was the life of alti-man glorious, but alti-man
marked an enormous step forward in human development. Obviously the direct descendant of the "great men" of the less distant future and also of the "one supreme mind" and his lieutenants, alti-man
"will develop into the great mental force that will direct humanity's
future movements." Ground-man, too, "will be infinitely superior in
intelligence to our present people." However, precisely because he remained on the ground, ground-man will not be the intellectual equal
of alti-man. Ground-man's role will be that of "the subordinate who

will carry out upon earth the orders and plans of the super-human above," whose evolutionary development in response to the thinness of the air around him would make him increasingly ethereal.

"From the top of the atmosphere the alti-man will be able to view and study the heavens with a clearness and breadth of range that the density of the air denies the ground-man and therefore great universal laws will be made known and made use of by him that present man has no way of understanding," Lawson prophesied. "Many wonderful things will be done by the alti-man of the future," one of which things will be to control the weather. But Lawson declined to give more examples on grounds that they "would hardly be understood or appreciated by this generation." Moreover, all that alti-man is and does by the year 10,000 will be superseded in greatness after that date, when "man will then begin to develop in real earnest." Inasmuch as these amazing developments can all be traced back to humanity's acquiring the ability to fly, there is irony in Lawson's concluding observation: "by that time, however, aircraft will have become an obsolete method of transportation."

As preposterous or repellent as Lawson's vision may seem to today's readers, it was nonetheless intended to be a vision of a utopian future, and indeed, it shared some important features with the utopia Lawson put forth earlier in his novel *Born Again*. A central characteristic of both, for instance, was the organization of humanity "as a unit," and another common feature was the incredibly advanced technology enjoyed in both utopias. Probably included among the unspecified "many wonderful things" which Lawson claimed alti-man will do were all those dazzling feats of Sageman which Arletta described to the awed John Convert.

In one very striking respect, however, Lawson's later utopia differed greatly from Sageland. In place of the equal participation by all citizens in public policy making which characterized Sageland, Lawson now envisioned the subordination of most citizens to the direction of a ruling class (or stratum, in both physical and sociological senses). Underlying this major difference were several others which should be noted.

First of all, Lawson's two utopias were built on contrasting assumptions about humanity, both as it is today and as it will be in the future.

Into the discussion of both utopias Lawson introduced a twofold division of humanity, but the specific categories and uses of the division differed. In *Born Again* he presented the two human types of Apeman and Sageman but looked forward to the overcoming of this division when all of humanity will have finally reached the advanced stage of Sageman. In contrast, in his aeronautical writings the change ran in the other direction. As humanity improved over time, it did so in increasingly divergent tracks, which ended in the emergence of two entirely distinct human types—the dominant alti-man and the subordinate ground-man.

Linked to these different views of present and future humanity were also some different views on how utopia will be reached. According to *Born Again*, the arrival at utopia hinged on the elimination of the "system of individual accumulation," and this in turn depended on the dislodging of selfishness from human hearts; thus, humanity's organization as a unit awaited the moral awakening signified by Apeman's transformation into Sageman. Lawson's editorials and articles in his aviation magazines offered another teaching, however. These specified a different route to utopia, in which the first steps were to be taken by dreamers and "great men" acting to exploit the exciting opportunities offered by aeronautics. Through their entrepreneurial initiatives large-scale organizations will be developed which will eventually produce the desirable result of mankind acting as a unit. No change of heart by Ordinary Mortal will be required as a precondition for this to happen; social behavior will necessarily improve, once the "great men" have changed social conditions and gotten Ordinary Mortal tucked properly into place in an improved organization of society.

As for the "great men" who will initiate these valuable changes, it is plain that their claim to act will not be based on anything like John Convert's advanced moral rectitude but on superior imagination, intelligence, and efficiency. Unlike Convert, they will not directly be moral reformers, nor will their actions be the result of altruism; the good which they do will be a happy by-product of their successful pursuit of ambition and opportunity.

One major consequence of the actions of the "great men," of course, will be a change in environmental conditions so drastic that it will in-duce the eventual emergence of a permanent ruling class of superior alti-man. But this event, too, will redound to the benefit of humanity, including the great mass of inferior ground-men below. The product of an evolutionary "selecting out" of the traits of high intelligence and great capacity for efficient action, alti-man will presumably long since have also been brought to virtue through an enhanced capacity to acquire knowledge of Natural Law. Thus, humanity will finally have attained what many philosophers from Plato to the present have sought: the union of power, knowledge, and virtue in rule by the minority of the absolute best.

The many unique features of Lawson's new position on utopian reform did not mean it was totally lacking in connection with other movements of thought of that time. For instance, that was the heyday of "technological utopianism," as Howard Segal has demonstrated, and therefore Lawson was definitely not alone in finding in the advance of technology the answers to the age-old problems of human life.[1] Lawson's call for "great men" to forge humanity into a harmonious unit by creating gigantic industrial organizations may also have been an echo of the voguish thought of the era hawked under such labels as "Taylorism," "scientific management," and "the science of administration"; in any event, Lawson was not the only theorist then to look at problems of human relations as amenable to solution through rationalized, hierarchical, large-scale organization. Finally, Lawson's thinking obviously also contained an element of Social Darwinism, an ideology which at that time still had proponents, at least at the level of popular culture and in certain business circles.

Noting the consistency or overlap of Lawson's new position with several contemporary strands of thought does not explain, however, why Lawson made such a major change in his position on utopian reform so soon after publishing *Born Again* in 1904. Lawson never said why, nor is there evidence of any intellectual influence so possessing his mind as to cause him to modify his position. It seems far likelier, in any event, that the explanation lay not in the influence of new ideas but in his "conversion" to the new "religion" of aeronautics.

Lawson was one of many to be excited about the advent of human flight and to predict that big changes in the human condition would

result from humanity's conquest of the air, as Joseph Corn has revealed in *The Winged Gospel*.[2] However, it was unlikely that anyone else
showed quite the degree of Lawson's enthusiasm or drew conclusions
quite as extreme as Lawson's. As *Born Again* showed, Lawson already
had a pronounced interest in the moral upgrading of human life, but
it was an interest which was at least equaled in intensity by his infatuation with the imagined technological marvels of the future, especially
technology having to do with off-the-ground transport. It is therefore
rather easy to see why the discovery of heavier-than-air flight would
have had such a profound effect on him. If humanity had already
taken the first step toward all the glorious technology of Sageland,
why could not more steps follow quickly? And surely the ensuing development of such a revolutionary new technology would also have
important social consequences.

Once Lawson's very ample imagination was put to work on exploring this possibility, it was not surprising that he came to some remarkable new conclusions, including the view that aeronautics will be the
vehicle for the utopian transformation of humanity and society. To a
certain extent, Lawson may not even have been aware of just how important a switch he had made in his position when he now had moral
and social reform follow upon technological change.

On the other hand, he may indeed have had a good understanding
of what switch he was making and why he was making it. If Lawson's
ardent pursuit of money and success in baseball conflicted glaringly
with the teaching of *Born Again* and called into question the sincerity
of his commitment to the cause of humanity's moral reform, this
would be no less the case as he ventured into the field of aeronautics.
However, the troublesome conflict would be nicely resolved by his
new line of thought. If the cause of humanity's moral reform could be
advanced by the progress of aeronautics, and if the progress of aeronautics entailed bold action by dreamers and "great men," then Lawson had all the legitimation he could possibly want for the pursuit of
his exalted ambitions. Already recognizing his talents as a dreamer,
he yearned also to be one of the "great men" meeting the challenge of
"the greatest task [humanity] has ever undertaken." Possibly at this
time he may even have had his mind set on becoming the "one human

brain [who] will direct the whole aeronautical machinery," if not in the whole world, then at least in the United States. How reassuring and inspiring it must have been, then, to know that in following such self-asserting ambitions he was really acting to further humanity's immediate welfare and also the glorious day when alti-man, perched in the sky, would preside over a perfected global society on earth.

Even in his earliest days as editor Lawson gave clear signs of aspiration to greater things in aviation, and in 1921 he acknowledged that he "did not go into the aeronautical movement to become a publisher, he merely did that work as a means toward an end. He had other plans. . . . It was to the founding of a great system of airlines that his mental energies were mostly directed."

This frank admission and the abundant evidence of his ambitions should not becloud the equally important fact, however, that in forwarding his own ends through his journals, Lawson also served the cause of aviation well during its infancy. No one came forward sooner to champion the cause, and no one could have done the job with more splash, energy, or enthusiasm. His longest-range views on aviation's development and its impact on society may have been bizarre, but his forecasts for aviation's development in the very near future were sound enough, as also were his editorial positions on the immediate issues and problems facing aeronautics. His magazines also played a valuable role as organs of communication among the scattered early devotees of flight. As editor, Lawson did much good work in promoting air meets and aero clubs, in encouraging American newspapers to give serious and accurate attention to aviation developments, and in making the case to Congress and the military branches for support of aeronautics as a vital matter in the national interest. Above all, Lawson was an early and effective advocate of the future military and commercial utility of aircraft at a time when such a future was not obvious, even among many aviation enthusiasts.

But it is unquestionable that his journals also served Lawson extremely well as means for furthering his own ends in aeronautics. Being at the center of an intelligence network, he acquired a complete knowledge of aviation developments throughout the world and a reputation as an authority on aviation. (For instance, his views were frequently solicited by magazine and newspaper editors, and in 1912 he prepared the glossary of aviation terms for a dictionary published by the National Press Association.) He also knew, and was known by, virtually everyone involved in American aviation and many active in aviation in Europe, too.

Very quickly, Lawson made earnest moves to exploit his reputation, contacts, and "insider" knowledge. As early as 1908—and then at times subsequently, he claimed—he tried to entice various rich men (according to Lawson, they included John D. Rockefeller and Henry Ford) into backing him in the manufacture of airplanes. In 1911 he was a major mover in the organization of the Aeronautical Manufacturers Association, of which he was elected vice president. In that same year he negotiated with the French airplane firm of Henry Farman to open an American branch, with Lawson as president—an arrangement which inexplicably fell through, however, even after it was announced publicly. In 1913 Lawson made another attempt—but again unsuccessfully—to enter the aeronautics industry in association with a European firm; this time his target was the Schuette-Lanz Company of Germany, with whom Lawson proposed to offer dirigible service between New York City and Washington, D.C.

A self-promotional activity of a different kind came in 1913, the year in which Lawson learned to fly. Purchasing an airboat, he began to fly daily the thirty-five-mile distance between his home in Seidler's Beach, New Jersey, and a landing place near his office in Manhattan. Although a Chicago businessman had beaten him to the distinction of being the first air commuter, Lawson could claim the honor of being the first to be his own pilot for the daily trip. The novelty of the achievement brought much publicity in the press for the pioneer air commuter.

Even greater publicity on a more heroic scale would have come Lawson's way if another of his projects in 1913 had come to pass. During that year the neophyte pilot made a vigorous search for the financial backing needed to build a monoplane of his own design and then to fly it solo across the Atlantic Ocean! Although Lawson claimed once again to have approached many prominent, rich men for the needed support, it was doubtless his good fortune that none was interested.

Lawson learned to fly in 1913. From *Lawson, Aircraft Industry Builder.*

Although this advertisement indicated that an enormous new Lawson factory (center) would open in Green Bay within a month, it was never built. From *Aerial Age Weekly*, March 25, 1918.

However, in Lawson's view, this was just one more instance of Ordinary Mortal being unable to grasp the out of the ordinary.

Lawson's activities during his first decade in aviation showed how determinedly he sought a breakthrough to greatness in his newly chosen field of endeavor—or at least an opening which would permit him to move beyond being merely a cheerleader and drum beater standing on the sidelines. But not until the entry of the United States into World War I was he finally able to get a foothold in the aeronautics industry. In 1917, securing financing in Green Bay, he founded his first aircraft manufacturing company, the Lawson Aircraft Corporation; in response to War Department encouragement, the firm then made prototypes of two military trainer planes, which were pronounced excellent by government inspectors. However, to Lawson's frustration and dismay, orders for large-scale production were maddeningly delayed, and his prospectus for a steel-plated plane, the "Lawson Armored Battler," was rejected outright.

Already well known as a leading advocate of military air power, Lawson now threw himself into an intensified campaign to awaken government officials to the crucial role of aircraft in prosecuting the war. In a barrage of sixteen bulletins issued serially to Congress and the press throughout the first half of 1918, he argued that the war could only be won in the air and that, in view of Germany's air superiority, the war would be lost unless a remedial effort on a huge scale was undertaken at once. Lawson proposed an immediate increase of the billion-dollar government appropriation for aviation to a staggering ten billion dollars. In order to meet effectively the German advantage in aircraft, he argued, the United States needed to have 40,000 planes in service in 1918; if the war continued into 1919, as Lawson confidently predicted it would, the American air fleet should be upped to 100,000 planes. But before the war was won, Lawson believed, even more planes would have to be sent to the front: "If my plans are followed quickly, 200,000, if not then 500,000."

Lawson acknowledged that his recommendations would be viewed as extreme, but in his fourth bulletin to Congress he explained that it was necessary to have a program that "will not only catch up with the Kaiser but . . . will go far beyond him," a program that "will surprise him, outwit him, swamp him." Lawson then described the kind of manager needed for successfully prosecuting a program on the scale he had outlined:

To even conceive of such a program will require the mind of a man who was born for the purpose.

It will require the mind of a man who understands aeronautics from top to bottom both in theory and in practice, a man with great organizing ability, foresight and a practical man with imagination, a real admiral of the air in every sense of the word.

No other man will ever be able to plan the conquest of the air but an airman. One who has been schooled in airmanship as a pilot and in industry as a builder; one who makes airology both a science and a religion; a man who breathes aeronautics with every breath he takes in and emits it from every pore in his body.

Lawson didn't suggest who would fill the bill, but had he been asked to take on the job of "admiral of the air" (or "air generalissimo," as he labeled it in another bulletin), he would undoubtedly have thought himself up to the task.

Orders for all those new planes should, of course, be placed only with American firms (e.g., Lawson's). In response to the argument that there would be a major problem moving so many planes to France, Lawson had an ingenious answer: fly them. He proposed stationing, every fifty miles across the Atlantic, the hulls of steamships having specially prepared flat tops for plane landings. Along the route of Lawson's "Transoceanic Float System," he maintained, planes could be safely flown to the front lines in Europe within forty-eight hours of factory completion in the United States. "Furthermore, if the United States Government cannot find any better man to supervise the job, I am willing to do it myself," Lawson offered, adding a guarantee to make the float system operational within four months.

Lawson's float system elicited official interest but was never tried during World War I. (Although Lawson always claimed thereafter to be the inventor of the aircraft carrier, his claim is subject to challenge. However, the first flight across the Atlantic Ocean was made using a modified version of his float system. The Navy seaplane NC4 made the flight in May, 1919, via a route over which destroyers were stationed at regular intervals.) Nor did Lawson make any headway with his argument on behalf of air power as the key to victory or with his campaign for increased government investment in airplanes. Finally, the Lawson Aircraft Corporation never got into production, for just as the company at last expected to get an order for one hundred planes, the war ended. Not only were Lawson's forecasts for the duration of the war and for America's aircraft needs far off the mark; his dreams of eventual domination of the American aircraft industry had still not gotten off the ground. But no one was more indefatigable. Not pressed into service as America's wartime admiral of the air, he nonetheless looked ahead to what might be accomplished along that line in peacetime.

5

THE

COLUMBUS

OF THE

AIR

Armistice Day, 1918, as Vincent Burnelli later recalled, brought high spirits and bedlam to Green Bay. Uppermost in Burnelli's mind on that day, however, was the question of what would happen to the Lawson Aircraft Corporation. He and the other employees had good reason for concern. The company's financial backers had been fetched by the opportunity to sell planes to the United States government during the war and, in anticipation of big sales, had authorized Lawson to build a new factory building. But now the war was over, before the company had even had a chance to start production. Probably the investors would be eager to pull out and declare their losses as a patriotic contribution to the war effort.

At an afternoon meeting at the factory, Burnelli reminded Lawson of a speculative discussion the two of them had once had about the potential of airplanes as commercial passenger carriers. Burnelli now proposed that the Lawson Aircraft Corporation stay in operation but convert to production of airplanes for peacetime passenger service. At the same time, he suggested, Lawson could create another corporation to operate the passenger service, using planes bought from the Lawson aircraft factory.

Burnelli hardly had to twist Lawson's arm. Perfectly aligned with Lawson's longstanding vision of aviation's commercial potential, Burnelli's proposal had probably already taken form in Lawson's mind. In any event, seeing the opportunity to make the planes, to operate the passenger service, and to get control of the next phase of aviation's development, Lawson enthusiastically concurred. When he spread the plan before the company's financial backers, however, the latter were not impressed and voted to dissolve the company.

Thoroughly fired up by his new dream, Lawson asked his employees to stand by without pay for several weeks while he sought new sources of financing among his many contacts in New York. One good prospect, he believed, was John McGraw, now manager of the New York Giants. With his old friend's help, Lawson confidently expected also to get funds from many baseball owners and players, "good sports in all respects," whom Lawson felt sure would "go for such a romantic venture." His instincts had misled him, however; the New York campaign proved to be a complete bust. Apparently baseball players were Ordinary Mortals too, unable to see the future. Of course, McGraw may simply have been holding to his vow never again to get mixed up in a Lawson scheme—a vow taken nearly thirty years earlier when Lawson had left McGraw stranded in New Orleans.

Although Lawson had no choice now but to lay off his factory employees, he continued the search for money. An increasingly frantic Burnelli put him in touch with one of Burnelli's relatives, John Koerner, a prominent businessman and civic leader in Milwaukee. Speaking to a group of the city's leading lights, whom Koerner had assembled, Lawson sketched a rose-hued picture of Milwaukee as the future Detroit of the aircraft industry. This time the Lawson charm and soft soap got results. Soon a syndicate was formed in Milwaukee to provide $100,000 to start up the reorganized Lawson Airplane Company on the understanding that major financing would come from sales of planes to a newly formed Lawson Airline Transportation Company.

Lawson had, in fact, gotten himself into a very difficult position, needing now to plan and organize an air passenger service (and to find the funding for it) at the same time that he began to build airliners. The tasks were made more difficult by the fact that no one had ever before operated an air passenger service on a large scale or built for this purpose the large planes which Lawson and Burnelli had in mind; in fact, no one had even heard the words "airliner" and "airlines" until Lawson introduced them at this time. But if the tasks facing Lawson were monumental ones, he had at least gotten the foothold he needed: the money with which to keep his aircraft company alive and to build his first airliner.

Lawson had something else going for him, too: the services of a first-rate technical staff, three of whom, in addition to Burnelli, had been with the Lawson company in Green Bay. Although Lawson always insisted that he was the inventor of the airliner, he was not a designer or engineer. At most, Lawson could sketch the main features of the plane he wanted but then necessarily had to leave it to others to reduce his vision to a detailed, workable plan. Precisely how the design of the first airliner was arrived at remains a mystery, but Burnelli and possibly others on the Lawson staff had to have played at least as large a part as did Lawson. In fact, the latter's greatest contribution probably was the recruiting and leading of such talented specialists. Most of them were much younger than the fifty-year-old Lawson; Burnelli, for instance, was only twenty-six. Like Burnelli, some of the others were to go on to distinguished careers in the aviation industry.

While Lawson devoted most of his time to the search for more capital, Burnelli secured space for the Lawson factory in the loft of the Cream City Sash and Door Company, hired the remaining technical staff, and got operations underway. Five months later, the airliner's components were completed and taken to the State Fair grounds, where Lawson had obtained the governor's permission to assemble the plane. The mayor of Milwaukee cooperated, too, by ordering the City Maintenance Department to prepare a runway to Lawson's specifications on city property. Within another month the plane was assembled. Following a public reception and the removal of the wings, the plane was hauled laboriously (with the help of brewery horses!) in a two-day trip to the runway five miles away, where the wings were put back on.

What Lawson and his colleagues had produced in such short order was a totally new kind of very large airplane. Nearly fifty feet in length, it had twin four hundred–horsepower Liberty engines, biplanes spanning ninety-five feet, an unfilled weight of six tons, and a capacity for two pilots and sixteen passengers. Although some military planes were larger, Lawson's plane was the largest non-military

LAWSON CREATOR OF THE **AIRLINER**

THERE HAS NEVER BEEN A PERSON HURT IN A LAWSON AIRPLANE

FACTS ARE BETTER THAN FANCIES

HERE IS A FACT — AN ACTUAL PHOTOGRAPH OF THE GREAT 26 PASSENGER CARRYING LAWSON AIRLINER PASSING OVER NEW YORK HARBOR ON ITS 2500 MILE HISTORY MAKING TRIP FROM MILWAUKEE TO WASHINGTON AND RETURN.

LAWSON AIRLINE COMPANY - MILWAUKEE, WISCONSIN, U. S. A.

An advertisement featuring Lawson's splendid sixteen-passenger airliner. Only when movable seats were placed in the aisle could it carry the twenty-six passengers claimed by Lawson. From *Aerial Age Weekly,* January 26, 1920.

plane built in the United States to that time. Elsewhere, enterprising persons had begun to convert much smaller war planes for use as passenger planes, but Lawson's was the first plane, certainly in the United States, and probably in the world, to be designed and built expressly for the purpose of hauling large numbers of passengers as a commercial undertaking.

The plane incorporated many novel features which became standard in later airliners. Thanks to the rigid construction of its walls, floor, and ceiling by the use of plywood paneling, the plane's cabin was kept totally free from the usual interior crosswires and bracing used at that time. Extending through the front half of the fuselage, the cabin measured approximately twenty-five feet in length, five and one-half feet in width, and seven feet in height. Its ample space accommodated seats for pilot and copilot at the dual controls at the front end, eight upholstered wicker chairs on each side of the cabin, an aisle running between the rows of chairs, and enough headroom for even a tall person to stand and walk freely throughout the cabin.

Next to each of the sixteen passenger seats was a large window made of celluloid. Enclosed in front and on the sides by celluloid windows and overhead by a roof, the pilots' section was entirely insulated from the elements—an innovation bordering on sacrilege in a day when pilots attached an almost mystical significance to flying in open cockpits. The pilots' section was open to the rest of the cabin, and the single door permitting entrance to the cabin was immediately opposite the pilots' seats on the left side; in all other major features of layout, however, Lawson's plane looked much like today's airliners, of which it was the clear original.

Of course, the question of whether it would fly remained to be answered. There was never any question about who would be captain when the flight tests were made. Uneasy about both Lawson's flying skills and his eyesight, however, Burnelli strove mightily to secure an expert pilot to share the controls. The problem was finding one willing to consent to Lawson's theory that the pilot would serve merely to steer, while Lawson, as "Captain in Command," would give flight orders and *control the engines*.

A pilot not too proud to put up with this bizarre arrangement was hard to find; several applicants walked out of interviews in a huff. But finally Burnelli had a live possibility in Charles L. Cox, a young man from Denver reputed to have been an RAF ace in World War I. When they met Cox, both Burnelli and Lawson had some reservations. A professional ballroom dancer who weighed one hundred and ten pounds, wore spiffy clothes and kid gloves, and shook hands delicately, he didn't fit their image of an air ace. Moreover, Burnelli found Cox's knowledge of the planes he had flown during the war curiously incomplete and inexact. Still, it was hard to get around the fact that Cox was reputed to have shot down nine German planes during the war, and he also was willing to give Lawson's concept of pilotage a try. Setting aside their doubts, Lawson and Burnelli hired him.

As a result of some heavy promotion by Lawson, a large crowd turned out on August 22, 1919, to witness the champagne christening of the plane. As Burnelli recalled, "Money was being bet all over the field—it was even money that the Lawson Airliner would never leave the ground." When Lawson and his colleagues got on board and started the engines, a representative of the mayor announced that the crew intended that day only to test engines and controls by taxiing on the runway. At least, that is what Lawson had told the mayor. But neither prudence nor caution was Lawson's long suit. Not even waiting for the engines to warm sufficiently, he shoved the throttles full forward for a fast taxi down the field. As the plane moved with increasing speed toward a bank of trees at the end of the runway, Lawson couldn't resist the temptation. "Steer for those trees and clear them by fifty feet!" he ordered.

While Cox and all others on board, except Lawson, held their breath, the plane lifted abruptly and cleared the trees by a wide margin. Soon the plane was moving smoothly over Milwaukee, its large control surfaces responding perfectly. Only when the gas supply ran low, about twenty minutes later, did the crew realize they didn't know where they were. Not able to find the field they had started from, Lawson ordered Cox to put the plane down in a pasture. As it hit the ground in a series of bounces, the plane lost all four tires to blowouts, which sounded like cannons going off. So much dust and noise were stirred up that fire engines and a huge crowd rushed to the scene. The plane was not damaged, however, and the crew emerged uninjured amid the settling dust, elated with the results of the unscheduled flight test. They had proved that their leviathan not only could leave the ground but was beautifully responsive in the air, even with Lawson and Cox at the controls.

Replacing the tires and refueling the plane where it sat, the crew took off from the pasture several days later, on August 27. After they had flown ten miles north of Milwaukee, Lawson suddenly ordered Cox to reverse direction and head for Chicago, where they set down fifty-eight minutes later at Ashburn Field. While relaxing on the field and basking in all the attention the plane was getting, Lawson's colleagues were astounded to hear him announce to reporters that the plane was on its way to New York City and Washington! Once again, Lawson had caught his partners off guard. Expecting to return to Milwaukee that same day, they had nothing with them but the clothes on their backs. Ecstatic about the continuing fine performance of their plane, however, they quickly fell into enthusiastic step with Lawson's impromptu plan and made arrangements by phone for money and clothes to be sent ahead. Possibly, too, they had already begun to share Lawson's vision of the incomparable opportunity and adventure which their airliner had opened to them. In any case, who could resist the vigorous direction provided by the self-assured dreamer and "great man" who was their Captain in Command?

During the next three months, Lawson and crew flew the plane on a two thousand–mile odyssey which took them to Toledo, Cleveland, Buffalo, Syracuse, New York City, and Washington, D.C., and then back to Milwaukee via Connellsville, Pennsylvania, Dayton, Indianapolis, and Chicago. As Lawson no doubt sensed from the start, the flight had a rare potential for helping him drum up publicity and support for his projects. At every stop, Lawson took up local notables and reporters from all the local papers, and the resulting newspaper coverage was immense. Lawson and his airliner were front-page material everywhere along the route.

Seizing the opportunities presented at every stop, Lawson laid out his vision of a transcontinental airline network, soon to be made available by the Lawson Airline Transportation Company. Cities acting quickly to cooperate with the effort by providing adequate airfields and other services and facilities could expect to be served in the network, he promised. But events were moving ahead rapidly, he stressed. As early as the spring of 1920, Lawson claimed in Chicago, he expected to have one hundred planes flying between New York and San Francisco and serving ten intermediate cities. No doubt his colleagues were amazed to learn, too, that in order to meet this huge demand for planes, the Lawson Airplane Company had already gone into full production. So great was the demand, in fact, that Lawson was reported in the Cleveland papers as "thinking of spending some of his money on his fleet of liners in the Martin factory here, if his own plant doesn't produce them fast enough." And Syracusans learned that in order to produce all the needed planes fast enough, he might open a branch plant in Syracuse.

These tantalizing prospects would materialize, of course, only if

The great flight of Lawson's airliner churned up much gratifying public notice for Lawson and his projected airline service, as in this story in the *Dayton [Ohio] Sunday Journal,* December 7, 1919.

Cleveland, Syracuse, and the other cities showed immediate, tangible support for what Lawson was trying to do. Individuals were also welcome to buy stock in Lawson's airline. Whether any did is not known, but his pitches to chambers of commerce and city government officials generally were very effective. Everywhere along the route of Lawson's grand flight, city officials fell into line vowing to provide fields, runways, and airports. All were eager to insure that their fair cities were beneficiaries of the next revolution in transportation history.

Because Lawson's newspaper coverage in New York was enormous (and also because Lawson had sent two publicity agents ahead), by the time he reached Washington, D.C., many government officials were eagerly awaiting the chance to talk with him and see his plane. Lawson was as eager to talk with them and in particular to lobby for a bill which would authorize the Post Office Department to let contracts with private persons for the carrying of airmail. Somehow Lawson had already managed to develop good contacts with several important members of Congress, including House Speaker Joe Cannon and Senator Warren G. Harding of Ohio. Through Harding's good offices, Lawson was able to arrange a visit on September 21, 1919, by a large group of dignitaries for an inspection of the airliner.

Included among the distinguished guests that day were General "Billy" Mitchell, Harding, six other Senators, Secretary of War Newton Baker, Mrs. Baker, the Bakers' young daughter, and the Reverend John Cavanaugh, former president of Notre Dame University. Lawson took this group (minus Mitchell and Harding, but plus five others) on board for an inspection and brief sales pitch. Overwhelmed by the opportunity for showmanship and glory afforded by that moment, however, Lawson suddenly ceased his lecture, ordered the engines revved up, and closed the door. His alarmed guests could not respond as quickly or effectually as their inspired host could act. Taking the controls himself, Lawson then shot the plane down the runway (again, without waiting for the oil to warm up) and seconds later the plane was airborne.

Totally indifferent to the wails and protests rising from his captive passengers, Lawson seemed intent on showing them the Washington sights from the air. But finally he responded to Father Cavanaugh's pleas and agreed to bring the plane down. When he tried to do so, however, he found that the heavy load greatly extended the plane's movement down the runway, the upshot of which was that the plane was about to end in a patch of tree stumps at the end of the runway. As Lawson jerked the plane aloft again, it nearly stalled, and then the engines began to backfire. Only Burnelli's fast action with a hand pump kept the engines from dying for lack of sufficient fuel pressure.

When the plane was finally brought safely to the ground, the terrified passengers quickly scampered out—all, that is, except Senator Hoke Smith of Georgia, who had passed out. Several men had to help the three hundred–pound Senator out of his seat and off the plane. In spite of their harrowing experience, however, the Senators and Secretary Baker expressed enthusiasm for Lawson's big plane. In the 1920 session, Congress passed and the President signed the law which Lawson had pushed, which would allow private contractors to haul airmail.

The scary moments over Washington were not the only ones to occur on the great tour. At Toledo, Cox almost had the plane on the ground at Maumee Park before noticing that the field was littered with debris—wooden stands and other remnants of the Dempsey-Willard heavyweight championship fight which had just been held there. Quickly taking the plane up, he barely got it over some trees and then immediately had to lift the right wing to clear the span of a bridge. And in the approach to landing at Syracuse, Lawson cut the throttles too soon, which brought the plane down short of the field in a cabbage patch; its right wing then skidded along the ground, making cole slaw. The plane ended in a ditch. This pitched it onto its nose at a forty-five-degree angle, tumbling all passengers into a heap at the pilots' seats and causing minor damage to the nose section.

More serious danger confronted the plane and crew during the first leg of the return trip from Washington. On the day Lawson had planned to leave Washington for Dayton, reports came in of very bad weather over the Alleghenies, causing the Army Air Service to ground its flights there. Lawson wouldn't hear of such a thing, however. By now he had announced that San Francisco was the plane's ultimate destination and he was eager to get on with the triumphal

The team which built and flew the first airliner in 1919. From left: Vincent J. Burnelli, chief engineer; Lawson; Charles L. Cox, pilot; Andrew Surini, mechanic; Carl Schory, mechanic. Photo courtesy of George A. Hardie, Jr.

flight. "The Lawson Airline will operate on schedule regardless of weather," he announced grandly.

The Captain in Command had made his decision, and that was that. Still his colleagues must have thought he was crazy, especially since an important fact had come to light while they were in Washington: the Charles Cox, RAF captain and ace, whom they thought they had hired was in Australia! The Charles Cox they had hired had been in the RAF, all right, but had been a second lieutenant and had not flown during the war. When he joined the Lawson team, he had had exactly *eight hours* of flying time, in single-engine planes after the war was over! Of course, by the time the crew learned this, their Charles Cox had logged many more hours at Lawson's side and had been doing a pretty good job. In spite of his alarming lack of experience, the plane had not crashed—at least not so far.

On the flight to Dayton, Lawson soon learned why the Army had canceled all flights. Flying into severe air turbulence and overcast skies, Cox took the plane (whose cabin was neither heated nor pressurized) to 17,000 feet, where he found no calmer air but at least was over the clouds. By the time the plane began to get low on fuel, about five hours into the flight, the clouds had dissipated enough for Lawson to make out a river below. Declaring it to be the Ohio River, he commanded Cox to follow it. Spotting no level places for a safe landing in the mountainous terrain, Lawson finally ordered Cox to put the plane down on a domed field. A sudden draft, however, brought the plane down early in a field filled with corn shocks. Although the corn shocks helped bring the plane to a quick stop, corn was strewn everywhere in the wake of the landing. The plane ended tail up, with its nose buried in a shock. Once again, all on board landed in a heap at the front of the plane and were rescued only when the tail had been lassoed and pulled down.

The flyers then learned that they were near Connellsville, Pennsylvania (which Lawson referred to afterward as "Collinsville," apparently not recalling that he had once managed the local nine there); the river they had followed was the Monongahela, not the Ohio. Upon learning this, according to Burnelli, Lawson quickly surmounted embarrassment by replying, "Of course. I changed the flight plan to Pittsburgh en route."

Because a takeoff was impossible anywhere in the vicinity, Lawson had the plane dismantled and sent by flatcar to Dayton, where it was repaired and overhauled. Before he was permitted to do this, however, the farmer whose crop had been destroyed (by both the airliner's landing and the trampling feet of gawkers) demanded settlement. Turning on the charm, Lawson got him to accept payment made in stock of the Lawson Airline Transportation Company. In fact, before Lawson and crew left Connellsville two weeks later, the previously disgruntled farmer had parted with ten thousand dollars for additional shares!

The flight from Dayton back to Milwaukee via Indianapolis and Chicago went without incident. When on November 15, 1919, the five weary flyers returned triumphantly to the city from which they had started nearly three months earlier, they received a welcome fit for heroes, including a reception by a large committee of bigwigs, a motorcade, and a banquet several days later. When the celebrations were over, Burnelli and Cox departed, ending their brief connection with the latest great saga in American aviation.

Surely this was the grandest moment of Lawson's life. He had been hailed everywhere on the trip with such accolades as "the man who made Milwaukee famous," the "new air magnate," the "air king," and most thrilling of all, the "Columbus of the Air." Now, as he returned home, he found himself described in the local press as "Milwaukee's genius of the air." At the banquet in his honor, Lawson declared that "the future of the airliner is assured. We have already demonstrated the practicability of it." If anyone should be so rash as to doubt it, Lawson had only to point to his thick file of press clippings, all of which soon were neatly pasted into a gigantic scrapbook documenting the sensational first flight of the first airliner.[1] All told, four hundred passengers had been hauled.

"My ambition," Lawson had declared in Indianapolis, "is to do for air transportation what Robert Fulton did for water navigation." Could anyone have doubted now that Lawson was, in fact, the "great man" who would push aviation to its next level of development? Certainly none at the banquet did. But the Columbus of the Air couldn't perform the herculean task unaided, he explained. "It is now up to the people of Milwaukee to continue to support the enterprise which promises to place Milwaukee in the van of airline passenger service," Lawson told the banqueters. He didn't need to press very hard. At that moment, all present were eager to shove more money into the hands of the genius whom they were certain would make Milwaukee the aircraft capital of the United States.

Up to a point, that is, they were eager to meet Lawson's money needs. However, there probably was an early limit on the amount of money which his backers—a large number of small-time investors in Milwaukee—were able to provide. Certainly their backing fell far short of the money needed to give reality to the glowing reports Lawson had been spreading of factories humming along in round-the-clock production. Indeed, Lawson had no more than enough money to keep

A commemorative march composed in 1919 by Edgar W. Croft, Chicago reporter and passenger on several legs of the flight of Lawson's airliner. Through Croft, who had connections with Wilbur Glenn Voliva of Zion City, Illinois, Lawson sought financial support from the famous community of flat-earthers.

going in the very short run. For all the elements of his ambitious schemes to mesh, he would need to bring in much more money soon from sales, new investors, or other sources such as government airmail contracts. But so strong was Lawson's faith in himself as a "great man" and in the soundness of his plans that he probably continued to believe that all difficulties would be surmounted. In the meantime, to help move matters along in the desired direction, he would continue doing what had seemed to work so far—that is, intensively hyping the wonderful new age of air transportation lying just around the corner, to be brought to realization soon by Alfred Lawson.

Lawson's announced plans were breathtaking, both in scope and in the speed with which they were to be executed. He reiterated his earlier announcement of daily airline service between New York City and San Francisco, with ten intermediate stops, to begin by July 1, 1920— that is, only about one-half year later. The trip would take thirty-six hours. Night planes would be equipped with showers and sleeping berths. Food service would be available on planes and in airports. A system of "lighthouses" (Lawson's word for beacons) at hundred-mile intervals would guide his night flyers. By July 10, ten planes would fly the Chicago–New York route daily. Business executives could expect to leave Chicago at 8:00 P.M. and be on Broadway the next day at 6:00 A.M. Soon there would be additional routes between Chicago and New Orleans, Seattle, Winnipeg, Quebec, and Washington, D.C., respectively. By 1921 passenger fares would be as low as rail fares.

In April, 1920, Lawson also announced what must have been soothing news to the ears of his backers: the Lawson Airplane Company had just taken orders for ten airliners. Four were to be delivered in June, three in July, and three in August. The selling price of each was fifty thousand dollars. No mention was made, however, of the fact that the buyer was the Lawson Airline Transportation Company, which was hardly in a position yet to use or pay for the airliners.

There were two problems with Lawson's hype: it failed to bring in the needed additional capital, and it was quickly belied by events. Lawson was put constantly in the position of having to revise plans previously announced, as due dates arrived but no planes were delivered and no passenger service was inaugurated. A big boost did seem

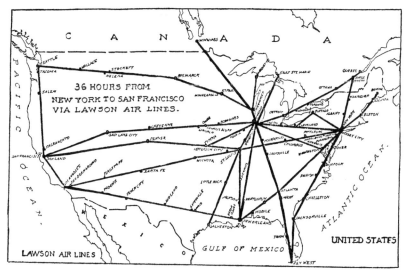

In 1919 Lawson envisioned this national airline network. From *Lawson, Aircraft Industry Builder.*

to come on September 13, 1920, however, when the Post Office Department announced it was awarding to the Lawson company the first
large airmail contracts ever awarded to a private firm. In return for
carrying daily mail for one year over three routes (Pittsburgh–Saint
Louis, New York–Pittsburgh–Chicago, and New York–Washington,
D.C.–Atlanta), the company would receive $685,000. If Lawson could
have those three routes in operation by March 15, 1921, the effective
date of the contract, the Post Office's money would start rolling in. It
was a big "if," but it was enough to keep hope alive.

A major aspect of the shortfall between Lawson's huckstered claims
and his performance was his delay in producing even one more airliner. Part of the delay resulted from his decision to relocate in a factory worthy of his grandiose dreams of full-scale production. After
buying the recently vacated Fisk Rubber Company building and an
adjoining three acres of land, he had spent several more months
equipping and organizing the factory, hiring additional workers, and
building a shed hangar for airplane assembly next to his factory.

But the major source of delay was Lawson's determination to make
his next plane even bigger and better than the first one. Although the

original airliner had generally performed well, it was underpowered; Lawson therefore decided to add a third motor. At the same time, he increased the wingspan to one hundred and twenty feet and lengthened the fuselage in order to accommodate space for airmail and a larger cabin capable of seating twenty-four passengers. Other novelties to be incorporated in the next plane were a restroom; a pilots' compartment divided from the cabin by a door containing a glass window; an adjustable pilot's seat and overhead sliding panel allowing the pilot to fly open-cockpit style, if he preferred; a chute allowing mail to be put on or taken off feeder planes while the airliner was in flight; and a door located on the right side at the rear of the cabin (instead of by the pilots' section, where the door in the first plane jammed everytime the plane upended). In addition, the new plane was to have a passenger compartment convertible into something like a Pullman sleeping car. Overlooking no attention-getting detail, Lawson even included a shower bath. Because only twenty gallons of water would be provided, however, no more than one lucky passenger would be able to enjoy this luxury.

The new plane, called the "Midnight Liner," obviously entailed a considerable amount of redesign; moreover, much of the experience gained in constructing the first plane could not be put to use in constructing the next one. For both reasons, by July 15, Lawson's revised deadline for delivering just a single plane, the Midnight Liner was nowhere near completion. In fact, it was not finished and ready to fly until early December, 1920.

By this time, Lawson's situation was a desperate one. A whole year had lapsed since his triumphant return flight from the east coast. Not only was he now far behind schedule; buying and equipping his factory and building the luxurious Midnight Liner had drained his money. But his need for more money merely to meet weekly payroll and other operating expenses collided with an ominous new reality—the tightness of money accompanying the major financial recession which began in the fall of 1920. If there had ever been any chance that Lawson could meet the start-up date of his airmail contract or post the required $100,000 performance bond, it now fell to zero, and he had no choice but to ask the Post Office to release him. Lawson's straitened circumstances were revealed by a full-page ad carried in the *Milwaukee Journal* of January 23, 1921, in which the self-proclaimed "wonder man of aviation" offered to pay 10 percent interest for money.

Apprehensive stockholders, at first only disappointed by Lawson's slowness, now went beyond the stage of polite inquiries. They demanded answers: Why hadn't the big things which Lawson promised happened? When were they going to see a return on their investments? Lawson could only plead for continued patience and support. The rough winter weather even made it impossible for him to fly the Midnight Liner and hope by that means to bedazzle his supporters into coughing up more money.

With no money at hand to continue operations, Lawson had to lay off most of his factory workers indefinitely. Now, as he awaited the spring and decent flying conditions, the long period of inactivity stimulated ever stronger and angrier demands from his stockholders. Finally, a revolt in early May among some of the stockholders produced an ultimatum to Lawson: get the plane in the air or resign.

With the coming of spring, Lawson had realized that unsuitable flying weather was no longer the major factor constraining the test flights of the Midnight Liner. The hard truth was that he didn't even have enough money to move the plane to the flying field. Anticipating the unlikelihood of more money coming in, Lawson had already decided on a great gamble: he would fly the plane from a makeshift runway behind the factory. To a man, his engineers and technicians were appalled, protesting that the three hundred–foot runway was far too short. In the face of the unanimous opposition of his staff, however, Lawson gave the order to prepare the runway. If the plane carried a minimum load and took off into a strong wind from the south, both he and his new pilot, Charles Wilcox, believed that they could get the plane up.

For weeks, while his men continued to roll the strip, Lawson waited for a south wind. But it never arrived before the ultimatum from his stockholders came. Now truly desperate, Lawson decided to fly the plane on Sunday, May 8, 1921. There was still no wind from the south, but his alternative was to be fired the next day. As Lawson climbed into his seat next to steersman Wilcox, possibly he was emboldened by recalling the dictum of the Columbus of the Air: "The Lawson Airline will operate on schedule regardless of weather." In the absence of a stiff wind to help lift the monstrous plane, however, Wilcox and the two mechanics on board must have been skeptical about the chances for the plane ever to leave the ground.

Its engines warmed and all other preparations completed, the Midnight Liner slowly began its takeoff roll down the runway. As the heavy plane strained to attain takeoff speed, however, it was resisted by the softness of the runway. When the end of the runway was reached, the plane still was not moving fast enough for a takeoff. Now beyond the runway, it was moving along a neighboring farmer's field. That was all right; the use of this field had been part of the contingency planning for the takeoff. However, nobody had taken into account that farmers plow their fields in the spring, and this particular farmer had just completed his plowing of this particular field. That, too, might have been tolerable—but unfortunately, the farmer had plowed in an east-west direction. Running athwart the north-south path of the plane, the furrows added one more impediment to the efforts to get the plane up to sufficient speed.

Lawson was determined to fly, however, and ordered Wilcox to take the plane up. Giving full lift to the elevator, the dutiful steersman got the plane's nose up and the wheels off the ground. Under the circumstances, getting the plane airborne was an achievement, but it was not a sufficient one: as the Midnight Liner slowly ascended, a farm house loomed ever closer ahead, and it was apparent the plane was still not high enough to clear it. When Wilcox banked left to avert collision, the left wing caught some tree branches, which next put the plane into a collision with a telephone pole. Now carrying a wooden pole and entangled in wires, within another several hundred feet the plane had been dragged back down to the ground. When it hit, so did the right wing, which spun the plane around in the opposite direction.

Although the plane sustained substantial damage, none of the four on board was injured. As onlookers came up to inspect the remains, Lawson emerged and calmly announced that the plane would soon be repaired, at a cost of ten thousand dollars. But Lawson's backers had had enough and refused to provide the money. Having run out of

Lawson's Midnight Liner crashed on takeoff on May 8, 1921, and his Milwaukee company followed soon after.
Photo courtesy of George A. Hardie, Jr.

stratagems and options and still unable to find money elsewhere, the
Columbus of the Air soon had no choice but to throw in the towel.
The Lawson Airplane Company was declared bankrupt in 1922. Just
like that, what had seemed only several years earlier to be the hottest
thing going in Milwaukee (especially after Prohibition had closed the
breweries) came to a surprising and sad ending.

No longer in the airplane business, Lawson turned his primary attention during the next three years to writing the first two volumes
of Lawsonomy. His faith in the airlines idea and in himself as the
man needed to bring the idea into reality did not die, however. Still
bedazzled by the prospect of fast coast-to-coast air service, he continued to ponder its requirements. If it were to attract customers, he
concluded, long-distance air passenger service would have to offer
amenities approximating those of rail passenger service. Even more
important, in order to get the air fares down while still keeping the

undertaking economically viable, planes would need to carry very large passenger loads. The requisite large planes were certainly congenial to Lawson's mind—but how could planes be designed to carry huge numbers of passengers in comfort? Finally he hit on the answer: put the passengers in double tiers.

In 1926, the Lawson Aircraft Company came to life for a third time, having in this incarnation a New York address and a factory near Plainfield, New Jersey. Soon news stories began to appear heralding the wonders of the forthcoming new two-tiered monster. Meanwhile, Lawson also proceeded to secure patents on his two-tier concept in the United States and the major European and British Commonwealth countries. Because the patents covered the application of the concept to boats, buses, and trains as well as airplanes, Lawson had hold of a potential moneymaker. Both the Pennsylvania and the Long Island Railroads were early licensees, and Lawson himself built a prototype of a two-tier bus. Characteristically, even while he was attempting to recover his foothold in aviation, he allowed his attention to wander to another great enterprise—the Shelf Bus Company, through which he aspired to operate a New York–Washington, D.C. bus service using two-tiered buses.

Lawson's bus service never materialized, but even if it had, the "super airliner" which he simultaneously pursued would have remained the truer expression of the Lawson genius. More than merely wonderful, the superliner was fantastic for its time. As Lawson envisioned it, the gigantic new plane would have a sixteen-seat officers' compartment, seats for one hundred and four passengers arranged in double tiers, dining room, library, sleeping berths, bathrooms and showers, and capacity for ten thousand pounds of mail or express matter. Having a wingspread of two hundred feet and a fuselage of one hundred feet, the plane would weigh fifty tons when loaded. It would be powered by twelve (!) four hundred–horsepower Liberty engines (six "pullers" and six "pushers"), which would drive the plane at one hundred and twenty miles per hour. Served by a crew of six, the plane would fly nonstop between New York and San Francisco in twenty-four to thirty hours. One intermediate refueling would occur in midair. Even more novel, mail and *passengers* destined for or originating at intermediate points would transfer to or from the superliner in flight through trap doors and chutes linked to feeder planes. As had happened once before in Lawson's career, however, several announced completion dates came and went; like the two earlier Lawson aircraft companies, the third one had chronic problems in obtaining adequate financing. Finally the cabin and fuselage were done in late 1927 and the beginning of service was projected for spring, 1928. But again the deadline was missed, and press coverage soon ended altogether. The plane was never finished, and by the end of the decade of the 1920s Lawson had severed his ties with aviation forever.

Albeit fascinating, Lawson's aviation work in the latter half of the 1920s did not have nearly the importance of his work in the early years of that decade. His later work is of interest today mainly for its disclosure of Lawson's continuing obsession with gigantic airliners and the pathos of his attempt to regain a lost initiative. Although his vision of airliners capable of carrying over one hundred passengers was prophetic, his large plane—constructed of wood, wire, and sheet metal and incorporating a cabin designed in two tiers—did not represent the wave of the future. Moreover, because he had had his usual money problems, he could not even afford to equip his new leviathan with state-of-the-art engines; unable to wheedle eight hundred–horsepower engines from the Army (whom he tried to interest in the plane's troop-moving potential), he had to settle for an offer of World War I–vintage four hundred–horsepower engines. In sum, if his great superliner was to be the means for recapturing his leading place in aviation, the quest was doomed from the start. Hindsight makes clear that his most creative and promising work in aeronautics was already behind him. So, too, was his greatest opportunity to achieve fame, power, and fortune in the aviation industry. If he had once seemed actually on the verge of becoming the Robert Fulton, Cornelius Vanderbilt, or Henry Ford of air passenger service, as he so often claimed, that possibility passed forever with the crash of the Midnight Liner.

An observer can't help but be struck by the common pattern discernible in Lawson's rise and fall in baseball in 1888–1890 and in aviation in 1919–1921. In both instances, he rose rapidly on the basis of demonstrated and celebrated achievement. In both instances, he

Drawing showing the Monmouth 12 engined Lawson super airliner with seats for 100 passengers, the first of it
kind in the world. It has a wing spread of 200 feet. Its length is 100 feet and its total weight is 100,000 pound
Upon this craft pasesngers can be carried at a profit at less than railroad rates.

Drawing showing the double tier cabin of a Lawson 100 passenger super airliner which doubles the seating and earn
ing capacity and makes possible carrying passengers at less cost by air than by railroad. Patents have been granted
upon this invention all over the world, which cover passenger compartments on either land, water or air vehicles

Publicity for Lawson's two-tiered, hundred-passenger "super airliner," which was never completed.
From *Scientific Age,* January, 1927.

seemed suddenly to have before him a rare opportunity to attain fabulous success. And in both instances, he faltered, failing to exploit an opportunity which would never come again. In the case of his baseball failure, it is not clear why or how he was able to rise so high, only to fall so fast. In the case of his aviation activities in Milwaukee, however, much more can be said about why things went wrong.

A post mortem examination can begin with the crash of the Midnight Liner. That seemingly trivial things often determine the outcome of historic events was certainly illustrated well in this plane's test flight. The main point to observe here, however, is that the crash need not have happened. Like Lawson's first plane, the Midnight Liner appeared to be well designed, well constructed, and made to fly. It was, in fact, off the ground and responding to Wilcox's control when the crash occurred. This promising plane—one of the largest and heaviest built at that time—was simply never given a fair test under proper conditions. And for failing to give the Midnight Liner a fair test, Lawson must take the full blame. Certainly his colleagues had ample grounds for resenting the imperious manner in which he overrode their collective technical opinion and exposed to grave risk the plane on which they all had worked so long and hard.

Unquestionably, here was bad judgment by Lawson. It has to be acknowledged, however, that his decision was a consequence of his desperate financial circumstances. If there had been any prospect of his backers providing more money, he certainly would have made a safer attempt to fly the plane. From Lawson's point of view, then, the problem he faced in this instance was the same problem he had faced all along: his backers simply had never provided him with sustained funding on a scale ample enough to get his airliner enterprise very far off the ground. As he saw the matter, the company's stockholders had bought his vision of making Milwaukee the Detroit of the aeronautics industry but then had refused to invest the funds needed to make the vision real.

There was, of course, much truth in Lawson's analysis of the cause of his failure. He was attempting to do something on a scale requiring an enormous investment of resources, and as a matter of objective fact, he had nowhere near the level of funding required. But one then has to look at this issue from the point of view of his backers. They were a multitude of small-time Milwaukee investors, daringly putting money into a completely new and untried venture. Moreover, they were doing this during a time of very major recession in the American economy. From their vantage point, they were taking a great risk on Lawson's say-so and had, in fact, cooperated fully, doing all that Lawson said needed to be done to get things humming. They might therefore have charged Lawson with misleading them about the ease with which production could be started and sales made to the Lawson Airline Transportation Company. If Lawson hadn't exactly misled them, they could have concluded, then he certainly had overstated the rosy prospects for success in the business of manufacturing airplanes.

From the start, Lawson's schemes had indeed been oversold, and if overselling had gotten him into a financial jam, his method of meeting the problem—more overselling—only got him in deeper. But did Lawson have any alternative to overselling? Perhaps in order to get anything at all started he had to oversell and then rely on the hope that the soundness of his vision would make everything work out right. Pushing the analysis in this direction, however, carries it beyond the question of why Lawson's effort failed to the question of whether it could have succeeded. Why were lenders and investors reluctant to part with the large amount of capital needed to support Lawson's schemes? The later tremendous success of the airline industry should not be permitted to cover over the fact that in 1920 the market potential for air passenger service was very problematical. Even if Lawson had been able to offer the nationwide air passenger network he dreamed of, it is far from certain that the patronage to sustain it would have been there. Moreover, it is even more questionable that aviation technology had advanced far enough to make air transportation a safe and realistic undertaking. As good as Lawson's planes were, sooner or later one of them probably would have crashed while carrying passengers (especially since Lawson proposed to stick to schedule and ignore weather conditions). In that early day a crash would doubtless have sent his airline company reeling and set back the cause of air passenger service for many years.

Only after Lindbergh's celebrated flight did the public become sufficiently air-minded and aroused by aviation to raise significantly the prospects for air passenger service. By then, too, many advances had been made in aviation technology, especially in greatly increasing the horsepower of engines, at the same time that their weight was reduced. Government interest in aviation (something Lawson had tried in vain to excite for years) also substantially increased. Finally, when the effort was made once again to essay air passenger service on the grand scale envisioned by Lawson, large corporations, not the single "great man" on the Lawson model, were on hand to generate the necessary financial support.

In sum, those who finally succeeded in making Lawson's dream a reality had many advantages—probably indispensable advantages—which were denied to him. It was Lawson's misfortune to have acted prematurely. He was nearly ten years ahead of others—and also ahead of a reasonable chance for success. Still, it is conceivable that Lawson might have succeeded if he had followed a different strategy of "smaller and slower." Instead of projecting the immediate development of a nationwide passenger service, he might have aimed at building slowly on successful experience acquired at first over several relatively short routes. In this more modest, initial service he could have used smaller planes to carry a few passengers and airmail. As his experience, the passenger market, aviation technology, and his claim on development capital matured, he would then have been in a better position to experiment with advanced airliners and expanded service.

This speculation is beside the point, however. Lawson could never have conceived or pursued such pintsized schemes. He was foredoomed by his very nature to think only big, to gaze far ahead, and to pursue heroic projects.

These traits clearly played a part in undermining Lawson's airline efforts; however, they were also the very traits which led him to aspire to great things in aviation. If they prompted him at crucial moments to make bad decisions, they also emboldened him to act in the face of the great difficulties confronting him. Without question, they lifted Lawson into high place as a prophet of and pathfinder for air passenger service.

Through the last phases of Lawson's life, the failures of his airline efforts and the rapidity with which these pioneering efforts were forgotten obviously gnawed away at him, and it is very easy to sympathize with his feelings of anguish about what might have been. In 1937 he published *Lawson: Aircraft Industry Builder*, a documentary history of his role in aviation. Also, his many other books usually carried in the back pages a large section devoted to his aviation exploits. The principal burden of these writings was to establish that Lawson was *the* father of the American aviation industry, who merely had left aviation when it was clear the child could survive on its own.

Even if Lawson's self-evaluation cannot be accepted, Burnelli's description of him as "one of the dynamic figures of the pioneer days of aviation" still sticks. Certainly some of Lawson's activities are entitled to much greater recognition than they have so far gotten—in particular, his valuable work as publicist in the earliest days of aviation, his role in the development of the airliner, and his early attempt to found a transcontinental air passenger service.

Even Lawson's prophecy of the alti-man, as extreme and balmy as it was, deserves remembrance, too, as an important and representative artifact of its time. No other person registered as graphically as Lawson the profound effect which humanity's acquisition of the ability to fly had on imaginations and intellects during the earliest years of flight. Nor did any other person express as clearly the new hope for humanity's destiny which human flight engendered.

Finally, if the world were a juster place, it would never have forgotten that, for good reason, it had once hailed Lawson as the Columbus of the Air. "It is a very easy matter," Lawson wrote in his second bulletin to Congress in 1918, "to sit down in a comfortable armchair and, like the poets, dream over fantastic things that ought to be, but it is an entirely different matter to show how these things can be done and then do them yourself." Unlike Columbus, Lawson ultimately failed, but like Columbus, he dreamed of a new "fantastic thing," showed how it could be done, and then did it himself. Lawson clearly can claim the honor of being the first in the United States to envision and then to demonstrate what others with more resources and advantages later made the commonplace reality of the present day.

Part Three

FROM

AVIATOR

TO

AVATAR

No sooner had Lawson returned from the great flight of his airliner than he eagerly added to all the burdens awaiting him a true labor of love—the writing of a celebratory account of the flight, of its place in aviation history, and of his life and ambitious plans. *The Airliner and Its Inventor, Alfred W. Lawson* was self-published by Lawson in 1921 under the name of "Cy Q. Faunce." (The choice of pseudonym was apt; say "Cy Q. Faunce" rapidly enough and it comes out sounding like "sycophant." If this little joke was intentional, it was the only instance of self-deprecating humor ever to appear in Lawson's writings and speeches.)

In this adulatory book Lawson not only spotlighted the greatness which he already had achieved in aviation but prophesied more Lawsonian prodigies to come: "But we believe he will do more, and if he lives another twenty-five years—and his strong athletic appearance and clean, regular habits give every indication of his doing so—then we can look forward to some of the most remarkable achievements and creations that the mind of a super-man is capable of devising." Lawson did live another twenty-five years—in fact, nearly nine more than that number. His forecast of future "remarkable achievements and creations" was on the mark, too. Although his greatest work in aviation was soon behind him, other realms of activity remained to engage the Lawson genius. Indeed, even as he wrote in 1921, he was preparing to stake a claim to greatness in another field.

A novel physical theory—a total replacement for orthodox physics—had been simmering in Lawson's mind for decades. The failure of his aviation activities in 1921 gave him an earlier-than-expected occasion to get it down on paper, a task which took up Lawson's next three years. The result was two treatises—the earliest works of Lawsonomy. In the preface to the first of these volumes, the irrepressible Cy Q. Faunce hailed Lawson as the "Wizard of Reason" and accounted his scientific achievement as greater than those of Copernicus, Galileo, and Newton, whose teachings were "like school boy information" compared with Lawson's.

Lawson's airline dream still beckoned alluringly, however, and because his superliner project brought him back to the pursuit of the dream from 1925 to 1929, he sometimes referred later to his 1921–1924 season of writing as only a brief "vacation from his business affairs." By the early 1930s, however, Lawson realized that his forced vacation had, in fact, been a providential event. In his view, it was God's way of putting him on the path to the true purposes of his life—elaborating his intellectual discoveries into a comprehensive scientific, moral, and religious system and, through the promulgation of this doctrine, leading humanity upward a notch on the evolutionary scale and toward a perfected social life. Once Lawson had abandoned his aircraft ventures forever in 1929, he was preoccupied exclusively with these goals for the rest of his life.

Lawson's movement toward messiahship came in two phases coinciding with the first and the second halves of the decade of the 1930s. He kicked off the first phase with publication in 1931 of *Direct Credits for Everybody*, which specified a "perfect economic plan" for dislodging "the financiers" from control of the American economy and ushering in utopia under the capitalist system. For sure, here was another "remarkable achievement and creation." By virtue of his plan's liberating effects, Lawson proclaimed himself to be the "New Emancipator."

To gain support for his plan, Lawson also founded in 1931 the Direct Credits Society (DCS), which soon had a large, far-flung membership. In keeping with these heady circumstances, Lawson adopted two other dramatic self-characterizations in this period—"The People's Coach" and, even grander, the "Man of Destiny."

But all the while that Lawson pushed his Direct Credits program and built up the Direct Credits Society, profound changes were occurring in his perceptions of his role and his goals. What lay behind his changing perceptions at mid-decade was his resumed attention to Lawsonomy, which he worked away at even while he built up the Direct Credits Society. Lawson's most "remarkable achievement and creation" in the 1930s was the completion of this multifaceted doctrine. As new treatises were added to the shelf of Lawsonomy in the latter half of the decade, they offered moral, religious, and economic teachings which didn't square with the Direct Credits doctrine, especially with the premise that utopia could be reached under capitalism. Returning to utopian views he had first enunciated in 1904 in *Born Again*, Lawson came to believe that institutional reform, as aimed at by the Direct Credits movement, was not enough. What was also needed was a reform of human nature through education in Lawsonomy.

Thus, as the decade of the 1940s opened, Lawson had attained another of his "remarkable achievements and creations"—a new and final *persona*. No longer merely the "great man" who had done so much for aviation, or merely the Wizard of Reason, who had put knowledge of the physical universe on a rational foundation, or merely the New Emancipator, the People's Coach or the Man of Destiny, who sought economic justice for humanity, Lawson was now all of these things and yet much more. He had become the First Knowledgian.

6

THE

WIZARD

OF REASON

AND THE

ORIGIN OF

LAWSONOMY

Anyone looking into *Born Again* and Lawson's magazine editorials will quickly spot Lawson's fascination with movement. "To learn how matter was forced to move about in space eternally," Lawson later acknowledged, was "uppermost in [Lawson's] mind, almost from the day of his birth." He found nothing mysterious about his preoccupation: "such an inclination was born in him and was but the effect of a preceding cause."

The "preceding cause" was the intense mental concentration which Lawson's father had summoned for the building of a perpetual motion machine during the three years prior to Lawson's birth. "Thus the thoughts passing through the mind of the father were generated into the seed from which the child was initiated during the year of 1868 and born . . . on March 24, 1869." That none of his brothers and sisters had similar preoccupations or scientific inclinations confirmed this explanation, Lawson believed.

However, in contrast with his father, whose focus was only on *perpetual motion*, Lawson was obsessed with *perpetual movement*. What causes movement? he wanted to know. Especially he sought an answer to this question: what can account for the movement of matter into transitory "formations" (for example, atoms, molecules, raindrops, trees, human bodies, the earth, the solar system, galaxies), the inevitable breaking down of the formations, and the subsequent movement of the same matter into new formations, world and time without end?

In a story which may well rank with those of Archimedes in the bathtub and Newton under the apple tree, Lawson explained how he got his first inkling of the answers to these questions. In 1873 at the age of only four years, confined with measles to a darkened room, he noticed in the air dust particles illuminated by the shaft of sunlight entering between the blinds and window frame. Swirling around, they suggested to his mind "a series of minute worlds moving about in space." Then came the decisive discovery: "By blowing out his breath against these particles he learned that he could push them away and scatter them apart by PRESSURE and that by drawing in his breath he could pull them in and hold them together by SUCTION."

The discovery made by the four-year-old boy remained at the forefront of his mind in subsequent years, issuing at last in matured scientific conclusions reached by the middle-aged man. Convinced that his youthful discovery could be generalized to account for all movement of matter, Lawson eagerly awaited the opportunity to work up his secret in a systematic statement. The opportunity came several years later with his "vacation from business affairs" imposed by the crash of the Midnight Liner. In another venture into autobiography, *Lawson: From Bootblack to Emancipator* (1934), he described his next undertaking and its significance as follows: "So he quickly forgot all about his property losses and buried himself for three years in a work of love without pay, that future generations would be benefited by his labors. And during those three years of super-labor, Lawson lifted the entire science of physics out of the quick-sands of theory and mysticism and placed it upon the solid foundation of absolute fact and reality."

Shortly into this three-year period of intellectual effort, Lawson was ready to present to the world his first announcement of his revolutionary conclusions. That came on September 19, 1922, the day on which Lawson informed the press corps of Washington, D.C., that he would receive them in his hotel and reveal a great scientific breakthrough. For the occasion, he prepared a statement, "The Key to Perpetual Movement: A Digest of the Causes and Effects of Universal

YOUNG LAWSON STUDYING THE MOVEMENT OF MATTER

At age four, Lawson made his first discoveries of suction and pressure. From Lawson, *Children*.

Laws," which he copyrighted at the Library of Congress and "telegraphed to all parts of the world" on the same day.

Of the hundreds of Washington correspondents, only three showed up. One who did was the *Milwaukee Journal*'s reporter, who probably was curious to know what Lawson had been up to since leaving Milwaukee a year earlier. In his dispatch published the next day, this correspondent took note of several strange new words he had heard at this press conference, including "Lawsonomy" and "Lawsonpoise." Trying to capture the significance of Lawson's performance, he concluded that Lawson had "attempted to 'out-einstein' Einstein."

Four days later, Lawson gave an interview to a *New York Times* reporter in the Vanderbilt Hotel in New York City. This time he dealt with the implications of his new physics for an improved understanding of the operation of the human body. Among other things, he described the heart's action and the circulation of blood in terms of his new "Law of Penetrability" and announced that a person maintaining the body's "Lawsonpoise" could live to be two hundred years old. Regrettably, the reporter had a hard time grasping all that Lawson said. In the September 24, 1922, newspaper story, he garbled the key concept of "Lawsonpoise" as "lost pause."

Lawson followed up these early declarations of the new science of Lawsonomy with a book, self-published in 1923, bearing the curious title of *Lawsonpoise and How to Grow Young* but then reissued that same year under the title *Manlife*. As both titles indicated, this was a volume in which Lawsonomic analysis was applied to problems of human physiology, health, and longevity. Why Lawson's first book-length exposition of Lawsonomy dealt with these applications rather than with the fundamental physical laws themselves is answered, perhaps, by the first sentence of *Manlife*: "To me, the most important thing in the universe is man—because I am a man." Moreover, ever since his "born again" experience, Lawson had had a keen interest in the maintenance of his bodily health. Now that he was in his fifty-fourth year, the conditions for sustaining the vigor and longevity needed to tackle future "remarkable achievements and creations" possibly figured even more urgently in his mind.

Turning next in 1923 to a treatise setting forth the axioms of Lawsonomic physical science, Lawson completed it within the same year and submitted it to a prestigious publishing house, G. P. Putnam's Sons, which rejected it. He then withheld the manuscript until 1931, when he published it himself under the title *Creation*.

In *Manlife* and *Creation*, the reader finds a strange new account of the physical phenomena of the universe. Lawson gives his attention in these books to a reinterpretation of existing scientific data and a reformulation of scientific concepts. Although he jettisons much of orthodox physics, chemistry, geology, and physiology, he presents no new experimental data or quantitative analyses but does introduce many new terms.

One learns in these books why movement has to be the central problem for Lawson: energy doesn't exist in Lawson's universe. In the past, he claims, "some fanciful mind" introduced the concept of energy, from which point onward the rule-bound scientists have accepted it "as a matter of course and beyond the jurisdiction of anyone to question." However, "there is no greater load of misconception that Science has ever had to shoulder than the unprovable theory that somewhere, somehow, and in some shape, there exists a substance called Energy that causes movement. No such thing exists anywhere and Science should expurge [*sic*] the fallacy without delay."

Having rejected the concept of energy, Lawson necessarily supplies an unusual account of movement. Space, he argues, is teeming with matter (that is, "substances" and the "formations" into which substances enter). In fact, there is no empty space; everywhere space has material contents. Included among the contents are the ether of outer space, air, other gases, solids, liquids, two newly heralded substances which Lawson calls "lesether" and "mentality," and heat, cold, light, sound, electricity, and magnetism, all of which are substances, according to Lawson.

A key fact about substances is that they have varying densities. "Because of this difference in density throughout Space, one substance is enabled to penetrate another substance and this act of penetration is movement." If all substances had equal densities, there could be no penetration and therefore no movement. *Penetrability* is thus the fundamental Lawsonian physical law.

When a substance moves, that is, penetrates another substance, it leaves behind it for an instant something like a vacuum or, as Lawson calls it, a "suction terminal," which immediately draws in new substances. And in its movement, the first substance puts pressure on the substance(s) toward which it moves, which pressure can cause still further movement. Hence the basic factors of movement in the Lawsonian universe are *suction* and *pressure*. Penetrability makes movement possible; suction and pressure actually cause things to move.

Or is it the other way around? In the Lawsonian texts (as in the preceding paragraph), suction and pressure appear to be as much the consequences as the cause of movement. Lawson also seems as often to treat penetrability as the cause rather than as the condition of movement. Because one substance *can* penetrate another substance, it *will* or *must* penetrate it, Lawson seems to say.

The movement accompanying any single event of penetration has effects felt throughout the universe—that is, "no one thing can move without everything moving." It is also the case, Lawson argues, that "in Space without size, shape, inside or outside, or directions, there is no foundation whatsoever for anything to rest upon. So everything must keep moving forever." Thus Lawson presents a mind-stretching picture of a universe of matter caught up in a system of necessary, never-ending, interdependent movements.

There are other stiff challenges to the ordinary mind in Lawson's physics. For instance, Lawson rejects the concept of gravitational energy and conceives of other forms of energy, such as heat, light, and electricity, as substances. But this would seem to leave suction and pressure in an uncertain status. They clearly aren't substances, and they can't be energy. Nonetheless, they do define "terminals" between which flow "currents" which cause movement. The beginner in Lawsonomy may struggle for a long while to overcome a feeling that suction and pressure are, in fact, forms of fluid energy and may also fail to understand at once why suction is a conceptual improvement over gravity.

Another puzzle is presented by the operation of the Law of Penetrability. Which way does penetration run? Lawson finds the basic pattern to be penetration of substances of lesser density by substances of greater density. For instance, greater-density iron can penetrate lesser-density water, but water can't penetrate iron. Yet this basic pattern is easily shown not always to apply, and even Lawson acknowledges that some substances of lesser density can penetrate some substances of greater density. For instance, both iron and water can be penetrated by electricity, a substance having an extremely low density, much less than that of either iron or water. In an attempt to salvage lawfulness in such cases, Lawson falls back on the argument that, on the microscopic level, these higher-density substances will be found to have "crevices" which permit penetration by the lower-density substances.

Two other important Lawsonomic concepts are needed to complete one's understanding of the complicated phenomena of movement in Lawson's universe. One of these is *zig-zag-and-swirl*, which Lawson defines as "movement in which any formation moves in a multiple direction according to the movements of many increasingly greater formations, each depending upon the greater formation for direction and upon varying changes caused by counteracting influences of Suction and Pressure of different proportions." What Lawson is saying here is something like the following: nothing moves simply in a single current between a single set of suction and pressure terminals. This is so because the universe is not simply filled with substances, but with combinations of substances in formations and, in turn, with formations composed of other formations. Movement occurs within formations, which in turn are moving within larger formations. This means there is much movement within movement and that the universe is crisscrossed with an enormous number of suction and pressure currents. Anything capable of movement will move with all these currents. The resultant path of movement is incredibly difficult to describe, but zig-zag-and-swirl comes close to capturing it.

Lawson gives a splendid illustration of his meaning. Consider, he says, that:

> . . . a germ moving across the surface of a blood corpuscle might think he is going in a certain direction in Space. If he could understand he would know that the blood corpuscle also moves him in another direction, and that the blood current was also carrying him in still another direction.

And still that would not end there, as the germ, corpuscle and blood current are all dependent for further movement and other directions in Space upon a greater formation, man.

But there is yet more complexity, for this man is walking in a westerly direction at two miles per hour in an airplane which is flying in an easterly direction at one hundred miles per hour and at a declination of thirty degrees to the surface of the earth. A forty mile per hour north wind is causing the plane to drift to the south. Finally, of course, the earth is revolving on its axis and in its orbit around the sun, and the whole solar system is also moving.

How else to describe the resultant movement of the germ but as a zig-zag-and-swirl? Lawson left it for posterity to devise the "system of superlative mathematics" which he said was needed to compute this complicated movement.

A concept of even greater importance in Lawsonomy is *equaeverpoise*, Lawson's final term for what he originally called Lawsonpoise. Lawson defines equaeverpoise as "a common level sought by substances of varying density that causes perpetual movement of matter." This is a tricky concept, because the words "common level" might mistakenly be thought to describe a tendency of penetrability to proceed until all matter has reached a uniform density and thereby come to a state of rest. In fact, equaeverpoise explains why these conditions will never happen. To put it another way, equaeverpoise explains why matter clusters and reclusters eternally—explains, that is, the origin, duration, and ultimate disintegration of formations and then the building of new formations from the substances of the old ones. In the sense that equaeverpoise, obtained within formations, prevents an ultimate homogenization of matter and a consequent cessation of all movement, it is for Lawson yet another cause of the perpetual movement of matter.

To reach an understanding of equaeverpoise, one must start with a current flowing from a pressure terminal to a suction terminal. When the current reaches the suction terminal, it cannot go farther; the substances carried in this current have run into higher-density substances which they cannot penetrate. But the substances want to keep moving; they obviously have momentum. At this point, according to Lawson, "a swirl is caused in which the moving substances rush round and round and cause extraordinary pressure in their attempt to reach space with lesser density."

Here is the first step in the building of a new formation; it organizes itself around an internal suction terminal. In the case of the solar system, the sun is the suction terminal; for the earth, the suction terminal is the earth's core; for humans, it is the heart. But the swirling matter from which the formation is made creates an internal pressure, which is also essential to the formation. Both internal suction and internal pressure are needed to resist the otherwise devastating operation of external suction and external pressure to which the formation is subject.

As long as internal suction and pressure are greater than external suction and pressure, the formation is in a state of growth. If internal suction and pressure are less than external suction and pressure, the formation is in a state of decline. However, "when a formation has reached a stage of maturity and internal Suction equals external Suction, and internal Pressure equals external Pressure it is then in a state of EQUAEVERPOISE and as long as it can remain in such condition it can live."

Manlife presents an analysis of the human body as a formation which goes through stages of growth, maturity, and decline dependent on the states of internal and external suction and internal and external pressure acting on the body. Lawson includes in this discussion prescriptions for diet, exercise, rest, and hygiene, which he claims will prolong the body's equaeverpoise, perhaps thereby doubling the normal lifespan.

In *Creation* Lawson's most striking illustrations of growing, declining, and mature formations are, respectively, Jupiter, the moon, and the earth. A closer look at what is happening in, on, and around the earth will aid the understanding of equaeverpoise.

In his analysis of the earth, Lawson raises two fundamental questions: what keeps the high-density earth afloat in the low-density ether? and what prevents the earth from being squeezed to death by external pressure? The answer to both questions involves a marvelous substance called *lesether*. Lesether is produced in the earth from sub-

stances drawn in by the earth's suction. These substances "are supplied directly by the Sun in currents of various density and also by
solid substances which are drawn into the Solar System, such as mete-
ors and other cosmic debris which are dissolved into gases by contact
with the atmosphere of the Earth."

Within the earth, these raw materials are converted to lesether,
which, because it has a lower density than ether, allows the earth to
float in the ether, in the same manner in which a battleship is able to
float in the water. The lesether also supplies the internal pressure
needed to offset external pressure. Thus, the earth remains in equaeverpoise. It has a healthy suction power to offset external suction,
and it has the capacity through its production of lesether to offset external pressure. Of course, someday internal suction will falter, whence
it follows that lesether production and, thereby, internal pressure will
also falter. When that sorry day comes, however, Lawson doesn't say
which will happen first: the crushing of the earth by external pressure
or the sinking of the earth in the ether, like a ship lost in the sea.

It is important to observe that, for Lawson, the processes of equaeverpoise are, in fact, *life* processes. All formations—earth and solar
system, no less than humans and microbes—are alive; they all go
through the life phases of birth, youth, maturity, old age, and death.
Lawson carries through the life analysis thoroughly in the case of the
earth. Cosmic debris is the earth's food; the earth's atmosphere begins
the digestion of it. This food enters through the earth's mouth, which
is located at the North Pole (which accounts for the northern lights).
In the interior of the earth, digestion is completed and the lesether is
pumped by pressure to all parts of the earth by arteries. Waste products are released through pores (including the earth's volcanos) or are
transmitted back to the earth's central channel through veins, where-
upon internal pressure causes them to be discharged at the South Pole
(thus the southern lights).

To say that the earth is in equaeverpoise is to say that all these life
processes are working well and that the earth is in a state of health.
But this state can't last forever. "Every time an earthquake takes place
it is mournful evidence of the fact that external Pressure has made
another encroachment upon the structure of the Earth and is gradu-

ally gaining the mastery over the Earth's power of Suction. It shows that the Earth is no longer expanding or growing as it did in its youthful state but is gradually settling down before age." Eventually, as is true for all formations, the earth will die.

This intermingling of physical and biological categories is a major characteristic of Lawson's thought. Life processes are explained in terms of suction and pressure—but physical processes are shown actually to be life processes. For instance, suction and pressure account for sexual mating; "the attraction of one sex for the other is but the attraction of Suction for Pressure." On the other hand, sexual activity is even more rampant in the universe than had ever been supposed, because all formations and, in fact, every particle of matter are either male or female, depending on whether pressure or suction predominates. "The male sex of a formation is caused by a super-abundance of internal Pressure. The female sex of a formation is caused by a super-abundance of internal Suction." On the basis of these sexual attributes of matter, Lawson explains, for example, the "so-called chemical affinities" and also claims to have discovered "the cause of sex."

But the most astonishing revelation of all about the physical universe is this: "There is no particle of density throughout limitless space that is not inhabited by living formations having consciousness." These conscious inhabitants, which are incalculable in number, submicroscopic, intelligent, and beneficent, Lawson calls "mental organisms." The presence of mental organisms gives consciousness and intelligence to all formations—that is, makes it possible for all formations to use mentality, the extremely low-density substance which flows in currents between suction and pressure terminals throughout the universe and makes consciousness and thinking possible. In fact, the presence of the mental organisms—the agents of equaeverpoise— gives life itself to all formations. Lawson explains the relationship of mental organisms to the very existence of formations as follows: "To keep the formation from caving in as a result of external Pressure, internal bracing must be built and internal Pressure developed, and to keep the formation from exploding from too much internal Pressure a suitable exhaust system must be arranged. All this work requires conscious planning by living, working creatures"—that is, the mental organisms inhabiting the formations.

Lawson also finds the "cause of evolution" in the activities of the mental organisms, who produced humanity as "the result of millions of years of constant laborious effort in which experiment after experiment and improvement upon improvement took place." The same laborious ministrations have also been given to that other living entity, the earth. And in the case of both humans and the earth, the work of the mental organisms is not yet done. As their tinkering goes on, the consciousness of both humans and earth will expand. When this has happened sufficiently, humans will begin to communicate with and learn from the mental organisms who populate the earth's interior. What they will learn from communicating with them and observing their operation of the earth's equaeverpoise is the necessity for humanity to develop "a world consciousness in which all men on earth will unite as one and think as one." That is, humanity will see the necessity and desirability of organizing into a single formation.

When the "world consciousness" and the global organization of humanity as a unit have been obtained, humans will have reached their destiny as "the chief governing factor of the Earth," supplanting the mental organisms in the role of "the Earth's captain and pilot." At that point, they will have acquired the capacity "to rearrange the structure of the Earth" and thereby tap the earth's "internal power." Among other stupefying feats, humanity will at last be able to do successfully what the residents of Sageland tried to do prematurely—that is, navigate the earth through the heavens by freeing the earth from the suction and pressure currents which now determine its movements.

A brief summary cannot do justice to all that is in *Manlife* and *Creation*. Illustrating or buttressing Lawson's main arguments is a wealth of other marvelous material—for example, his display of the falsity of the conventional understanding of vibration, including an account of how the bow squeezes sound (a substance) from the violin's strings; discussions of the sex particles of magnets, the eyes' power to draw in light by suction, and the endless divisibility of matter; explanations of capillary action, thunderstorms, walking, eating and defecating, the functioning of the heart and circulation of blood in terms of suction and pressure; proofs that the moon was not once part of the earth or the planets part of the sun; demonstrations that more of the earth's heat comes from the earth than is furnished by the sun and that the speed of light is not a constant but depends on the variable force of suction and pressure terminals; and finally, Lawson's bold dispatching of atomic physics: "If all the force within a single electron, atom, or molecule should be released at once there would not be enough of it to move a hair on a flea's back."

The stunning originality, ingenuity, and colorful terms put on display in these books, the architectonic grandness of their depiction of a suction-and-pressure universe, the systematic manner in which they unfold the awesome story and handily account for everything in terms of penetrability, equaeverpoise, and zig-zag-and-swirl—these are qualities which yield a high standing for *Manlife* and *Creation* as classics of unorthodox science. Like many other works in this genre, *Manlife* and *Creation* give much space to faulting the conventional scientists' alleged goosestepping and trained incapacity for fearless inquiry (a clear echo of a major theme of his aviation editorials). True to the tradition of unorthodox science, they also exhibit their author's passion for replacing "fanciful theory" with "hard facts" and his triumphant conviction of having caught the Truth where all others have failed. In brief, one can't read these books without concluding that Lawson was in the front rank of independent thinkers; his clearly was, as Wordsworth wrote of Newton's, "a mind forever voyaging through strange seas of thought, alone."

Like many other unorthodox scientists, Lawson also took pride in believing that he had exposed as mystifying nonsense the arcanum of the scientific priesthood and had made scientific knowledge accessible to the laity: "Lawson brings to the average thinking man or woman in simple, beautiful expressions the greatest secrets that the universe contains." Indeed, "his masterful works can be understood by the thinking child if but studied and pondered over carefully." On the other hand, perhaps Lawsonomy really wasn't as easy to grasp as this last statement suggests, for Lawson (Faunce) also asked, "Who is there among us mortals today who can understand Lawson when he goes below a certain level? There seems to be no limit to the depth of his mental activities." He recognized, too, that most orthodox scientists would work fiendishly to thwart general acceptance of his work. Thus, he concluded that "posterity alone will be able to fully appreciate the value of this brilliant contribution."

Only a year before the publication of *Manlife*, Lawson had written in *The Airliner and Its Inventor*, "If he never does anything more the invention and demonstration of the airliner is enough to ingratiate him in the hearts of all men." Now, however, he was ready to stake his claim to lasting fame and humanity's gratitude on his latest achievement: "If Lawson should die today (1922) posterity will honor and glorify him as no other mortal, because he has given mankind the true base from which to start an edifice of super-knowledge of the universe and its laws." Indeed, "the birth of Lawson was the most momentous occurrence since the birth of mankind. His coming will establish the beginning of a new order in the development of man." Lawson also repeated his earlier prophecy of more great things to come: "Lawson says that his great work is only begun and that he has formulated plans that will require fifty years to complete."

"His great work" still included establishment of an airline, of course, the project to which Lawson returned from 1925 to 1929. (Here is a tantalizing question: Did Lawson actually design and fly his airplanes on the principles of suction, pressure, and penetrability?) For the duration he shelved the further development of Lawsonomy. However, he had no intention of abandoning it permanently. Indicating in *Manlife* that he already had in mind other great writings extending Lawsonomy beyond physics and physiology, he made good on their delivery in the 1930s.

Lawson's high regard for his scientific discoveries and his intellectual brilliance launched him on a journey from which there was no turning back. The occasion for the resumption of his trek toward his destiny was his final abandonment of aircraft work following the failure in 1929 of his second effort to found an airline. As he picked up his pen again, he turned from physics to economics.

7

THE NEW

EMANCIPATOR

AND HIS

PERFECT

ECONOMIC

PLAN

"In order to thoroughly understand ECO-
NOMICS one must know something about
PHYSICS," Lawson confided in a speech
delivered in 1935. Through his plumbing
of nature's physical laws, he added, he had
come to see that economics was a "side
partner" of physics—or as he said on another occasion, "physics and economics are
like a couple that can't be separated." This
meant that one must also know something
about economics in order to understand
physics. Sometimes, as in the following vol-
ley (one of his least intemperate) loosed
against university professors, Lawson even
seemed to give the highest place among the
sciences to economics: "How could they
teach you physiology when they do not
understand physics? How can they understand physics when they know nothing
about economics?"

To Lawson's mind, the most striking feature of the operation of the physical laws
was the manner in which they achieved a
recycling of matter. As every particle of
matter was moved about by suction and
pressure, it entered endlessly into successive formations and was never "wasted."
From this observation Lawson arrived at
what he called "God's first Natural Law,"
namely, "the utilization of everything without the loss of anything." This—"one of
the unchangeable laws of the equaeverpoise"—was as much an economic as a
physical law; in fact, Lawson adopted it as
his definition of economics. Coming at a
point of intersection between physics and

economics, the law enabled Lawson to attribute purposefulness to nature's physical processes and at the same time claim to derive economic norms from the study of these physical processes.

In *Manlife*, Lawson had promised to say more about economics in future writings. What he planned to address were the principles of "natural" economics gleaned from his Lawsonomic studies, not economics as it was actually practiced in human societies. Natural economics would, in fact, be the basis for the critique and the reform of "man-made" economics. The onset of the Great Depression of the 1930s then made Lawson's attention to economics urgent. The first fruit of his effort was a book, *Direct Credits for Everybody*, published in 1931.

This was probably not the book on economics Lawson would have written under more leisurely conditions. Not a treatise systematically setting forth the fundamentals of natural economics, *Direct Credits for Everybody*—a book of only sixty-five pages—was skewed toward offering an explanation of what had gone wrong with the American economy and proposing reforms which would make things right again. Clearly Lawson's first foray into economics had been powerfully shaped by the circumstances of emergency to which he was responding.

It would go too far to conclude that *Direct Credits for Everybody* simply generalized from Lawson's personal financial difficulties during his airliner years or was written merely to retaliate against those who had made problems for him. Nonetheless, the central argument of the book does coincide strikingly with Lawson's account of his own tribulations. Just as greedy people controlling money had undermined his creative entrepreneurial efforts, so they had, in Lawson's judgment, undone the whole economy. Dealing with the problems of the Great Depression meant knocking out the power, position, and privileges of the financiers.

Direct Credits for Everybody rests on the premise that economists go woefully wrong in assuming only two main classes in society—capital and labor. The error arises from their lumping of finance with capital. But "there is as much difference between Capital and Finance as there is between Milk and a Sponge." Economists have also assumed that the interests of capital and labor are in conflict, but this, too, is false. Wealth is a social product produced by capital and labor working together. Each is entitled to a fair share which would assure economic security and comfort for all. Unfortunately, however, neither gets its fair share, because the largest share is filched by finance. Hence capital and labor have a common interest in breaking free from the bondage imposed by a class which itself creates no wealth, steals wealth, and even interferes with the production of wealth.

According to Lawson, "at present Finance is swallowing Capital and crushing Labor." This system which finance has created has become not only "so rickety that it . . . endangers the foundation and stability of modern industry" but also "so decayed that it undermines and degrades the mentality, morality, and spirit of everybody." But even though the people know that something is radically wrong with it, they submit to the financiers' system because they don't see clearly the source of their plight. Moreover, the financiers are clever. They keep the people "arguing and quarreling over everything except the fact that [the financiers are] skinning them." Thus, the financiers promote the popular delusion that the people rule through elections contested by competing political parties—both of which they control, however. They also encourage struggles among citizens over the distracting issues of race and religion and over "endless minor disputes," such as Prohibition. Because the financiers control all the media of communication and the institutions of education, they can make sure, too, that no heretical ideas which challenge their position get very far abroad.

But how did such a pernicious system ever get started? It arose unintentionally with the introduction of money. Money began merely as a convenience—a medium of exchange and a measure of value—to facilitate trade. But from the start, there was a problem: money was based on gold, which is scarce. The supply of gold could not keep pace with the expanding need for money as population and trade grew. The resulting scarcity of money soon brought a perversion of money: it came to be regarded as value or wealth itself, not simply a neutral means to measure wealth and facilitate trade.

The scarcity of money also brought another perverse development: the rise of persons who "made it their business to get control of [money] and make everybody pay for its use in the shape of interest."

Their depredations were enormously enhanced, too, when they succeeded in putting over "the credit system": this made it possible for
them to extend credit far beyond the amount of money in their possession—and, of course, to charge interest on this credit as well. But
because the collective debt of the American people has come to ex-
ceed by far the amount of money in circulation, it can never be paid
off. National, state, and local governments find that they have to impose ever higher taxes merely to make interest payments on the ever
growing governmental debt. Individuals and businesses, lacking a tax
power, have no choice but to submit to the dictates of the financiers or
go under, or both.

In order to consolidate their power and holdings, periodically the
financiers withhold credit and call up loans, thus setting off increasingly severe business depressions. Accompanying foreclosures on
homes, farms, and businesses, widespread joblessness and personal
misery, and a falloff in the production of wealth are a steadily increasing ownership and control of productive property by the financiers.

In 1931, when Lawson wrote, he believed the problem had become
intolerable. In his view, the money supply of the United States was
absurdly inadequate—only one-twentieth of the annual income from
the products of American industries, he claimed—and "to make Five
Billion Dollars in money do the work of more than One Hundred Billion Dollars in business puts a tremendous premium on money and
gives to those who own it control of industries, and trade generally,
through loans upon which interest must be paid." In Lawson's estimate, already "ten percent of the population of the United States control ninety percent of the money," and "the heads of 300 corporations
control the finances of 600,000 corporations." Given the inexorable
working of compound interest, he predicted that it would not be long
before one percent of the population "or a fraction thereof" would
control the money of the United States as "the big schemers . . . swallow up the little schemers." Worse still, the real controllers of the
American economy would be foreigners pulling strings from abroad,
especially in London. Already the banking and financial operations of
the United States were increasingly carried out at the behest of the
"international financiers."

Lawson's program for remedying the iniquities and malfunctions of the American economy consisted of fourteen points. Two called for alleviating the scarcity of money through the abolition of gold as money or as backing for money and the issuance by the government of paper money in "sufficient quantities for all purposes." The amount of currency needed, Lawson concluded, was equal to "the annual income from the products of the industries of the United States"— in 1931, by his reckoning, $100 billion. This worked out to about one thousand dollars per capita, he calculated—certainly an astounding increase over the fifty dollars per capita which he claimed was then in circulation. But this great influx was just the tonic needed to stimulate industry and trade, he argued. Because the new paper currency was to be backed by "the entire productive wealth of the United States," he foresaw no problem about its being honored both at home and abroad.

Four more of Lawson's proposals were designed to eliminate the market in money and the finaglers who had gotten rich by controlling that market. The charging of interest, insurance companies, and private banking were to be prohibited, and all banks and other financial institutions were to become agencies of the government, which would have total control over money and a monopoly of the right to make loans. The interest-free loans made by the government would be extended directly to borrowers (hence, "direct credits") in order to eliminate the possibility of intermediaries unjustly getting a cut on the transactions.

As a consequence of all of the foregoing steps, the status of money would dramatically be changed, Lawson believed. No longer the commodity it had previously become under conditions of scarcity, money would be restored to its true roles as a convenience of trade and a measure of value. Because it was backed by the ample wealth of the United States and no longer had value in itself, new money could be issued in huge quantities without having inflationary effects, Lawson serenely proclaimed.

Most of the remainder of Lawson's proposals covered the kinds of credits which the government would make available to citizens and the conditions governing their availability and use. The government credits were to be of two types—loans and grants. Although one point of his program specified that "everybody must be entitled to basic equal credits given by the government," he meant only that the claims of all for loans and grants would be considered fairly and equally, not that all would receive equal-sized loans and grants. In fact, in the case of only one kind of government credit—what Lawson called a limited credit—would citizens receive absolutely equal benefits.

In Lawson's scheme a limited credit was a small loan not requiring security. All citizens proposing to undertake some "constructive" project or investment would be equally eligible for loans up to a specified amount. What that amount would be Lawson didn't state in *Direct Credits for Everybody*, but in a later publication he suggested the figure of one thousand dollars. Every citizen would be eligible indefinitely for renewals of these small unsecured loans as long as he or she had paid off all earlier ones.

All other loans would have to be secured, and because the need for money and the capacity to put up collateral would vary enormously among individuals and businesses, the amounts and the availability of government loans would also vary greatly among borrowers. Loans would be made only in support of wealth-producing activities involving "actual service"—that is, work or entrepreneurship—by the borrowers. Presumably these loans, if not repaid, could be foreclosed by the government. However, Lawson said nothing about foreclosure policy or about how property collected in foreclosures would be disposed of. He also was silent on the question of what degree of discretion the government would have in approving or rejecting loans—a crucial question, because borrowers whose applications were rejected would have no alternative sources of capital to turn to.

Lawson's program included three important grant or entitlement provisions, affecting children, those unable to work, and the aged. Because he proposed to have the government pay all expenses of the persons in these categories (not merely fixed allowances applicable to all equally), the benefits paid to recipients would vary as widely as their actual needs and expenses varied. In the case of all three entitlement programs, Lawson gave some further unique twists.

As an investment in the nation's future, the "upkeep and education of children up to 21 years of age" would be paid for by the government, and in the case of bright youths who wish to pursue advanced education beyond the age of twenty-one, "special additional credits" to cover the cost would be arranged. However, in order to assure that no one would start adult life having had the benefit of unfair advantages, parents would be forbidden to spend any more on their children than was provided by government credits or to pass on property at a parent's death to heirs. All property would be confiscated by the government at the death of its owner, although Lawson was silent about the details, especially about what disposition the government would then make of the property.

In order to abolish charity and replace it with justice, government credits would be issued to provide for the sick and the infirm. Only in a later publication did Lawson reveal that he also intended the abolition of the private practice of the health professions. The incomes received by practitioners would come exclusively from the government via the credits issued to the sick and be determined in the case of each practitioner by both the quantity *and the quality* of the services provided. Obviously many questions about the health care system remained unanswered in *Direct Credits for Everybody,* but in a subsequent statement Lawson did specify that the supervision of health professions and the determination of the fees and incomes to which each practitioner was entitled would be in the hands of "a board of knowledgians having had practical experience along those lines." Of course, here the word "knowledgian"—one of Lawson's earliest uses of it—raised further questions about precisely what Lawson had in mind for the operation of the health care system.

A further important element of Lawson's reform program called for the provision of government credits, "if wanted," for all living expenses for everyone older than sixty-five years, even if the recipient chose not to retire. In Lawson's view, this provision was a simple matter of just treatment for those who had contributed forty-four years of their adult lives to the creation of the wealth of the nation. Of course, justice also required that "the size of such credits [ought] to be proportionate to the value of the services rendered by the beneficiary prior to that age." Although Lawson never specified, in *Direct Credits for Everybody* or elsewhere, how these determinations of entitlement were to be made, perhaps he again expected to leave the decisions to a board of knowledgians having the requisite insight and expertise.

The final two provisions of Lawson's program were also unusual. One prescribed that in all court proceedings, the government would provide lawyers for both sides. Believing that the present legal system had been corrupted by the financiers' ability to hire high-priced shysters to defend their swindling, Lawson hoped to reorient lawyers toward the pursuit of truth and justice by having the government pay their salaries and prohibiting them from accepting private fees.

The last of Lawson's fourteen points required that "everybody must furnish sworn statements periodically, showing the amount and character of wealth possessed and the manner in which it was obtained." In a later amplification, he specified that these reports would also include data on expenditures and be required at least once every six months. Sworn statements would make it possible for the government to know whether citizens had earned their incomes honestly or fraudulently, spent their incomes in a reasonable manner or hoarded them, treated their employees fairly or exploited them, or illegally attempted to transfer wealth or money to friends or relatives. These statements were crucial to the enforcement of Lawson's program, because "the penalty for willfully breaking any of these laws will be the loss of all wealth by the law breaker. There will be teeth in all Direct Credits laws."

Among the many practical benefits which Lawson claimed for the Direct Credits program would be its salutary impact on taxation. Taxes could be drastically reduced, once governments were freed from the obligation to pay tribute to the financiers in the form of steadily accumulating interest. In fact, Lawson argued that taxes should be eliminated altogether; he proposed instead that the costs of government operations (which he blithely assumed would remain modest) simply be added to the costs of manufactured articles and the revenue raised in this manner then be transferred by manufacturing corporations to the government. But wouldn't immense costs be entailed by the credit programs run by the government? Because the government would have complete control of the money system and the ability to issue money as needed, it is easy to see why Lawson didn't think it necessary to discuss the amounts and means of finance required by his program.

Other practical benefits which Lawson claimed for the Direct Credits program included a gigantic increase in productivity, the stimulation of invention, an outpouring of new consumer products, falling prices, full employment, and high wages and profits. But to his mind, even more important than these substantial benefits were the evils it would eliminate and the moral improvements it would produce. Gone forever would be the capricious ups and downs of the business cycle, the insecurities engendered by unemployment, the strife between capital and labor, the inequitable distribution of the social product, the cruel denial of just treatment to children, the sick, and the aged, and the irrationality of destroying wealth in the form of "surpluses" when many remained in want. Not only would Direct Credits "make wealth as cheap as water and eradicate the cause of human beings quarreling over it," but "it will reduce the number of hours workmen toil, and afford them more time for intellectual pursuits." In sum: "The system of Direct Credits will work for everybody. It will give work to everybody, opportunities to everybody, credit to everybody, money to everybody, nourishment to everybody, comforts to everybody, education to everybody, character to everybody, intelligence to everybody, and justice to everybody."

There is today no way of knowing what reading in economics Lawson may have done prior to writing *Direct Credits for Everybody* or what authors may have exerted special influence on his thinking. For instance, did he get his fundamental dichotomy between industry and finance from Thorstein Veblen? Had he read the Social Credit treatises of the Scottish engineer, Major C. H. Douglas?[1] Lawson didn't say. On several rare occasions in later writings he did refer to Marx and Henry George, but only fleetingly and by way of contrasting his ideas with theirs. Undoubtedly Lawson would have insisted his ideas came full-blown and freshly minted out of his own mind. This seems unlikely, but even if it were so, at least the snug fit of his ideas into the long tradition of American financial reform agitation could hardly be overlooked.

Among the devotees of the Greenback, Populist, and other crusades preceding Lawson in the cause of financial reform were many who had been fetched by simplified, easily grasped, unicausal analyses of economic and political problems and by various panaceas for their remedy. These earnest reformers often shared a view that the ideal

republic of widely distributed power and equal opportunities bequeathed by the founders had been upset and was in the process of
being permanently destroyed by a small handful of manipulators of
concentrated wealth and their touts and lackeys. However, if only
"the people" were rallied to enact a few narrowly confined and relatively marginal changes, they could usher in a new order of justice or,
as the issue was often presented, restore a lost order which had been
subverted. The recommended steps varied—destroy the Bank of the
United States, adopt the single tax, abolish the gold standard, coin
both silver and gold at a sixteen-to-one ratio, print more greenbacks,
pass usury laws, nationalize the banks—but always the money panacea
would solve the most serious political and economic problems. Clearly
the patterns, as well as some of the specific content, of Lawson's analysis
and prescriptions closely matched those of these earlier movements.

Of course, Lawson's program did project an activist and regulative
government role probably going beyond anything ever proposed earlier. Rising as steeply as the power of government under Lawson's
plan would necessarily be a bureaucratic pyramid of unprecedented
size and a mountain of paperwork. And yet for all the initiatives for
radical change which it contained, Lawson's program, like those of his
predecessors in the American financial reform tradition, remained
fundamentally limited and conservative in its objectives.

For example, Lawson sought no change in the American system of
government, politics, and individual liberties. In traditional American
fashion, he rejected notions of the permanent division of society into
classes and the inevitability of class conflict, finding instead a basic
harmony of interests between labor and capital which would come au-
tomatically to the fore once the small artificial class of the financiers
had been eliminated. Under the Direct Credits program, Lawson believed, even the financiers would become useful and honest citizens.
In Lawson's America, as in the ideal America desired by most Americans before and since, all citizens would be middle-class property
owners and all would share fairly and bounteously in the abundant
collective product. Most important, the means to achieve the largest
social product and its equitable distribution were traditional ones: as-
suring equal opportunities for all and then letting all go as far as they

can by virtue of their own self-reliance, industry, and entrepreneurial skill. In other words, Lawson's Direct Credits program, like those of most earlier movements, was intended to shore up the American capitalist system and implement the ideas concerning democracy, equality, rights, individualism, and justice which Americans had always associated with it.

What Lawson hymned was a distinctively American capitalist utopia: "ideal conditions can be established under capitalism if ['financialism'], its deadliest sting, is taken from it." There is ample reason, however, to question how thoroughgoing Lawson's commitment to this position really was. Certainly his new vision of a capitalist utopia clashed with the one recommended in *Born Again*. Recognizing this, he addressed the shift in position frankly: "My book, 'Born Again,' published in 1904, opposed capitalism entirely. But practical experience gained in many ways during the past quarter of a century causes me to look very carefully into the matter from all of its different viewpoints before introducing Direct Credits for Everybody."

During most of those twenty-five years he had, of course, acted in conformance with yet another utopian vision—that of a world restructured in huge global organizations by "great men" of daring entrepreneurial audacity, of which he knew he was the principal example. There definitely were connections, too, between this utopian vision of his aviation editorials and his latest utopia. Both rested, for instance, on the same strategic premise concerning the relation between human nature and institutions: make institutions better and human conduct will be better. Lawson stated this view explicitly in *Direct Credits for Everybody*: "It is the system that must be altered or abolished if improved conditions are to be had. . . . A bad system makes bad men, while on the other hand, a good system will make good men." "There is little use condemning individuals for faults bred into them by the system they are forced to live under," he added. Although this message ran counter to that of *Born Again*, in which Lawson had not hesitated to condemn individuals for their faults and had argued for the moral regeneration of humanity as the prelude to utopia, the message was consonant with the utopian position taken in his aircraft magazines.

Too, the utopias of the aircraft magazines and of *Direct Credits for Everybody* were both capitalist utopias. In his Direct Credits treatise, Lawson even recommended, on grounds of greater efficiency and productivity, a government credit policy which would promote the growth of the huge corporations he had called for in the earlier magazine writings. Certainly also appearing to share the spirit of the aviation editorials was his projection that "those who are more industrially inclined and have more ambition and ability, will rise above the average in station and become leaders in every line of human effort. The fittest will assume authority."

On the other hand, Lawson now showed a new concern about concentrated economic power, which led him to stipulate in *Direct Credits for Everybody* that the government must prevent ownership *and control* of large corporations from resting in the hands of "individuals, families, or cliques." Even though distributed ownership does not necessarily prevent concentrated control by management, Lawson still was prescribing corporate conditions uncongenial to the freedom of action of the freewheeling "great men" he once had celebrated. By calling for widespread ownership and control of the new economic entities, he appeared to be seeking a twentieth-century expression of the ancient American ideal of a wide distribution of modest economic holdings. Moreover, the traditional forms of these holdings—farms and small businesses—were to be no less recognized and served than were large corporations under the regime of Direct Credits. In fact, anyone giving *Direct Credits for Everybody* a quick reading would likely conclude that these traditional small enterprises were the primary objects of Lawson's solicitude. In the end, Lawson's new capitalist vision seemed to be built around not so much bold action by "great men" as expanded opportunities for action afforded to multitudes of little people.

Lawson's reservations about his new utopian vision rested not on a lingering yearning for the utopia he once had called on the "great men" to create but on a conviction that his new vision really was only a second-best alternative to the true utopia outlined in *Born Again*. His experience of twenty-five years had apparently reinforced his earlier convictions of the depravity and squalor of contemporary civilization and the need to reform it through the moral regeneration of humanity. But that same experience had also brought him to see how difficult the thoroughgoing revolution in human life which he sought would be to achieve. As a result of the learning acquired from experience over a quarter of a century, he was now ready to pursue the best he could hope to get under existing conditions, even though it wasn't absolutely the best: "Although the author's ideals are the same now as when he wrote 'Born Again,' still he has learned from experience that it is better to retain the benefits that have come through capitalism, and merge with them the greater benefits of improved economic humane methods; than to condemn everything in connection with capitalism and advocate the hasty extermination of the whole system, which if executed, would throw the entire machinery of mankind out of order and cause terrible suffering for everybody for many years to come." Shortening his sights, he was willing to adjust to the impediments to change presented by the American people, who "will suffer much before they will turn against their masters. They would much rather take half a loaf peacefully than to try and get the whole loaf through turmoil." The Direct Credits program was that possible half-loaf which he hoped he could persuade his fellow citizens to seek.

Although Lawson may have made his extreme and sweeping claims about the benefits of the Direct Credits program partly to coax the approbation of his readers for the program, no doubt there was a genuine sense in which he had come to believe these claims, including even the premise that "ideal conditions can be established under capitalism." Yet an undertone of uneasiness about this premise and his commitment to half a loaf remained. For instance, after declaring at one place that "capitalism can be made to work," he added this important qualification: "At least it can be improved if purged of its worst faults." At another place, he argued that "to try and socialize land and industry in America, as radical economists advocate [and as Lawson advocated in *Born Again*], would be impractical *right now*" [emphasis added]," as if to suggest that he hadn't abandoned hope that someday the whole loaf might be obtained.

His Direct Credits treatise also contained passages exhorting humanity to a moral awakening—passages which were reminiscent of those found, more appropriately, in *Born Again*. For example: "Mankind has a duty to perform here on earth, the first part of which is self-development and self-restraint." For another example: "Everybody must learn to be moderate in the use of wealth and look upon it as a means with which to perform a duty." At one point, Lawson even fell back on his earlier view that institutional reform must await a change for the better in human behavior: "A little less selfishness on the part of all of us; a little less jealousy that others may succeed as well as ourselves; a little more big-heartedness in which we want others to enjoy the same luxuries that we do; will go a long ways toward the establishment of a worthy economic system."

Statements of this kind suggest that Lawson, essentially a moral reformer, sensed a fundamental flaw in his economic reform plan: capitalism—even as it would be at its most enlightened under the Direct Credits program—encouraged materialism, acquisitiveness, and indifference to others and the common weal, not spiritual elevation, moderation, and altruism. Because he sought these latter ends most of all, he had good reason to be troubled about his new commitment to the Direct Credits program. By the end of the decade of the 1930s his reservations figured larger than ever in his mind, finally causing him to break away from commitment to the program.

Throughout most of that decade, however, Lawson threw himself wholeheartedly into the cause of the Direct Credits Society, which he founded in 1931 under the stirring motto of "Justice for Everybody Harms Nobody!" Touting the Direct Credits program as the "perfect economic plan" (even while he also acknowledged it was a compromise), he proclaimed himself to be the "New Emancipator," whose plan would free humanity from the shackles of the financiers.

Lawson also frequently identified himself as "The People's Coach," who would lead the team to a rout of the financiers; *Direct Credits for Everybody* outlined the game plan. But the metaphors of coach and game were really not apt and couldn't hold firmly, because to Lawson's mind, much more was afoot than merely play or even a conventional clash between political forces or economic interests. Always one to view the world as a scene of struggle between the forces of good and evil, he depicted the financiers as no ordinary political interest but rather a

sinister power, which had rigged the game against the apostles of justice and would continue their cheating play until the moment of their
complete capitulation. If God's purposes and the forces of good were to
prevail, more than an emancipator or an able coach was needed, and
hence the more fitting image of "Lawson, the Man of Destiny" eventually worked its way into Lawson's publicity campaign. As the members of the Direct Credits Society flocked to the opportunity to vest
control over their destinies in the Man of Destiny, Lawson took another
giant step toward his ultimate destiny as the First Knowledgian.

8

THE

MAN OF

DESTINY

AND THE

DIRECT

CREDITS

CRUSADE

In the last chapter of *Direct Credits for Everybody* Lawson called on readers to join him in the effort "to promote and educate everybody to want and vote for Direct Credits" and ended with a hopeful forecast: "We shall now see how many will join the movement to make Direct Credits for Everybody a live issue that will work constantly for everybody's good. I predict that when everybody understands this subject . . . interest-collecting financiers will cease to enslave us longer." According to a document which Lawson filed with the United States Patent Office on October 14, 1931, he resided at that time at the Hotel Douglas in Newark, New Jersey. He first spread his traps for members of the Direct Credits Society (DCS) in Philadelphia, however, for reasons not now known.

Lawson later claimed that in 1931 he made a pledge to God, as had John Convert before him, to give himself over entirely to unpaid service to humanity. Did he also, one wonders, take to the street-corner preaching which Convert had used to win souls to the latter's Natural Law Society? Lawson's strong identification with Convert raises this as a real possibility, and the few comments which Lawson later made about his first year in the Direct Credits campaign make it seem all the likelier. There was the precedent, too, of the soap-box speaking which he had done on behalf of a "radical party" in New York City twenty-five years earlier.

Lawson likely had little personal wealth

to bring to his organizing effort in 1931, although his assignment in that year of a patent on his two-tier passenger compartment possibly produced some funds for support of his new organization; he may also have had continuing royalty income from his licensing of the two-tier invention to several railroads. Throughout the 1930s, Lawson often claimed to live a simple, frugal life supported only by proceeds from the sale of his publications. On many occasions, standing before his officers, he would turn his pockets inside out to show that they were empty. The claims and the symbolic displays were somewhat disingenuous, however, because for most of the decade of the 1930s, Lawson had ample funds available to him, including funds donated in substantial amounts by his very generous followers. True enough, these were organizational funds, held by the Humanity Benefactor Foundation, the financial arm of the Direct Credits Society. But because Lawson controlled the Foundation, he had access to whatever money he needed—with no questions asked—to support his living expenses (including those of his family in the 1940s) and his heavy travel expenses. All the while, of course, he could still claim to be a "penniless, propertyless man."

But these were his circumstances during the palmy days of the Direct Credits Society. In 1931, before the organization was a going concern, Lawson's personal condition may actually have been as bleak as he later described it—for instance, requiring him, so he claimed, to use ink to color over the faded and frayed parts of his suit. Perhaps he really was forced to rely on pamphlet peddling to eke out a meager existence. Whatever were the facts about the hand-to-mouth condition which he claimed, Lawson found in it spiritual ennoblement; as he later recalled, "The Creator tried me out by nearly starving me to death the first year."

But his initial selling efforts apparently drew customers, although how many he never said. Having tested the market for depression-era reform agitation and finding it promising, he resolved to go all out in the promotion of the elixir he had on tap. As a follow-up to this decision, sometime in 1932 Lawson relocated the Direct Credits Society and the Humanity Benefactor Foundation to Detroit, the city of his boyhood. To the Society's headquarters at 606 Woodward Avenue was later added an auditorium, located at 4248 Woodward Avenue.

The Direct Credits Hall, Detroit, national headquarters of the Direct Credits Society in bygone years. Photo (taken in 1945) courtesy of the *Des Moines Register.*

Once his organization was set up in its permanent headquarters, Lawson went to work in earnest to build up its membership. A Direct Credits publication dated September, 1932, described the Direct Credits Society as "a non-political association founded primarily to eliminate pauperism" by promoting the adoption of the economic plan outlined in *Direct Credits for Everybody.* By "non-political" Lawson meant that the Direct Credits Society would not affiliate with a political party, sponsor candidates for office, take stands on other, non-economic issues, or allow these peripheral issues to divide the membership. Members were to be free to hold and act on whatever other political affiliations and policy views they wished, so long as they stood behind the Direct Credits program without deviation from a single feature of it.

In this manner, Lawson later claimed, the Direct Credits Society was acting to "separate economics from politics." But of course, on a more conventional understanding of terms, the Direct Credits Society was obviously an interest group engaged in political action. Lawson declared the object of the Society to be "to secure as large a membership as possible," in order that the members might then "express their economic convictions collectively through their officers before Congress for the enactment of laws beneficial to Everybody." Lawson's preoccupation with the membership drive, almost totally to the exclusion of other political activity, derived from his strategic premise that as soon as at least half of the voters in at least half of the congressional districts had given their support to the Direct Credits plan, Congress would enact the plan.

The organization and procedures of the Direct Credits Society were set forth in the Society's *General Orders,* put into final form and published in 1934. The most prominent organizational feature stressed in *General Orders* was the hierarchical principle for which Lawson had already disclosed great fondness in earlier writings. To Lawson's mind, the ideal social arrangement was an organization in which a single person made organizational policy and all other participants carried out the policy. The crucial task of leadership by the chief executive was organizing participants in such a manner that each was put in the proper niche, doing what he or she did best in complete conformance with orders transmitted from above along a chain of command. "Leadership" at all lower levels meant faithfully following orders.

About the issue of authority and its source within the organization, no misunderstanding was possible. As Article 47 specified, "There will be but one Commander-in-Chief of the Direct Credits Society— Alfred Lawson. During his absence from mortal life the Board of Trustees will act with the same powers as if he were present in person." And during his presence in mortal life, Article 7 directed that "all instructions of officers of the Direct Credits Society must come through General Orders by order of Alfred Lawson, the Commander-in-Chief. All rules or regulations of any nature whatsoever are subject to his approval." Much of *General Orders* was taken up with descriptions of other entities of the organization, including, in addition to a Board of Directors, an Executive Committee, a National Committee, and numerous functional departments, but in every case their members were to be appointed by, and also were subject to removal by, the Commander in Chief.

Any person, regardless of "race, nationality, religious belief or political affiliation," could sign an application for membership. Two kinds of membership were specified: passive and active. The active member was one "who contributes his or her services to building and operating the organization." All active members were officers of the Direct Credits Society, appointed pro tem until such time as they had proven themselves worthy of receiving permanent appointment by the Commander in Chief. Lawson made explicit that the phrase "contributes his or her services" was to be understood literally: "The Direct Credits Society has honorary officers who contribute their services without pay. Services, time, or material of any nature whatsoever, must be contributed to the Direct Credits Society free from all expenses."

Not surprisingly, *General Orders* specified military ranks (also official uniforms) for DCS officers. Each new active member would begin as a corporal, but Article 42 explained how he or she could advance: "When an Active member signs 50 new applicants and takes charge of a BLOCK, he or she becomes a Sergeant, pro tem; 100, a Lieutenant, pro tem; 250, a Captain, pro tem; 500, a Major, pro tem; 1,000, a Colonel, pro tem." As officers advanced in rank, they also would become eligible for management of larger geographical areas. Block leaders reported to sector leaders, who in turn reported to district leaders, who reported, finally, to state leaders. (The districts, identified more fully as "economic districts," coincided with congressional districts.) One had to be a brigadier general to be a district leader and to have attained the rank of major general to be a state leader. Of course, "all appointments and promotions of officers are subject to General Orders, or revocation without notice, cause, or explanation by the Commander-in-Chief of the Direct Credits Society."

The conduct of officers while on duty was closely prescribed. Discussions of politics, religion, and public persons were prohibited at DCS meetings. "Economics must be the main thing discussed at all meetings and Direct Credits for Everybody must be the main principles taught." Only Direct Credits literature could be used in the organization's educational activities; lecturers were not to refer to material in any publications other than those of the Direct Credits Society. While dressed in official uniform, officers could not "drink, smoke,

visit beer gardens or questionable places" and at DCS schools or meetings "no smoking, chewing of tobacco, liquor drinking, spitting or
using vulgar language will be permitted." Nor at any public meeting
sponsored by the Direct Credits Society could debates, general discussions of economics, answering of questions from the platform, or use
of parliamentary rules be allowed. The meeting chair, as "sole judge
of who may speak and the time that he or she may occupy the floor,"
was to be mindful that the purpose of meetings was "to teach Direct
Credits for Everybody and not to argue about anything." While officers were granted the right *individually* to file *with Lawson* written complaints against other officers, any attempt to combine or coordinate
with other officers for this purpose would be considered a "conspiracy," punishable by "suspension, demotion, or dismissal."

The final major topic addressed in *General Orders* was organization
finance. Article 40 prohibited membership fees or dues. One reason
for the ban was to ensure that no one would be barred by financial
circumstances from joining, but another reason was to assure that "the
Direct Credits Society has no assets or liabilities." This condition was
needed, Lawson explained on later occasions, to eliminate an allure-
ment to "the slickers"—agents of the financiers—and the risk, if they
ever did get a foothold in the organization, that they might harm the
Direct Credits Society by stealing its funds or committing it financially.

But Lawson knew full well that there would be large costs involved
in running the nationwide organization which he aimed to create—
costs going far beyond those met by the contributed labor and personal expenditures of members (although the value of these proved
to be enormous). Article 31 barred direct solicitation of funds from
the public but did prescribe "four ways of financing operations for the
benefit of the Direct Credits Society"—freewill offerings at meetings,
contributions from DCS members, proceeds from the sale of Direct
Credits literature, and the sale of advertisements in Direct Credits
publications. The key phrase above is "for the benefit of the Direct
Credits Society"; although he didn't say so explicitly here, the money
raised in these ways would not be funds of the Direct Credits Society
but rather funds available to it (under Lawson's total control, of course)
which, in order to thwart "the slickers," would be legally held by the
Humanity Benefactor Foundation.

It is the rare organization which will as frankly avow as did the Direct Credits Society the principle of one-person rule. In doing so, Lawson was doubtless running athwart a norm of American political culture and also was expecting from his members a more serious kind of commitment than Americans will usually give to political organizations. None of these considerations appears to have inhibited Lawson's success, however. Although the absence of organizational records today makes it difficult to say much precisely about the DCS membership, the available fragmentary evidence strongly suggests that the number of passive members was huge and, more significant, that Lawson also succeeded in drawing in a very large number of active members.

The six issues of a Direct Credits magazine which Lawson published from 1932 to 1936 recorded, by names and ranks, the promotions of DCS officers, from which lists it is possible to get some feel for DCS recruitment and growth in the early days of the organization. The June, 1932, issue of *Humanity* (all subsequent issues were entitled *Direct Credits*) reported 132 promotions in seventeen states, but over half of these came in the two states of Michigan and Indiana. Other states having 7 or more promotions were Ohio, Pennsylvania, New York, West Virginia, and Tennessee. Three months later, in the September, 1932, issue of *Direct Credits*, 398 promotions were reported in twenty-eight states. Over half of these (240) occurred in Michigan, while 27 came in Indiana. All of the other states listed above also advanced significantly in promotions, and three new states—Maryland, Texas, and California—made it into the circle of those having at least 7 promotions, which indicated that DCS was in process of establishing the far-flung outposts which would qualify it in form, at least, as a national organization.

Yet these same data also showed that the center of DCS strength already was Michigan and nearby states, a fact made even clearer in the first issue of the DCS magazine published in 1933. Here eleven pages were given over to listing promotions of about 7,800 officers in Michigan alone. At the end of the list, Lawson also claimed that the total officer corps in Michigan numbered more than 10,000. In the next issue, published later in 1933, he advanced the claim to 20,000 officers in Michigan.

15 cents

DIRECT CREDITS

VOL. I   NO. 3

TYING YOU UP FOREVER

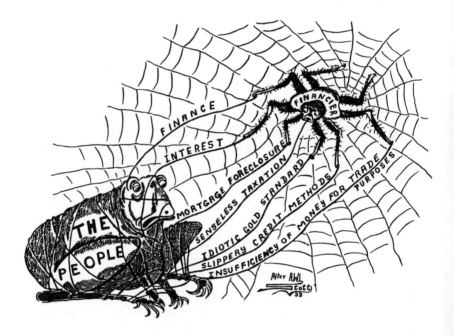

What Are YOU Going To Do About It?

The cover of an early (1934) issue of Lawson's first Direct Credits serial publication.

By the end of 1933, according to Lawson, the Direct Credits Society had members in all forty-eight states. These, of course, must have been mainly passive members, but doubtless there were active members, or officers, in most or all of these states, too. In the 1934 issue of *Direct Credits*, Lawson claimed 75,000 officers nationwide. Two years later, in the 1936 issue, the number had jumped to 150,000 officers.

In these last two numbers of the DCS magazine, Lawson no longer listed all promotions but only promotions of officers (not identified by states) to the ranks of major general and brigadier general. The 1934 issue identified 113 and 242 elevated to these two ranks, respectively. The comparable lists in the 1936 issue included 276 and 399 names, respectively. Since to reach these high ranks these officers must each have recruited at least 1,000 members (the number required to become a colonel), they alone must have accounted for about one million members, and of course the numerous other officers at lower ranks would have added many more members, probably also numbering in the millions. In Michigan alone, in 1936 Lawson claimed the total active and passive membership of the Direct Credits Society was one and one-half million.

There is no way to verify Lawson's figures, but even allowing for the possibility that he may have puffed them up a bit, one can still safely conclude that he got a very substantial response to his membership drive in the first half of the 1930s. Further evidence of this is supplied in the Direct Credits magazines by the numerous photographs published there showing uniformed DCS officers by the hundreds marching in parades or by the thousands attending to Lawson's speeches in huge auditoriums in such cities as Cleveland, Toledo, and Detroit.

The greatest concentration of DCS members was found in the Midwest, especially in and near the cities of Michigan and the states immediately adjoining—Ohio, Indiana, Illinois, and Wisconsin—because Lawson concentrated his most strenuous recruiting effort there. Why he did so can't be known for sure today. However, the scope of Lawson's recruitment activities probably was to some extent constrained by his decisions on the role he would play and the methods he would use in the effort to reach new members.

Maintaining that the financiers had barred his access to radio (but

A decorated truck publicizing an appearance by Lawson in Cleveland in 1934. From *Direct Credits* 1, no. 5 (1934).

more likely because he found cheering, adoring audiences spread before his eyes more gratifying to his ego and more congenial to his speaking style than were unseen radio audiences), Lawson took to constant travel and speechmaking in public halls in order to publicize the Direct Credits Society and its program. Neither his skill as a public speaker (about which more later) nor the success of DCS in getting a large membership in the towns and cities where he spoke is a matter for doubt. However, the serial speaking which Lawson adopted as his main propaganda method did have implications for the efficiency of his effort; being frequently on the road and living out of a suitcase required a huge expenditure of time, money, and bodily ergs, yielding in return a shorter outreach than might have been obtained by use of radio. In the end, Lawson's speechmaking campaign appears rarely to have gotten very far from home base in Detroit.

The relatively narrow geographical range of Lawson's stump-speaking tours is confirmed today by a collection of tickets in the possession of one of the Lawsonomists. What these tickets reveal is an effort confined to an area of the United States swept by a radius of only several hundred miles out from Detroit. Of the eighty-six tickets for Lawson's appearances for which locations can be identified, one is for a speech given in Buffalo, New York. All the rest are for speeches presented in eight Midwestern states, and three states account for seventy-two of these eighty-five Midwestern speeches—Michigan, forty; Ohio, twenty-two; and Indiana, ten. The remainder are distributed as follows: Illinois, five; Wisconsin, three; Iowa, three; Missouri (Saint Louis), one; and Nebraska (Omaha), one.

In spite of the heavy burdens involved in a relentless routine of travel and public speaking, however, over the seven years (1933–1939) covered by these tickets, Lawson could certainly have made more forays than he did into new and more distant territory. That he apparently didn't do so may be linked partly to another peculiarity of Lawson's promotional methods: believing that the financiers also controlled all newspapers in the United States, Lawson refused to advertise in them and relied instead on his officers to publicize his appearances and line up the crowds for him to address. As one consequence of his refusal even to give advance press releases to the newspapers, his speeches and rallies would usually come and go unheeded by the press, a result which then served to confirm Lawson's conviction that the financiers had conspired to blank out all public mention of him and the Direct Credits Society. But Lawson's chosen method of publicizing his speeches only through the efforts of his officers obviously had another flaw, which was its dependence on the presence of a well-developed local DCS organization to serve as his advance agent. This left Lawson in an anomalous position: while the purpose of his travels and speechmaking was to gain new members and build the organization, he could not count on putting on a successful show where he didn't already have a strong organization and many active members. Under these circumstances, it is easy to understand that he would stick close to the well-plowed ground of the Midwest.

Lawson was well aware of the ethnic and nationality differences among his audience in the Midwest and took steps to accommodate them by issuing foreign language translations of his published speeches and of *Benefactor*, his official DCS periodical after 1935. At one time in the late 1930s, in fact, *Benefactor* appeared in Polish, Italian, Hungarian, Romanian, German, Croatian, Serbian, and Ukrainian editions, as well as in the principal English edition and a French edition for use in Canada. However, there is no evidence that Lawson focused his member recruitment campaign on particular ethnic or nationality groups, and certainly he never altered his Direct Credits message, or otherwise fashioned special appeals, in order to play up to one or another of these limited audiences. On the surface, the DCS promotion lists do seem to disclose a preponderance of names of Western European origin. However, even if a more detailed analysis showed that persons of Eastern and Southern European origin (that is, persons deriving from later waves of immigration and therefore lower in the American pecking order) were disproportionately underrepresented among Lawson's officers, clearly it was not the result of policy. Lawson also appears to have made no more special effort (directly or covertly) to appeal to members of any particular religious group than to appeal to members of any ethnic or status group. In both respects, he differed considerably from Father Charles Coughlin, who was out beating many of the same bushes at the same time with much the same doctrinal stick.

Mention of Father Coughlin also brings to mind the anti-Semitic strain found in the Catholic priest's movement and prompts the question of whether a similar strain was found in the Direct Credits movement. Coughlin and Lawson certainly agreed about who the devil was—the "international financiers"—but there is no evidence that Lawson, like Coughlin, intended this to be understood, or at least was willing to let it be understood, as "Jewish international financiers." Not once in his writings and published speeches did Lawson ever let slip any overt or coded anti-Semitic statement. Moreover, in the many cartoons found in DCS publications, portrayals of the financiers employed no Shylockian stereotypes or other hackneyed cartoon conventions meant to suggest Jewishness. In sum, it seems reasonably clear that Lawson's mind was free from anti-Semitism and also from a willingness to exploit it to advance his cause. What may have been in the minds of his followers is another matter, of course, and it is possible that Lawson's increasingly fervent attacks on the "international financiers" may have unintentionally tapped anti-Semitic attitudes among some in his audiences and drawn a favorable response on that basis (just as his identification of London as the principal seat of the international financiers may in some instances have engaged anti-British sentiments).

Were there Jewish members of the Direct Credits Society? When asked this question in recent years, several long-time Lawson followers insisted that there were; each recalled knowing or working with some members who were Jewish. However, affirmative responses based on a few examples suggest that Jewish members were not numerous.

About the racial composition of the Direct Credits Society one can draw a conclusion with a greater feeling of confidence; the most striking common feature of the hundreds of DCS officers depicted in the many photographs which Lawson published in his Direct Credits magazines is the whiteness of their skin. Lawson, of course, insisted that DCS membership was open to persons of all races, and at least one former DCS activist today recalls having carried the DCS sales pitch to blacks, both individually and in group meetings, on more than one occasion. However, this person also recalls that the efforts yielded no black recruits and, along with another long-time follower of Lawson, has no recollection of ever encountering a black among the active members. Perhaps there nonetheless were some blacks among the passive members; after all, such cities of DCS strength as Detroit, Chicago, and Cleveland already had large black populations, and signatures by blacks on membership applications would be as valuable as any others for indicating the ground swell underway for the DCS program. Supporting this surmise is a document in Lawson's FBI file, which mentions the existence in 1940 of a DCS "Bureau of Information for Colored People Only" in Chicago.

Another important characteristic of DCS membership disclosed in the photographs is the large number of women who were DCS officers. The openness of the Direct Credits Society to women is not surprising, in view of Lawson's claim that the enactment of the Direct Credits program "will make women the equals of men, physically, mentally, morally, and spiritually." On the other hand, the largest proportion of the female DCS officers who are identified by name seem to be wives or other relatives of male officers. This suggests that the Direct Credits Society, its doctrine, and its leader may have had

The Direct Credits Society had many female officers, a battalion of whom are here shown on parade in Detroit in 1933. From *Direct Credits* 1, no. 5 (1934).

special attractiveness not so much for women as for whole families or even groups of families within particular economic strata and ethnic and religious communities located in the industrialized and urbanized parts of the Midwest. Certainly a very large number of DCS photographs show families—husband, wife, and children (both adult and minor)—decked out in DCS uniforms (Lawson provided a junior officer corps to accommodate the youngsters). The lists of promotions and of officers involved in various DCS meetings and other activities also contain a considerable overlapping of names.

The DCS membership application form asked applicants to identify their political party affiliations and pledge to work within their parties for enactment of the DCS program, but no information is available today about either the party identifications of members or their affiliations with other significant organizations, such as labor unions. Neither can anything be found out about the members' educational backgrounds. About the economic characteristics of DCS members, however, a few conclusions can be worked up from miscellaneous fragments of information.

Certainly the DCS ranks included members who were assembly line employees, farm hands, and other kinds of unskilled workers—or at least had been until the calamity of the depression of the 1930s may have stripped them of their jobs. For some of these, full-time organizing and recruiting work for the Direct Credits Society appears to have provided an unsalaried employment alternative which at least provided food, shelter, and other basics from organizational resources.

For the most part, however, the Direct Credits Society was distinctly not an army of the poor, the unskilled, the unemployed, or the demoralized and destitute. It is safe to say that DCS members were not, by and large, among the most economically vulnerable in American society or those hit the hardest by the depression; both in flusher times and during the Great Depression, they probably fared better, on the average, than did most Americans.

All of the available evidence, fragmentary though it is, points to this conclusion. Consider, in the first place, that active membership in the Direct Credits Society was not cheap. Members carried most of the financial burden of their local DCS activities, including such costs as those involved in maintaining local headquarters, recruiting new members, and buying uniforms. When Lawson came to town and a parade and rally were called for, the members participating footed the largest share of the costs; the numerous elaborate parade floats which they provided are documented in the photographs in the DCS magazines, as also are the many vehicles made available by members for use in the parades and for extended recruiting drives by DCS crews.

Although members did not pay dues to DCS, probably most contributed frequently at weekly DCS meetings when the hat was passed around. The totals raised by this means were often substantial. According to a former DCS officer speaking in 1945, the take at the weekly meetings at Benefactor Hall in Detroit once ran to over $1,000 per meeting, and collections at neighborhood meetings could net $90 to $100. Many members also made special "voluntary donations" to DCS. For example, a special fund drive made by Lawson in 1943 brought in over $84,000 within six months. On that occasion, ten of the contributions were in amounts of $1,000 or more.

The money contributed sometimes reflected extraordinary generosity and genuine sacrifice on the part of contributors. A *Des Moines Register* reporter in 1945 dug up many examples among former Lawson followers in Detroit. "My family gave Lawson $8,000 over 10 years time," one former DCS officer claimed. "That's the reason we don't have a home of our own today." Other officers described in the reporter's story allegedly cashed in their insurance policies or sold farms, cemetery lots, stores and businesses in order to make substantial contributions to Lawson.

Other evidence points in the direction of a reasonably well-off and substantially middle-class membership of the Direct Credits Society. According to the testimony today of several longstanding followers of Lawson, for instance, the DCS ranks definitely included owners of farms and small businesses and members having substantial wealth. The advertisements carried in DCS publications document the membership in DCS of many operators of small businesses, as also do the inscriptions of sponsorship on some of the parade floats depicted in the DCS magazines. Scattered through the pages of these magazines also are discussions of or references to members who were public school teachers, church ministers, contractors, school board members, and other local officials, including a municipal judge, as well as owners of small businesses. Finally, the present or pre-retirement occupations of the small band of DCS members surviving today tell much the same story; included among the handful attending annual Lawsonomy reunions in recent years have been, for instance, an osteopathic doctor, an accountant, a professional engineer, an owner of a small metalworking firm, a school teacher, a farmer, and several members of skilled-craft occupations.

Looked at from one angle, the success of Lawson's recruitment among persons of middle-class standing might not seem surprising. After all, their numbers included many—farmers, small businessmen, would-be or actual entrepreneurs—who stood to benefit the most from the enactment of Lawson's economic program. Rational calculations of self-interest might seem, then, to be the obvious main factor accounting for their attraction to the Direct Credits Society.

But more than pursuit of material self-interest was involved in their enlistments. Indeed, if DCS members had been responsive to material incentives only, far fewer would have joined, because Lawson actually offered to them a *negative* balance of material costs and benefits. On one side of the ledger, Lawson expected active members to pay enormous costs, including out-of-pocket expenditures and donations, many hours of unsalaried organizational work, acceptance of strict control over the conditions of their participation in the organization, and a foregoing of any opportunity to share in the shaping of Direct Credits policy. But on the other side, the only thing of material value which Lawson could dangle in front of potential members was the *prospect* of free loans *if* the Direct Credits program was ever enacted. On a severely rational calculation of self-interest, many would-be active members would have chosen instead to be "free riders," reasoning that their participation could not be crucial to the success of DCS and that if DCS did succeed, they would benefit anyway without having to bear any of the costs.

In the face of the disinclination of most people (at least most Americans) to pay very high, or any, costs to achieve a *collective* benefit, many organizational entrepreneurs seeking a mass membership have resorted to providing *selective* benefits also—that is, benefits which only organization members can receive, such as attractive and valuable publications, useful "insider" information, or discounts on purchases of such things as prescription drugs, trips to Europe, and health insurance. Lawson offered nothing which could be plausibly construed as a selective material benefit. However, it is clear that his followers did perceive in DCS membership important selective benefits of a non-material sort.

According to the testimony of many DCS members, for example, reading Lawson's treatise or hearing his message for the first time had been for them like the sudden lifting of a veil from their eyes. Thanks to Lawson, at last they thought they understood how things had gone wrong in the United States and what should be done about them. Enlisting in the cause of Direct Credits, they concurred, was the obvious next step to take in order to give expression to their newfound, supercharged convictions. Of course, the free-rider logic holds that few would actually have followed through to pay the costs of membership merely because they had strong feelings about the rightness of the DCS program. The 1930s were not normal times, however. The widespread perception then of unprecedented crisis gave rise to a larger than usual number of persons alarmed about their country's fate and ready to enlist in the cause of one sure cure or another. Among the many groups and movements springing up to compete for the satisfaction of this widespread yearning for *expressive* benefits was the Direct

Credits Society. Lawson's appeal was ably crafted to hold its own in the competition, counterbalancing as it did a call for radical changes with a simplistic explanation of problems and a soothing affirmation of many hoary American verities, of conventional moral and religious sentiments, of patriotism and law-abiding respectability.

For the many true believers in the Direct Credits doctrine, the missionary work which they were called upon to perform also brought substantial *solidary* benefits—that is, gratifications derived from participation itself. Over the course of the 1930s Lawson gave increasing emphasis to the theme that the DCS officers were a new cognoscenti from whose learned and well-disciplined ranks would come the leaders of tomorrow's better world. Features of the organization which contributed powerfully to the élan and sense of special community found in DCS included the many local chapters built on networks of friends, entire families, and neighborhoods, the availability of many local DCS headquarters and meeting halls as social centers for members, the military ranks which accorded status and offered incentives to advance in service to the organization, the camaraderie developed by crews of DCS officers in their extended recruiting forays undertaken in new territory, the almost endless singing of an enormous repertoire of Direct Credits songs, and the many elements of pageantry provided by the organization, including uniforms, marching bands, and parades featuring spectacular floats.

What Lawson succeeded in doing was to make some of the costs of DCS membership into sources of benefits for the members. In normal times, the demanding requirements, strict discipline, and considerable encroachments on members' private lives and personal autonomy would probably not have been perceived by many as benefits or even as an acceptable price of DCS membership. In the circumstances of the 1930s, however, not only was Lawson able successfully to buck the usual indifference of Americans to appeals made on behalf of collective benefits, but he also overcame the usual reluctance of many Americans to make political activity a central and determinative part of their lives. As a result, he made of DCS not so much a conventional interest group as an organization which smacked of being a blend of military order, fraternal lodge, and church.

Direct Credits parades featured large, dramatic floats, as in this "All Nations" float in Cleveland in 1934. From *Direct Credits* 1, no. 5 (1934).

Fervent seekers warming to an organization of this kind or to the DCS ideology, however, would probably also have felt the tug of a third source of attraction to the Direct Credits Society—Lawson himself. For if they believed the DCS doctrine was eye-opening Truth, were they not also likely to revere the man whose towering intellect had produced this great gift? And if they found emotional balm in participation in the Direct Credits Society, would they not also feel a profound sense of debt owed to the benefactor who had built the organization and continued to endow it with beneficence by his presence? Indeed, the very conditions of membership—unswerving fidelity to Lawson's doctrine, unquestioning subordination to his direction—insured these results; members who didn't wax enthusiastic about Alfred Lawson would necessarily have found continued involvement in DCS unsustainable.

The evidences of the DCS members' adulation of Lawson are abundant. They can be spotted, for example, in members' testimonials to Lawson published in the early DCS magazines, in the slogans adorning the gaudy parade floats depicted in those same magazines, and in the accounts of several mass meetings, which reported that the cheer-

ing didn't stop for fifteen minutes after Lawson had been introduced
and walked on stage. No visitor to a reunion of the surviving Lawsonomists could fail to notice, too, the undiminished place which Lawson continues to hold in their hearts and minds; although dead for
over thirty-five years, Lawson somehow is still there, still the major
orienting factor in their lives, still referred to in hushed and reverent
tones simply as "Commander," the affectionate name bestowed on
him in the glory days when he was with them bodily. But probably the
most revealing evidence of the singular response of the members to
their leader is found in the lyrics of the DCS songs which once were
sung so heartily and interminably.

In 1940 the Direct Credits songs, all written by Lawson's followers,
were gathered in a songster entitled *Songs That Will Be Sung Forever*.
Of the fifty-one songs published there, no fewer than ten make the
claim that Lawson had been sent by God to lead humanity to justice
through the Direct Credits program or Lawsonomy, and in some of
these songs, Lawson is expressly identified as God's answer to humanity's prayers. In a few instances, Lawson seems to be depicted, like
Moses, simply as the agent of transmission of a plan whose author is
God—for example, "The plan we stand for is God's will to be done /
And he chose Alfred Lawson to do it" and also "Lawson's Plan, eman-
cipation / 'Twas a God-sent inspiration." Oftener, Lawson is given lavish credit for a more creative intellectual role, but in those instances it
still is clear that it was part of God's plan to dispatch the "greatest
mastermind" of all time to discern God's intentions for humanity—as,
for instance, in this line: "Creator of all, within His law / Sent a mastermind to teach Natural Law."

All of the foregoing themes are brought together nicely in the lyrics
of a song entitled, "Economic Freedom":

> We cannot change a wicked past but we can all agree,
> To follow Alfred Lawson on to save humanity.
> We asked for guidance and expect an answer to our call,
> So recognize this man God sent to teach and lead us all.

The theme of saving humanity recurs frequently, too, throughout the
entire corpus of songs. As one lyric puts it, "Lawson a leader bold

came forth mankind to save," and in another song, the message is hymned as follows:

> Lawson will save us, yes, save us forever,
> His name forever all mankind will remember,
> Mankind will honor, his name will live on,
> Telling posterity what he had done.

But the most extraordinary lyrics are those which deal with relations between Lawson and his officers or declare the personal significance of Lawson for his followers and their lives. In these lyrics, expressions of love for Lawson are offered repeatedly, as in "Lawson, we love you, your name we proclaim," or as in "He's our great Commander, and we love him true," or finally, as in this verse:

> Alfred Lawson, how we love thy name,
> Posterity will bow to thy fame.
> Alfred Lawson, how we love thy name,
> Loyal to you we will ever remain.

And some of the songs offer assurances that the great man is not some stern and distant authority figure but an accessible, friendly human being who reciprocates the love heaped upon him—for instance, "He's our friend and leader, always he will be / Here to guide and help us through Lawsonomy." Moreover, the great man's love for his followers is seen as transforming:

> He came into our lives so drear,
> This wonderful man we know.
> He came with words of love and cheer,
> And set our hearts aglow.

Not only are hearts lit up by Lawson's presence and his love for his followers but his Great Message gives point and direction to anomic lives—for example, "We need your teachings evermore for without them what would we do?" and "With our commander, we will never falter." A similar sentiment is sent forth in another song: "With our Commander leading on before / With him to guide us we can feel secure." And yet another song picks up the theme with dithyrambic abandon:

Listen! Listen! Alfred Lawson's come.
Oh have no fear for Lawson's here,
He's come to aid humanity.
Happy now are we! Oh happy now are we!

But if the great teacher and leader is to work his wonders in lives otherwise "so drear," powerless, and adrift, his followers must repose complete, undoubting trust and faith in him: "Our faith that Alfred Lawson will lead us all the way / Should ever urge us onward and his commands we must obey." In making the same point, another song— "The Friend of All"—neatly combines with it a résumé of virtually all the emotions ignited in Lawson's officers when they contemplated their great leader:

Our Commander, how we love him!
We have put our trust in him.
We'll obey his orders, follow where he leads.
He's our leader, he's our teacher, and he is our comrade dear.
Yes, Lawson is the friend of all.

Can these song lyrics leave any doubts about the comfortable fit here of that overworked (and often misused) concept, charisma? The extraordinary qualities attributed to Lawson in the DCS songs were precisely of the kind indicated by Max Weber in his pioneering work on the subject. Belief in the reality of those qualities legitimated for the DCS officers their complete submission to Lawson's guidance, a conduct both prescribed in the songs and acknowledged in Weber's account of charisma; and on the basis of his followers' voluntary submission, Lawson was enabled to exercise over them a profound influence exactly matching that called charismatic by Weber.[1]

Leaping out of the DCS songs is evidence suggesting two of the major ingredients in the response of Lawson's followers to their leader: a stress-inducing sense of personal inefficacy, unequal to the task of contending with the events impinging on their lives, and a stress-relieving determination to find in and through Lawson the control over events which they felt to be lacking in themselves. Both inner states would seem to characterize fairly a person who could sing such remarkable lines as "Lawson will save us," "with him to guide us we can feel secure," "without [his teaching] what would we do," and "have no fear for Lawson's here." If this be granted, then Lawson's followers could be described as engaging in a kind of coping behavior which psychologist Albert Bandura has identified as the search for "proxy control." In Bandura's account, proxy control is a surrendering of the dependents' personal control or power to a proxy, who is thereby empowered. In the case of Lawson (and probably of all charismatic leaders), this was precisely what happened. But, again in line with Bandura's specifications, the empowerment of Lawson was part of an exchange in which his followers expected in return an improved control over the circumstances of their lives through proxy control. In short, Lawson's followers surrendered power and agreed to submit to power—but in order to acquire power, or at least the sense of having enhanced power.[2]

On his side of the charismatic relationship, Lawson played a part tightly entwined with the ecstatic response rising from his followers. Quite willing to accede to their belief that the hand of God was upon him, he took on the new self-proclaimed title of the "Man of Destiny" and acted accordingly. Certain that he had hold of the whole truth, demanding complete subordination of others to him, and always ready to eject from his organization those judged to have defied his total control, Lawson poured out in ever-increasing volume the most extreme claims imaginable concerning his accomplishments, selflessness, and intellectual genius. Outsiders might scoff at his claims and denounce him as a megalomaniacal authoritarian, but to his followers, Lawson's imperious conduct and utterances were perfectly consistent with their exalted estimation of the man and perhaps were even proof of the validity of that estimation.

Although in later years some of Lawson's followers were to recall in him a penetrating power of the eyes (in the words of one, "He could see right through you to your soul") and an uncanny ability to read their minds, outsiders looking at photographs of Lawson taken in the 1930s will miss these preternatural qualities and see nothing else extraordinary or exciting about the man. He was trim, erect, and tall (about six feet), but advancing years had robbed him of the strikingly handsome face, the athletic appearance, and the air of immense vitality always disclosed in photographs taken in his younger years. His

A Friend of the Children

ALFRED LAWSON
Commander-in-Chief of the
Direct Credits Society

Lawson in the 1930s. From Lawson, *Creation*.

silvery hair especially betrayed the fact that he was now in his sixties. Moreover, his apparel had suffered a marked decline in recent years; once a natty dresser, now he usually went about in a cheap, plain suit, discordantly accented by unbuttoned shirt collar and absence of necktie. But of course, his undashing appearance was perfectly in keeping with his claim to be the penniless servant of humanity.

If one may generalize from the accounts of several surviving Lawsonomists who were privileged to hear Lawson speak in the 1930s and 1940s, Lawson's speechmaking ability was a prime asset for rousing the enthusiasm of his followers. These long-time members agree that Lawson possessed a powerful voice, which he could project far out into an auditorium. Although they claim he never spoke from a prepared text or even from notes, his fluency and loquacity apparently never faltered.

Lawson published transcriptions of several of his speeches in booklet form, giving them such titles as *Manufacturers*, *Watch the Slickers*, and *Hey, Farmers, Know the Game*. Transcriptions of many more of his speeches ended up in *Benefactor*, his newspaper, under screaming headlines composed of huge, boldface letters—for instance, FINANCE IS THE BUNK, CIVILIZATION IS THE STAGE OF SKINNERY, DOCTOR FINANCIER AND HIS LIVE CORPSE, THE DICTATOR IS JUST AROUND THE CORNER, DEMOCRACY NOW HAS ONE FOOT IN THE GRAVE, and PEACE? NOT WHILE FINANCIERS RULE THE WORLD. Anyone reading these speeches will be ready to believe that Lawson must indeed have been a gifted speaker—especially so, if these speeches really were extemporized on the stump.

A portion of most of Lawson's speeches consisted of non-technical elaboration of teachings found in *Direct Credits for Everybody*, presented in terms which connected his general ideas to the lives and personal concerns of his audiences. Appearing in the speeches were many concrete and homely illustrations of how the present financial system worked against the interests of farmers, workers, merchants, and manufacturers—the "producers"—and of what difference the DCS program would make to persons in each of these groups. A major theme was the common interest of all producers in opposing

BENEFACTOR

"For the People, Of the People, and By the People"

Vol. 2 — No. 7   27   Justice for Everybody Harms Nobody   Three Cents

JUMP

WHENEVER THE FINANCIER PULLS THE STRING
COPYRIGHT, 1939
BY ALFRED LAWSON
Address at Masonic Temple, Jackson, Michigan.   Taken Verbatim by B. Freese, M. G. D. C. S.
UNLESS YOU KNOW THESE THINGS YOU ARE NOT EDUCATED

Part of the first page of the 1939 issue of Lawson's second Direct Credits serial publication, showing a typical screaming headline.

the financiers and not falling prey to the financiers' attempts to foment civil war among them.

But stirring up civil strife was just one of the numerous crimes of the financiers which Lawson detailed in his speeches; his listeners were regaled with blood-boiling illustrations of the heartlessness of the alien financiers. The eyes of his audiences were also opened to some startling facts which they probably hadn't known before—for instance, that the global conspiracy of the financiers had engineered the Russian Revolution and the Spanish Civil War and was the true power behind every dictatorship in the world, including that of the Soviet Union. Over and over again Lawson exposed the alien financiers' secret control in the United States of the major and minor political parties, of the press and radio, of the public schools and the colleges and universities, of local, state, and national governments, of labor unions and trade and manufacturing associations, and of all reform organizations except the Direct Credits Society.

Lawson's fulminations against the alien financiers constituted the largest part of all of his speeches and were productive of much colorful abuse, probably delivered with great sarcasm and crowd-tickling effect. Among the vituperative names which Lawson loosed at the financiers were "gold worshippers," "devils," "parasites," "wolves," "swindlers," and "two-tailed monkeys" (in reference to the swallow-tailed coats which they allegedly wore). However, the term he used most often to describe them was "slickers," of which there were three types—"mastodon," "second-story," and "pee-wee"—and always associated with the "slickers" were their "touts," who included professorial lackeys and "theorists," also referred to as "donkeys." Many times Lawson invoked the familiar image of the carnival shell game, in order to make the point that only the gullible could believe that they could beat the slickers and touts at their swindling enterprise.

As an assist to his main effort to stir up his audiences' wrath and focus it on the alien financiers, Lawson often resorted to scare tactics, as is hinted at in the frightening titles of some of his published speeches (and even graphically conveyed in the disturbingly large, bold headline letters used to spread these titles across the pages of *Benefactor*). Referred to many times was a diabolical ten-year, five-point plan by which the alien financiers were moving to transform and subjugate America. Already accomplished, he ominously observed, were the first three points: 1) withdrawing most of the money from circulation, thus forcing foreclosures as debtors found it impossible to make interest payments; 2) imposing unemployment on a large percentage of the work force, reducing the wages of those still working and fostering jealousies and strife among the entire work force; and 3) revaluing gold, thus doubling the capacity of the financiers to make loans while at the same time halving the purchasing power of the income of the "producers." Just ahead lay the achievement of the final two points: 4) replacing the American form of government with a dictatorship; and 5) after eliminating all freedoms and educational institutions, creating a financial aristocracy to rule over an ignorant, illiterate population "with the sword, gun, gas, and bayonet."

Already Lawson professed to see the signs of coming events. For example, he asked his listeners, why was the United States Army undertaking to recruit fifty thousand additional soldiers? And what were the real reasons for proposals increasingly heard (evidence of which not cited, however) to limit press freedom, allegedly in order

In Direct Credits cartoons, the financiers were depicted as either ghoulish or diabolical, as in this 1935 cartoon showing a DCS officer applying the brake to the "devil men's" five-point plan for subjugating America. From Lawson, *Powerful Editorials.*

to curtail the "yellow press," and to reinstate the whipping post, allegedly in order to punish wife-beaters and drug addicts? And lest his listeners be taken in by current gabble about centralizing or nationalizing the banking system, Lawson hastened to point out that, unaccompanied by other fundamental reforms, this step would merely enhance the control of the financiers, just as had the Federal Reserve System. Finally, Lawson disabused his audiences of any wishful thinking about improvement in the economy. The financiers had planned and hatched the depression, he often averred; because their fiendish interests were not yet fully served, the depression was far from over and would, in fact, get much worse, unless or until the financiers' grip was broken and interest was abolished.

But the malefactors had finally met their match. "The financiers are afraid of Lawson," Lawson boasted, adding that his fearless postings of the truth about them drove them into wild frenzies. Goodly portions of many of his speeches recounted his experiences with the financiers during his aviation years, when they had tried to co-opt him and buy him off. Now they were doing all that they could to deny him access to the public. But his voice would not be silenced. The people finally had a champion who would not let them down. Having hob-nobbed with the financiers and spurned their allurements in the past, Lawson was proud to be back with the common people with whom he had started life. As "The People's Coach," he would lead them to final victory in the titanic struggle, now in its last critical throes, between the forces of good and evil. Not power, privilege, or wealth, but the opportunity to serve the people was the object of Lawson's quest. In return for his selfless dedication to the interests of the people, the only things he wanted were their love and respect. That this last point expressed a longing urgently felt by Lawson is evidenced by the great frequency with which it appeared in his speeches and writings.

In the fervency and devotion of his members, as well as in their large number, Lawson appeared to have made a very respectable showing—in the face, moreover, of a fierce competition from many other expert anglers in the streams of discontent. Yet merely to sum-mon back to memory the names of the celebrated demagogic giants of that period is enough to plant a doubt about Lawson's stature and impact as a depression-era agitator. Father Coughlin, Huey Long, Gerald L. K. Smith, Dr. Townsend, "Liberty Bell" Lemke—these, but not Lawson's, are the names remembered. The same pattern holds for the many agitational organizations and movements of the era. Almost everyone having an interest in the history of the 1930s will know about Coughlin's National Union for Social Justice, Long's "Share-Our-Wealth" movement, the Townsend Plan crusade, the Union Party, the Silver Shirts—but who remembers or has ever heard of the Direct Credits Society?

This failure of Lawson and the Direct Credits Society to secure a niche in the consciousness of most Americans, then and now, is matched by a complete inattention by the historians. Picking up any of the many general histories of America in the 1930s, one will look in vain for even brief mentions of Lawson or DCS, nor are the omissions corrected in any specialized historical monographs. But the blackout goes still farther: even the major magazines and newspapers of the

1930s had little or nothing to say about Lawson or his organization. Because DCS was primarily a Midwestern-states phenomenon, the absence of entries in the 1930s, for either the organization or its leader, in the index of the main newspaper of record, the *New York Times*, may not seem unaccountable. But is it not puzzling that only a few short, not very informative articles can be dredged up from the clipping files of the *Detroit Free Press* and the *Detroit Daily News*?

Lawson and his followers have always had a ready explanation, of course: the financiers, controlling the newspapers, the book publishers, and academic institutions, blocked all public recognition of Lawson, his message, and his organization. The thoroughness of the financiers' ban presumably could also be cited to explain the failure of the Direct Credits crusade to achieve any of its goals. But a more plausible line of explanation runs in the other direction: the dearth of journalistic and historical coverage of Lawson and the Direct Credits Society is actually accounted for by the political ineffectiveness of the movement. For the DCS crusade did not merely fall short of reaching its goals; it failed to have any impact at all on the politics of the 1930s.

Lawson often claimed that DCS agitational work in the First Congressional District of Michigan (that is, Detroit) did win over the support of the district's representative for the Direct Credits plan and that the votes of DCS members thereafter enabled him to win bloated majorities in the Democratic primary, the effective election. If this was so, the Detroit press apparently never got wind of it. But even if it was so, this electoral triumph would remain conspicuous by its uniqueness; Lawson never claimed other electoral successes, and there is no evidence that there were any others. Moreover, the Direct Credits Society played no role in the presidential elections of 1932 and 1936.

Lawson's organization was also of no direct account in affecting Congressional decisions, inasmuch as Lawson never lobbied for or against any legislation before Congress, even when bills happened to overlap provisions of the DCS program. Although Lawson always denounced the revaluation of gold as a standard trick of the financiers, he never said a word about Roosevelt's abandonment of the gold standard or any New Deal measures. In fact, the only controversial bill up for action by Congress on which the Direct Credits Society appears ever to have taken a stand was the veterans' bonus, payment of which Lawson endorsed.

In view of the Direct Credits Society's apparently complete failure to be a factor affecting the politics and policies of the period, it hardly seems surprising that it should have fallen beneath the notice of contemporary journalists or, later, the historians. Yet in view of Lawson's success in attracting a large, dedicated following, one might wonder why he failed to make more political waves than he did. For certain, some of the factors deflating the very possibility of political impact by Lawson and DCS were well within Lawson's control. A good way to bring these factors into clear light is to contrast Lawson's leadership with that of a man—Father Charles Coughlin—who did succeed in shaking up American political life in the 1930s.

As it happens, Lawson and Coughlin both began their agitational careers in 1931, in each case setting up shop in the Detroit metropolitan area. The arsenals of the two leaders were also stocked with many doctrinal and rhetorical weapons of identical bore and caliber. For instance, each spoke darkly of a financial conspiracy executed by devilish domestic and alien financiers and attributed the Great Depression to that conspiracy. Both also denounced the financiers' "credit money," called for a greatly increased supply of "real money" backed not by gold but by "the productive wealth of the United States," advocated a central bank firmly under control of the national government, claimed to be the special champion of little children, "feeble old folks," dispossessed widows, and so forth, and called for financial and welfare reforms which were radical up to a point but would not disturb the capitalist system or existing property relations (except, of course, for the unjust property takings of the financiers).

While Coughlin's movement declined abruptly after 1936, Lawson's movement chugged along for many more years. However, at about that same time Lawson began to dilute the doctrinal octane of DCS with large infusions of Lawsonomy and ever more extreme claims for his personal greatness. As he did so, it is very likely that DCS also passed its high point of membership and commenced a steady decline in which it would lose more old members each year than it gained new ones. Unique coincidental factors were the most obvious ones ac-

counting for the slipping vitality of the two movements after 1936: in
Coughlin's case, the dismal failure of the Union Party in the presidential election that year and growing opposition from superiors and
prominent lay members in the Catholic Church; and in Lawson's case,
his increasing infatuation with Lawsonomy and the consequent blur-
ring of the Direct Credits Society's focus. But another factor, intrud-
ing from without, may have taken its toll on both movements, too—
that is, the falling prospects for agitational movements generally following the smashing success of Roosevelt and the Democratic Party in
the 1936 elections.

The overlap of programs, the similar chronology of origin, growth,
and decline, and the identical geographical bases of the two movements are so striking that one might wonder whether there was some
relationship between the two. Did Lawson and Coughlin compete
only or also collaborate? Did the efforts of each reinforce the agitational work of the other? Or did one rob the other of ideas and members, consistently benefiting at the other's expense?

Bearing on the question of collaboration is a statement made in
1979 by a long-time DCS member who was an active recruiter for the
organization in the 1930s. Claiming that Coughlin "approved of"
Lawson and authorized his followers to join DCS, this veteran recalls
working side by side at a member recruitment booth with local agents
for Coughlin's National Union for Social Justice (NUSJ). On this occasion, the latter allegedly assured new NUSJ recruits that they could
also join DCS and welcomed the enlistment of DCS members in NUSJ,
too. It is impossible to know which organization would have benefited
more by this arrangement. However, it clearly could have worked to
DCS's benefit only with respect to passive members; the active members of DCS could not also have had more than a nominal affiliation, if
any at all, with NUSJ, and in fact, NUSJ would have been DCS's rival
for the recruitment of active members.

Probably what the old-time DCS member recounts was only an iso-
lated incident of interorganizational cooperation not likely to have
been authorized by either Lawson or Coughlin. In a 1940 investigation, the FBI was unable to find any connections between their organizations. Extensive cooperation from Lawson's side was, in fact, al-

THE MAN OF DESTINY

most inconceivable. Although Lawson never mentioned Coughlin's name, the "radio priest" must have ranked high among the smooth talkers whom Lawson frequently denounced for crooning false economic doctrines over the airwaves. Lawson never once cited the National Union for Social Justice by name, either, but certainly it fell under Lawson's condemnation of all reform organizations which failed to advocate the total abolition of interest. For his part, Coughlin might have been readier than Lawson to enter into cooperative relations, but there is no evidence that he ever made inquiries.

With respect to the question of whether either man may have stolen doctrinal and rhetorical baggage from the other, at least one point can be made with certainty: Lawson cannot be charged with having lifted anything from his competitor. Until he began to pump large doses of Lawsonomy into his movement after the midpoint of the decade, Lawson never departed from a position which was fully formed and clearly stated in 1931 in *Direct Credits for Everybody*. In contrast, Coughlin's position steadily shifted and evolved, and some of his proposals—for instance, centralization of all banking functions in the national government, issuance of massive amounts of new, unbacked currency—came only long after Lawson had been pushing them as major components of the DCS program. If there was any swiping of ideas, Coughlin was the guilty party.

Unquestionably, the doctrinal flexibility of Coughlin gave him advantages over Lawson, who stuck stolidly to the Direct Credits doctrine in its unadulterated original form. But more than doctrinal factors figured in Coughlin's success in building a politically formidable movement and in Lawson's failure to do so. Especially important were Coughlin's superior efficiency in casting lines to potential followers, his greater skill in reeling them in, and the better political uses which he made of his movement.

As is well known, at the heart of Coughlin's success in rallying followers was his skillful, pioneering use of radio. Lawson's refusal to exploit the advantages of radio meant not only that he was still trudging around the Great Lakes states making personal appearances long after Coughlin had established weekly contacts with a national audience but also that he had to give far more time and attention to organization-building than did Coughlin. In fact, the latter did not even launch the National Union for Social Justice until late in 1934, more than three years after Lawson had begun the Direct Credits Society. Two weeks after Coughlin had made his initial sales pitch in a radio broadcast, 200,000 persons had responded, and one scholar concludes that NUSJ soon rose to over one million members.[3] But Coughlin's recruitment job was an easy one. In effect, he already had achieved, through radio and with great economy of effort, a mass membership of a kind which Lawson would have envied—enormous in number, distributed throughout most of the United States, and completely in the thrall of the leader. In spite of the seeming impersonality of radio communication, Coughlin had succeeded in eliciting through his broadcasts a highly personal response from hundreds of thousands of listeners, and they were as inclined to hang adoringly on every utterance of "Father" as Lawson's legions were to hearken to the inspired thoughts of "Commander."

Coughlin's political career was short-lived, his victories were few, and his lasting impact on public policy was negligible. During his few hours upon the stage, however, he could not be ignored and was a significant factor in American politics. Might Lawson have made a similar political splash if he had copied Coughlin's methods and activities—for instance, lobbying, electioneering, exploiting the mass media, entering into alliances, speaking out on current issues and events, criticizing the Roosevelt administration, attacking foes vigorously? The question is unanswerable, but at least it can be noted that Coughlin's choice of methods and activities rested on no more occult a foundation of knowledge than common sense could provide; he merely did things which should be obvious to any political entrepreneur eager to rally a large following and put it to political uses. A more apt question, then, is why Lawson didn't attempt to do some of the things which Coughlin did so effectively and which one would expect of any leader of a mass interest group.

The answer is that Lawson did not see himself as an ordinary leader of a typical interest group. Not willing to accept piecemeal policy changes extracted by pragmatic politicking, bargaining, and compromise, Lawson aimed only at the enactment of the Direct Credits program, unchanged and in its entirety. His was necessarily a strategy of the long range: patiently striving to win majorities to the Direct Credits program in the congressional districts until a majority of these districts had been won over, at which point Congress would enact the will of the majority. In the meantime, it would hardly make sense to electioneer, to lobby, to comment on current events and policy controversies, because all of current politics was merely epiphenomenal, directly serving the interests of the financiers or distracting attention from the reality of their power. Until that power was broken, any apparently desirable reform would be a sham and any effort at genuinely needed reform would be defeated.

Possessing not so much a program of desired ends to be pursued by standard political means as the Truth about changes needed to produce a just and ideal society, Lawson set out on what was essentially an educational mission. Because radio, newspapers, and magazines were under the thumb of the financiers, he reckoned that he could not use them without risking entrapment and distortion of his message and fell back instead on delivering his message through an endless series of face-to-face meetings with the public and through his own publications. Always addressing local audiences in his speeches, he was spared the relentless pressure Coughlin was under week after week to produce novel fare for his national audience. But probably Lawson would have relied, in any event, on variations of the same basic speech. Whether he was speaking in Detroit, Cleveland, or Indianapolis, repetition was always in order, because it was the definitive and unchanging Truth which he was hawking.

It is to Lawson's credit that, unlike Coughlin, he rejected the exploitation of anti-Semitic and regional prejudices; in doing so, possibly he failed to tap some of the steam powering the Coughlin movement. On the other hand, in their place, Lawson put an ample exploitation of anti-intellectual prejudice; his attacks on conventional learning, the professors, and institutions of higher education were numerous and egregious. In few other respects, however, did Lawson's speeches have the resentment-eliciting force of Coughlin's speeches. Perhaps his exposé of the financiers' five-point, ten-year plan for subjugating America brought a rush of blood to the heads of some listeners. For the most part, however, his discussions of the financiers and their touts eschewed specificity, attributing diabolical deeds of only a general sort to a malevolent force which remained disembodied and abstract. In result, his attacks lacked the punch which could have been there if, like Coughlin, he had named names, offered up-to-date details of the latest atrocities of the financiers, or exposed their hand in current legislative struggles or in the policies of the Roosevelt administration.

But Lawson had what he considered to be a principled reason for avoiding such content in his speeches and writings. Because people only did what they were encouraged or constrained to do in roles determined by an unjust economic system, Lawson argued, attacking specific persons would be both unfair and misleading. His quarrel was not with persons, but rather with bad institutions. Thus Lawson proudly noted on several occasions that he never attacked specific persons, and indeed, one can read hundreds of pages of his speeches without encountering a proper name or even a description of an event or a policy dispute involving unnamed but identifiable persons. Perhaps Lawson can be credited with high-mindedness in this respect. On the other hand, his policy prevented him from even trying to match the colorful show which Coughlin staged regularly and worked against his chances to be heeded in the political life of the 1930s.

Had a familiar pattern in Lawson's past once again asserted itself? That is, just as Lawson muffed his big chance in baseball and blundered at the brink of success with his brilliant airliner work, had he also undercut his opportunity to achieve effect and renown as a depression-era agitator? One could easily line up the evidence to support this conclusion.

Although Lawson may have expected to arrive quickly at a point of decisive influence on American political life, the terms on which he demanded, and also expected, to make his presence felt politically were absurdly unrealistic. The problem wasn't just that he would accept nothing less than the enactment of the total DCS program as a package; as improbable as attainment of this objective was, it still could have been pursued with more attention-getting effect, had Lawson not eschewed the use of radio, refused even to acknowledge the existence of the Roosevelt administration as the vital center of American politics, or failed generally to offer any commentary on current policy controversies.

Lawson's all-or-nothing commitment to the DCS program also led him, one could easily argue, to a wrongheaded rejection of many of the standard activities by which interest groups make their presence known and draw attention to their goals. By failing to do the conventional things, he forwent achieving valuable publicity for his organization and himself and called into question the potency and credibility of DCS as a significant reform organization; in brief, he undermined his effort to publicize DCS and the DCS program and provided no reason for politicians, the press, or informed opinion generally to pay any attention to him and his movement.

Finally, and probably the most significant consequence, by staying off the main stage of American politics, he let other gifted performers steal the show. Coughlin, Huey Long, Gerald L. K. Smith, et al., hogged the limelight, leaving none for Lawson. This consequence alone, one might claim, showed up the flawed political sense of the would-be Man of Destiny. Failing to hook his undoubted talents more effectively to the requirements and possibilities of political entrepreneurship in America, he was completely beat out by a very formidable competition.

However, harsh judgments of Lawson's political ineptitude are fair only if one can be certain that he really did steadfastly aspire to the role of the Man of Destiny. Certainly at the outset Lawson did aim to rally the American people for deliverance from their bondage to the financiers, and this remained his publicly stated objective throughout the 1930s; in fact, he never expressly or officially repudiated his pursuit of the Direct Credits program. By the midpoint of the decade, however, there was good reason to question the singlemindedness of his commitment to this goal, and by the end of the decade, even better reason to believe that he retained little commitment to it at all.

Even before 1935, Lawson had resumed his explorations in Lawsonomy; this was indicated by his publication in that year of *Lawsonomy*, designated as volume I of a projected trilogy on "the physical, mental, and spiritual manifestations of life." Volume II, *Mentality*, followed in 1938, and in 1939 came both volume III, *The Almighty*, and

Penetrability, an elaboration of Lawsonomic physics. Issues of *Benefactor* were also well larded with Lawsonomic content during the latter half of the decade.

Unquestionably, the new infusion of Lawsonomy blurred the focus of Lawson's DCS effort. However, perhaps this was not simply another tactical mistake by Lawson. Lawsonomy probably was his first love, to which he had itched to return ever since writing *Manlife* and *Creation* in the early 1920s. Once having resumed work on Lawsonomy, Lawson found his attention increasingly absorbed by the masterwork for which he expected to be accorded standing as history's greatest sage and moral leader—a goal which one can believe could readily become more important to him than stirring up the American public to support the Direct Credits program. With his increasing shift of focus to Lawsonomy also inevitably came a reawakening of his earlier commitment to the moral upgrading of humanity and a truly radical reorganization of social life going far beyond the Direct Credits panacea.

The wholeheartedness of Lawson's effort on behalf of the DCS program was diluted by yet another major concern drawing his attention in the latter half of the 1930s. Clearly causing him great anguish were both the finality of the failure of his airliner work and the alarming speed with which his contributions to aviation had been forgotten. To set the record straight, in 1937 he published *Lawson: Aircraft Industry Builder*, a documentary history of his aviation activities and accomplishments. All of his other books, too, began to carry a lengthy back section covering his aviation exploits. As of 1940, readers of *Benefactor* were also bombarded with documentation of Lawson's career in aviation; here was a clear indication that the Direct Credits movement had become a vehicle for carrying other matters of competing concern for Lawson.

By the end of 1936, it must have been apparent even to Lawson that the Direct Credits Society was going nowhere as a financial reform organization; thanks to the peculiarities of Lawson's leadership methods, the organization was politically impotent and unheeded, and even if it sustained the rate of growth achieved during the first six years, it would take many more years before a majority of Americans would ever be won over to the DCS program.

Whether or not Lawson was aware of the fact, however, further growth would have caused a major problem for him. He had created an organization built on the military hierarchical model, but in reality the central organizational fact about DCS was the direct, personal allegiance which each member gave to Lawson. If DCS were to continue to grow in size and geographical spread, however, this would necessarily change. Once it was no longer possible for Lawson to communicate personally with every member or to supervise and inspect in person every organizational unit, he would have had no choice but to place increasing reliance on the bureaucratic structure of DCS. In other words, if DCS had ever taken off in numerical and geographical size, Lawson risked facing up to the consequences of what Weber called "the routinization of charisma." For Lawson, those consequences—especially the possible challenge to his leadership and the ending of the members' personal fealty to him—would surely have been intolerable.

The looming crisis was averted, however, when Lawson, whether in recognition of the problem or fortuitously, changed his primary goal from advancing the cause of Direct Credits reform to seeking recognition for his aircraft work and perfecting and promulgating Lawsonomy. Lawson continued to hawk the Direct Credits line throughout the decade of the 1930s; not only did inertia keep him on this course, but he also had little choice but to recognize the strong attachment of his members to that program. No longer, however, was a steadily expanding organization or the forward movement of the Direct Credits campaign an appropriate measure of his success. His efforts in the first half of the decade had brought him a large membership devoted to his person; now the test of his success was intensifying and expanding their personal commitment to him to include celebration of his great aviation achievements and of his even greater intellectual and moral achievements in Lawsonomy. Here, in fact, may lie the best explanation of why Lawson never pushed his organization beyond the limited extent of the Great Lakes states—that is, beyond his capacity to ensure that the Direct Credits Society retained a membership tightly under his control and linked to him by personal allegiance.

Slowly, without fanfare, Lawson set out to steer his members to his new organizational purposes. Officers who may have thought that understanding the Direct Credits doctrine was sufficient for their good performance now began to find that they were expected to know something also about the much more abstract and difficult Lawsonomy. Lawson even began to talk about a commitment of thirty years to the study of Lawsonomy by his officers. Other new requirements were imposed, too. Lawson had originally insisted only that officers not drink, smoke, or chew while on duty or in uniform; as of January 1, 1940, however, members were forbidden at any time to indulge in these vices. DCS officers heard increasingly that they were the nucleus of a coming, improved human race. And of course, members were steadily encouraged in their inclination to find in Lawson "the gift of grace," only now the Lawson they were called upon to revere and celebrate was a much more august figure even than the Man of Destiny.

Very likely the rate of recruitment of new active members fell off in the latter half of the 1930s, and almost certainly many former members began to pull out or were ejected by Lawson. But even though the total membership may have declined, it hardly mattered. Except for a few years in the early 1930s, Lawson had never truly looked outward, as Coughlin did, toward the end of achieving political goals through an ever-expanding organization. Even when he talked this way, most of his efforts actually had always been directed inward, toward perfecting an organization of adulators. In the second half of the 1930s, this characteristic merely became more pronounced and evident.

In sum, if Lawson can be charged with muffing his opportunities and falling far short of his potential as a conventional political agitator and reformer, it must still be acknowledged that, in another sense, he was far from inept and, in fact, did not fail. Under the guise of the Man of Destiny, he had achieved what he most wanted—a large band of followers prepared to sing his praises and shower him with the love and respect for which he yearned. Moreover, this was precisely the kind of following most likely to stick with him as he set out in a totally new direction of utopian reform after 1940. As Lawson began to catch ever-clearer glimpses of the New Jerusalem based on Lawsonomy, he quietly retired the title of Man of Destiny and prepared to assume his final, magnificent standing as the First Knowledgian.

9

THE

FIRST

KNOWLEDGIAN

AND THE

UPGRADING

OF

HUMANITY

By the mid-1930s, Lawson's accumulated lofty self-appraisals already pressed hard against the outer limits of greatness imaginable for a mere mortal. Even so, he was nowhere near the end of hatching either prodigies or claims; indeed, he was only at the threshold of completing and publishing what he considered his intellectual masterpiece, the Lawsonomy trilogy. As the volumes of the trilogy issued from the press between 1935 and 1939, Lawson found justification for positing new, breathtaking dimensions of his greatness. In these pages, he disclosed a cosmic significance in his appearance on earth and claimed a place as first among the equals comprising the tiny band of authentic emissaries from God.

Strong hints of these latest convictions about the meaning of his life can be found in *Lawsonomy*, published in 1935 as the first volume of the trilogy. However, Lawson's earliest explicit discussion of the special role which he had been called to play in God's scenario of human progress did not appear until 1938, in *Mentality*. In this second volume of his magnum opus, Lawson noted that God always sends a lone precursor to point the way to human advancement. Moreover, he adjudged Lawsonomy to be just the ticket needed to lift a person "right out of the petty misunderstandings that miseducate humanity today and [to] actually TRANSFORM him into a superior being." However, in another passage in *Mentality*, Lawson still seemed puzzled about whether God had got the timing right: "When I look into the vastness of space and see the marvelous workings of its contents and ponder over the great opportunities for man's intellectual advancement I sometimes think that I was born ten or twenty thousand years ahead of time."

With the publication one year later of *The Almighty*, the final volume of the Lawsonomy trilogy, Lawson finally had pinned down precisely the meaning of his sojourn in this world: "About every two thousand years a new teacher with advanced intellectual equipment appears upon earth to lead the people a step or two nearer the one God of everybody." Lawson's appearance meshed with the divine schedule, after all. Yet, even as Lawson compared himself with Jesus and other unnamed predecessors, he made out a case for his uniqueness: he was better qualified to make a long-lasting, major dent on humanity's conduct than were previous teachers, who "lacked knowledge concerning the physical, mental, and mechanical laws to establish their teachings upon a sound and lasting basis." In other words, Jesus and the other great teachers of the past had been handicapped by knowing nothing about suction and pressure, equaeverpoise, and mental organisms.

Although it was his achievement of Lawsonomy which gave the advantage to his prospects as a reformer of humanity, Lawson generously shared the credit for his masterful scientific and moral discoveries with God. In an opening statement in *Mentality*, he beseeched God to "kindly accept my humble thanks for the privilege of presenting this magnificent gift to mankind." He also expressed a hope that God would continue to allow him to be God's agent by giving Lawson the further time needed to complete the teachings of Lawsonomy. His wish fulfilled, Lawson published *The Almighty* in 1939. The "magnificent gift" from God to humanity, via Lawson, had now reached the fullness of an integrated, definitive account, in three volumes, of God's physical, mental, and spiritual manifestations.

In truth, the opening volume of the trilogy, *Lawsonomy*, is little more than a reworking of the contents of *Manlife* and *Creation*. However, its first chapter, entitled "Lawsonomy," does give this material on "God's physical manifestation" a new context of significance, which is also intended to apply to the material to be discussed in subsequent books. Here Lawsonomy is exalted as a comprehensive doctrine consisting of nothing less than "the knowledge of Life and everything pertaining thereto." It is, Lawson asserts, "a formula that proves all things." Unlike other doctrines making the same claim, however, "Lawsonomy treats of things as they are and not as they are pretended to be." "Theory, as espoused by so-called wise men or self-styled scholars has no place in Lawsonomy. Everything must be provable or reasonable or it is not Lawsonomy."

Those who earnestly seek the truth, Lawson assures, will find it easy to understand Lawsonomy, which is "the opposite of the tricky stuff taught by those who feed on falsity." Those educated in Lawsonomy will find that it gives a "stimulus for great future deeds and a tremendous advantage over those who are mis-educated according to present-day falsification." In a broad hint of the direction in which his mind was already tending, Lawson observes that "God has decreed that mankind must move onward and upward to a much higher plane of intelligence than heretofore reached. Lawsonomy is the means by which mankind can reach that higher plane."

Resorting to hydrological metaphors, Lawson also describes Lawsonomy as "an oasis of Truth in the midst of a desert of lies" and as "the fountain of intelligence." Indeed, a figure included in the prefatory pages of *Lawsonomy* (and republished in all later books by Lawson) gives a stylized depiction of a fountain labeled "Lawsonomy," from which spout forty-seven streams of specialized knowledge. Included among the streams are, for example, history, chemistry, government, psychology, and surgery—but also such peculiar ones as "transformation," "attraction," "prophecy," and "micro-organism." (Strangely absent is a gusher marked "hydrology.") The inscription below the figure, "Growth Draws to and Expands from the Center," makes Lawson's intended meaning clear: Lawsonomy is the master study which subsumes and unifies all specialized fields of knowledge and provides the orientation needed for real advancement in those fields. It is also the means by which they can be purged of their harmful infestations of "falsification" and bogus "theory" put there by the "so-called wisemen or self-styled scholars."

If *Lawsonomy* reported little which was new in Lawson's thinking, this was certainly not the case for *Mentality* and *The Almighty*. Correlat-

FOUNTAIN OF INTELLIGENCE

GROWTH DRAWS TO AND EXPANDS FROM THE CENTER

Lawson depicted Lawsonomy as a fountain feeding forty-seven streams of specialized knowledge. From Lawson, *Lawsonomy.*

ing with Lawson's growing conviction of having a divinely appointed mission was his extension of Lawsonomy into the realms of ethics and religion. This extension brought some startling elaborations of Lawsonomy, and his emerging sense of being charged by God with the task of upgrading humanity imparted an impassioned, hortatory, even prophetic, quality to his writing. In result, not only did *Mentality* and *The Almighty* offer new Lawsonomic teachings but they also were quite different in tone from *Lawsonomy*. In their pages appeared another novelty, too: all these books carried glossaries of Lawsonomic terms, but unlike the glossary found in *Lawsonomy*, the glossaries published in the later books carried a striking new word—"Knowledgian," defined as "a certified teacher of Lawsonomy" or, in another place, as "one who knows the Truth." No other single feature of these books registered so simply or neatly the decisive change which had occurred during the brief space of three years in Lawson's sense of his destiny. He had finally become the First Knowledgian.

Of major significance in *Mentality* and *The Almighty* is Lawson's greatly expanded discussion of the mental organisms or, as Lawson now designates them, the "menorgs." Here he adds much detail to what he had written earlier about the importance of the menorgs and elaborates on a new theme: menorgs are the agents through whose activities God reveals norms for human conduct and attempts to bring all creatures to their perfection in accord with the divine will. Lawson's expanded discussion of the menorgs highlights their crucial function in his thinking: they are the point of intersection among Lawson's scientific, moral, and religious teachings. Thanks to them, he can claim Lawsonomy to be a comprehensive doctrine which anchors a complete normative teaching in a complete scientific account of the universe.

These books, *Mentality* especially, are a veritable paean to the menorgs. Here Lawson hails the menorgs for being, among other things, "real thinkers and planners," "masters of physics, economics, metaphysics, mechanics, and chemistry," and "great laboratorians" (that is, experimenters). In this last respect, Lawson marvels once again at their creative role in evolution. Receiving their charge from God, menorgs constantly tinker with formations, trying thereby to produce some variations which will bring all types of formations closer to fulfillment. ("Nature does not begin with perfection but aims to finish with it.") Some menorgs are brighter than others, however, and to them Lawson attributes credit for the most progressive genetic advances. Lawson proclaims as a genius, for example, the menorg who conceived and built the first blade of grass, for this menorg had hit upon a prototype of many formations which eons later would serve nicely as humanity's food. He also has high praise for the menorg who first toyed with making a plant walk and thus made the first step toward the emergence of animal life.

All menorgs deserve praise, however, for in addition to making things work, building well, and laboring diligently and cooperatively, they are perfect economists. That is, they follow the first law of "natural" economics: "the utilization of everything without the loss of anything." For instance, they made humans and all the plants and animals from the waste products expelled by the earth's internal pressure.

In view of the brilliance and ingenuity of the menorgs, sooner or later some exceptional menorg would surely have conceived and built a prototypal human. According to Lawson, however, God didn't wait for this to happen but instead gave a special order to the menorgs. As Lawson describes it, "God wanted a supervisory agent to manage the Earth and all that it contains therein and so He directed the menorgs to design and build a superconscious being upon humane principles that would be capable of executing such orders, and performing such duties, as He would from time to time prescribe."

Because the menorgs had already been doing such a superb job of supervising and managing the earth, one can imagine that they were puzzled by God's command. Nonetheless, they dutifully rose to the challenge of their new assignment. "It was a very crude thing that the menorgs first produced which was designated as man, but they continue to improve him with the object in view of constantly increasing his intelligence and enlarging his consciousness until eventually he will become acceptable in the sight of God."

Humans are therefore enormously in the menorgs' debt. The inventive menorgs built humans with opposable thumbs, upright, two-legged posture, vocal cords for speech (that is, for squeezing sound out of the air), and capacity for reason and have provided them in abundance with all that is needed to sustain life. The menorgs continue their efforts to improve humans. They repair them when higher density substances penetrate their bodies. They coordinate the operation of all the suction and pressure terminals in their bodies, including those within all the constituent cells. They operate the sensory, motor, and intellectual faculties. In sum, the latter could not live without the constant attention of the menorgs. Lawson speculates that one hundred billion understates their number within each human body, adding that there may be more than that number in the brain alone. "If those unknown numbers of menorgs would leave your body, it would fall to the ground like a dead chunk of putty."

But here a problem arises. Under the tutelage of the benevolent, competent, and watchful menorgs, one would suppose that humans would behave properly. But so much evidence, which Lawson documents at length in *Mentality* and *The Almighty*, runs the other way. How can this be? One possible answer would seem to flow from Lawson's speculations to this point: the menorgs haven't finished their job of perfecting the human species. But this would imply that the many shortcomings of humans are not their fault, and Lawson will have none of that. He offers a different line of explanation, which ends by pinning the blame for human depravity directly on humans.

In the first place, it turns out that humans are exposed to the influence of yet another species of mental organism in the universe, which Lawson calls the "disorgs." Disorgs have exactly opposite qualities from those of the menorgs. Menorgs are benevolent, helpful, altruistic, and intelligent; disorgs are malevolent, harmful, selfish, and ignorant. Menorgs build up; disorgs tear down (disorganize). Menorgs offer good example and guidance; disorgs deceive and mislead.

Like the menorgs, disorgs are submicroscopic and so can't be seen by humans. But Lawson has no doubt that they are there; their existence is established by Lawson's Law of Opposites—that is, everything in existence has its opposite. If there are menorgs, there must also be disorgs. Lawson nowhere speculates about their number and distribution, but presumably they are as numerous and far-flung as the menorgs.

Whereas menorgs everywhere do good work, however, it appears that disorgs can do their dirty work only where they are permitted to do it, and it further appears that the only formations which permit them to enter and destroy are humans. Humans, in other words, have free will and choose to be depraved. Human will and the disorgs together have produced the appalling degradation of humanity, which Lawson depicts so luridly in these pages.

Counterposed to Lawson's claims for the vast role of the menorgs in the design and operation of human beings, Lawson's assertion of human free will comes as something of a surprise. How free will and determinism (of menorgs) can be jointly accommodated remains a mystery of Lawsonomy—but no more so, perhaps, than it is in some other, better known philosophical and theological systems. In any event, according to Lawson, humans constantly have real, not apparent, choices to make, and they usually make bad ones.

Sad to say, the menorgs are powerless to intervene or resist as humans become addicted to "immoral thoughts, vulgar stories, or obscene pictures for pleasures" or give themselves up to "drugs, strong beverages, tobacco and candies, or dancing, night parties, licentiousness, obscenity, brutality, cheating, foul language, gluttony, and misrepresentation." The menorgs know what humans learn too late or not at all: these pollutions, and also "the lies that man fills his brain with nowadays from newspapers, magazines, books, radio, screen, and hearsay," are "food for the disorgs," who greedily move in for the free lunch and become permanent boarders.

At one point in his lengthy recounting of contemporary humanity's depraved condition, Lawson adds a pinch of Rousseauean savor by his adaptations of a "savagery/barbarism/civilization" triad introduced by ethnologist Lewis Henry Morgan (and also used by Marx and Engels). All that the menorgs have done to bring humanity through an early Age of Savagery, then through a higher Age of Barbarism, and finally to an (allegedly) even higher Age of Civilization, has come to naught, he concludes. More than the ages preceding it, the Age of Civilization has turned out to be an "Age of Skinnery," of institutionalized and legalized murder, theft, swindle, corruption, miseducation, waste, and godlessness. Although it is uncharacteristic and probably unintended, a wonderful Swiftian bite also accompanies one of Lawson's many depictions of civilization's shortcomings: "Savages have done much better [than civilized humans]. Cannibals do not let their food rot while their children starve."

But Lawson's most obvious spiritual predecessors are the ancient Hebrew prophets. In the manner of the prophets he throws down dire warnings of God's retribution for humanity's transgressions. The disaster will not come, however, through the direct intervention of a wrathful God. That would be uncharacteristic of Lawson's God, who has a rather impersonal and abstract nature: "Supreme beyond human understanding, HE is all pervading essence with power of transformation, magnification, condensation, and simplification of existants [sic]." Elsewhere, Lawson identifies God as a formation who "balances and perpetuates HIMSELF, spiritually, according to the rules of Equaeverpoise." Such a God is likely to keep a fastidious distance from humans, no matter how provoked God may be by their waywardness.

It is not surprising to learn, then, that God works a scheme of punishments and rewards through an impersonal law, called the "law of reaction" in *Mentality* but given final expression in *The Almighty* as the Law of Maneuverability. Hailed by its discoverer as "the great balancing wheel between right and wrong actions," the Law of Maneuverability is an application in the moral sphere of the physical principle of "for every action there is a reaction." "If things go wrong with one it is but the reaction of a wrong action. If things go right, it is because the previous acts of one have been what was right." Thus, wrong action will always be punished and right action rewarded. Lawson also describes the law more simply as, "As you give, so you receive."

"It is dangerous to break God's provable laws," Lawson warns. On the other hand, "follow God's positive laws and nothing negative will happen." But what are the right laws of conduct? How can humans know what God expects of them? The conduct of the menorgs provides the standard. "To keep well and alive, so that you may have the strength to do your duty as God expects it to be done, you must throw your full spiritual influence on the side of the constructive Menorgs." When humans, individually or collectively, team up with the disorgs, however, the Law of Maneuverability insures that punishment and destruction will follow.

Doubtless Lawson was well aware of the many apparent exceptions to the Law of Maneuverability. For example, he had acted nobly but still had suffered injustice at the hands of the financiers; had the law protected him? Implicit in the question, however, is a fallacy—the fallacy of placing an early time limit on the law's operation. In fact, sometimes reward or retribution comes swiftly, but sometimes it is delayed.

But even if it never comes in a lifetime, reward or punishment is certain to come after death. It will not come through eternal assignment to heaven or hell, however, because this would imply a direct, personal involvement by God in judging each person's fate. Instead, God has ingeniously built an automatic fail-safe mechanism into the Law of Maneuverability to ensure that just deserts are finally meted out: "A Soul that has proved trustworthy in the passing creature is attached to the body of a more progressive being during the next life. A Soul that proves unworthy in the passing creature is attached to the body of a retrogressive creature during the next life."

In other words, souls, unlike formations, are indestructible and only take up temporary residence in transitory formations. At the death of the presently inhabited formation the soul transmigrates to another formation. And God has arranged matters through another law—the Law of Disqualification—to insure that each soul "progresses or retrogresses in exact proportion to the constructive or destructive efforts displayed in each succeeding life." For example, "the soul of the rich tyrannical father who defrauds and abuses weaklings to-day may become attached to the body of a weakling to-morrow and be defrauded and abused by the son [to] whom he had previously bequeathed his ill-gotten wealth."

But souls on a downward course "may not even inhabit bodies of the same species" in their next incarnations. Thus, one could plausibly imagine that the soul of a glutton might depart to the body of a hog, or that a whining cur could be the next place of residence for the soul of a particularly heartless financier.

Lawson's exhaustive survey of the universe's moral and physical lawfulness moves him to offer this gloss on his awesome subject: "Nature does not recognize magic in any form. It bases its entire work upon immutable laws; laws which are well defined and certain. Nature knows no pity and shows no favors; it follows the rules and they must be obeyed or the consequences must be taken." Throughout *The Almighty*, however, Lawson is at great pains to make a clarifying point: lawfulness governs the *consequences* of human conduct but not human conduct itself. "It is . . . within the power of all creatures to decide whether the constructive menorgs will construct them with the right thoughts and materials or whether their opposites, the disorgs, will destroy them with the wrong thoughts and materials," Lawson proclaims. Although he acknowledges that humans will be "influenced to some extent by putrid social conditions," the primary determinant of their conduct is an essentially unconstrained volition. In adopting this line, Lawson throws overboard the contrary position advanced in *Direct Credits for Everybody*. That he does so he never acknowledges, however.

Between the axis of deterministic natural law and the axis of human free will Lawson plots the curve delineating the human predicament today: guided by faulty moral precepts, most humans have fallen into the clutches of the disorgs, and in result, contemporary civilization is on a downward suicidal course. In the face of the impending disaster, what is most urgently needed is a "readjustment of the spiritual lessons now taught to mankind." Lawsonomy, of course, offers those readjusted lessons—ones established, for the first time in history, on "a sound and lasting basis," thanks to their being well-grounded in the "physical, mental, and mechanical laws."

If these claims constituted the whole of Lawson's pitch to his readers, his message could not be considered particularly novel or worthy of note. While the specific Lawsonomic content of his claims is obviously unique, the pattern or essential message of his doctrine is a familiar one preached by exhorters from biblical times down to the televangelistic age of Billy Graham and Jimmy Swaggart.

But, in fact, when Lawson berates contemporary humanity, he is not merely demanding that humans end their sinful ways and return to the path of righteousness from which they have wandered. Lawson aims instead at an evolutionary advance in humanity which will secure a permanent improvement in human nature: "The time is now ripe for the birth of a new species," he proclaims. Taking over from the faltering and stymied menorgs, the prophet of the new species proposes to lead humanity in a big jump up the evolutionary scale.

In setting forth this startling project, Lawson goes back thirty-five years to take up his original utopian position found in *Born Again*. The treatises provide some new concepts and terms—menorgs and disorgs, the Law of Maneuverability, the Law of Disqualification, the

new species—but these only permit Lawson to express in a new way
ideas already presented in *Born Again*. (And in at least one instance,
Lawson retains in the treatises a term first encountered in the novel—
"Apemanism," a word used in both sources to describe the present degraded stage of human development.)

When Lawson refers in *The Almighty* to "this horrible nightmare
called civilization," his characterization conveys all of the anguish also
felt by John Convert and much of the documentation found in *Born
Again*. And in *The Almighty* Lawson gives this explanation of the source
of the problem of civilization: "Selfishness is the root of all evil; eradicate selfishness from humanity and the Earth will be heaven." If this
sounds familiar, it is because it is, word for word, the major moral insight which Convert acquired during his sojourn in Sageland. Also recurring in the 1939 treatise, again in unchanged wording, are the
major strategic reform principle found in the earlier novel ("The surest way to make the human race better is to begin by making oneself
better") and the major moral prescription which Arletta leaves with
Convert shortly before her death ("You should always consult your soul
for advice and do no act that your conscience will not sanction").

Other prominent features transported into the Lawsonomy treatises from *Born Again* include the doctrine of transmigration of souls,
the conception of natural law operating to mete out just deserts to the
virtuous and to the depraved, and a pronounced Manichaeism (now
menorgs and disorgs give vivid embodiment to the principles of good
and evil jousting in Lawson's universe). Lawson says little in the treatises
about the future way of life of the new species, but he says enough to
make clear that the utopia he anticipates is the Sageland described in
Born Again—a utopia characterized by stupendous technological marvels, by the everyday use of "telementy" (telepathy) and "transproces-
sion" (teleportation), and also by humanity's sharing with God in the
management of the Earth, the solar system, and the "other great cosmic formations."

All of the great things lying ahead for the new species will come by
virtue of humanity having at last learned to live and act cooperatively
"as a unit," the sine qua non for human development first broached in
Born Again. But now Lawson has the example of the menorgs to give

greater authority to his teaching and to make clearer his meaning. The new species, he avers, will "follow the example of the menorgs," whose most striking characteristics are unselfishness and cooperativeness. Here, given by nature, are the norms for human conduct: "Nature expects human beings to work together as a body with the same unification of purpose as the Menorgs work together as a body."

But still more is needed to ensure the accomplishment of stupendous menorgian projects; a well-articulated scheme of coordination and direction is also employed among the menorgs. At several places Lawson reports that in any formation, all the rest of the menorgs are under the command of one leader menorg. In a complex formation like a human being, composed of many formations, there is a hierarchy of command, culminating in one supreme commander: "There is located in a tiny cell of man's brain a thinking creature so small that no microscope is powerful enough to bring it to man's sight, but still it is powerful enough to manage the several trillion menorgs required to operate properly the machinery and the body of man."

"Following the example of the menorgs" includes, then, the adoption of this scheme of social organization. In fact, so excited was Lawson by the prospect of organizing the new species in the manner of the menorgs that he was brought to a fantastic vision of the future. That is, just as from those trillions of hierarchically organized menorgs emerges a new, more complex formation called a human, so from humanity, similarly organized and directed, Lawson looked for the emergence of a new, more complex formation. This vision Lawson first announced in *Mentality*: "I have given considerable thought to a plan by which can be designed, built, and operated a huge cosmic animal in which would be used human beings as supervisors instead of menorgs." And in *The Almighty* he returns to the fabulous idea, calling for human beings to join ranks toward the end of producing the "cosmic creature" as a "conscious workable machine." Doubtless the supreme commander menorg of the huge cosmic animal will be Lawson—or rather, the soul of Lawson residing in some later formation— for who else could be counted on to have the requisite knowledge and managerial skills? It also is likely that the blueprint for the needed command system is already laid out in the autocratic *General Orders* of the Direct Credits Society. Fortunately, when the time comes, the stupendous job of coordinating and directing the entire human race will be greatly facilitated by the availability of telementy as the principal means of communication.

Lawson's concept of the "huge cosmic animal," it must be conceded, is an unusual contribution to utopian thought. Even so, the concept is really no more than an exotic extension of the basic ideas found in *Mentality* and *The Almighty*, and in turn, those ideas are only new expressions of ideas first brought to light in *Born Again*. Does Lawson's fourth and last utopian phase come down, then, to being simply a repudiation in his old age of the capitalist utopias of his Direct Credits and aviation days in favor of a return to the socialist vision of his younger years?

If Lawson's only purpose had been to generate a soul-stirring and bedazzling vision of a radically reorganized world of the future, then this characterization of his final utopian phase would be accurate and sufficient. But with the arrival of the Direct Credits phase of his utopianism, Lawson revealed a much livelier concern about the questions of how his utopian vision could be realized and what role he should play to hasten its realization. As he returned to the utopianism of *Born Again*, he took with him the same serious interest in these questions. It is his new conclusions about the issues of implementation and his personal role which make his final utopian phase distinct from his first phase, even though both phases center on the programmatic goals found in *Born Again*.

The task of implementation lying before him, as Lawson now discerns and describes it, is to "plant the seed for a new species" of humanity, which certainly sounds like an insuperable task or at least one as difficult as any confronting John Convert. Lawson elaborates on what this task entails: "We must sift and choose the best living creatures that we can find now and educate them with the principles of Lawsonomy. We must inspire them to plant in their own seed, by their own thought and acts, the desire of their offspring to improve from generation to generation."

Lawson is undaunted by the stiff challenge presented, however. In spite of having found an extensive rottenness in contemporary hu-

LAWSONOMY

BY
ALFRED LAWSON

Author of
"MANLIFE"
"CREATION"
"BORN AGAIN"
"DIRECT CREDITS"
AND MANY OTHER BOOKS

Inventor of
THE AIRLINER
TRANS-OCEANIC FLOAT SYSTEM
TWO-TIER PASSENGER COMPARTMENT
AND MANY OTHER MECHANICAL DEVICES

The Discoverer of
THE CAUSE OF SEX
THE CAUSE OF GROWTH
THE CAUSE OF EVOLUTION
THE CAUSE OF ATTRACTION
THE CAUSE OF CONSCIOUSNESS
THE CAUSE OF CAPILLARY ACTION
ZIG-ZAG-AND-SWIRL MOVEMENT
CONTINUOUS MOVEMENT OF MATTER
THE LAW OF PENETRABILITY

The Founder of
LAWSONOMY—The knowledge of Life
THE DIRECT CREDITS SOCIETY

HUMANITY PUBLISHING COMPANY
PUBLISHERS
606 Woodward Ave., Detroit, Mich.

Beginning in 1935, the title pages of Lawson's books always summarized his claims and achievements. From the first edition (1935) of *Lawsonomy*.

manity, he believes that "there are enough unselfish people on earth now to plant the seed for a new species." In order to carry off the momentous project, he writes in *Mentality*, "we who believe in the higher principles of life must get together and *breed an unselfish animal* [emphasis added] that will rise as far above the pig-biped as he thinks he is above the pig-quadruped." One year later, in *The Almighty*, he adds that this saving remnant, in order to "create sufficient force to establish the birth of a new species," must also acquire "combination, coordination and concentration of action." But it is only in the final pages of this final book of the Lawsonomy trilogy that Lawson at last states clearly what he has in mind: "So, we will start the birth of a new species with our plans within the seed of *a self-perpetuating social body* [emphasis added], that will continue to grow until man has not only made himself capable of managing the affairs here on Earth, but until he is capable of getting off of the Earth, and managing the Solar System and greater cosmic formations."

What Lawson projects under the heading of "the self-perpetuating social body" is, in other words, an ideal or "intentional" community. However, this community will be more than simply a place of refuge at which the saving remnant of a degraded humanity can cultivate improved lives. Far more important to Lawson, his imagined community will be, quite literally, the seed from which the new species will grow. Obviously, then, the first requirement must be to make the community a microcosm of the future society of the new species—that is, to organize the residents "as a unit" and ensure that all aspects of life there will be based on and regulated by Lawsonomy principles.

Lawson also gives many hints that the community he envisions will give high priority to formal instruction in Lawsonomy; in order for life to be lived properly, minds must be drenched with the correct principles acquired through constant study. "By reading over and over again and again these Lawsonomy books, hundreds of times, the cells of consciousness will gradually grow in intellectual strength," Lawson maintains.

And finally, the community-as-seed means, as Lawson says, that it must be capable of renewing itself perpetually. Residents of the community, when properly prepared in mind, body, and spirit by the study and practice of Lawsonomy, will produce offspring, who also will be subjected to the complete shaping power of the community, and so on indefinitely. According to Lawson, whose views on biological evolution were Lamarckian (that is, when he didn't credit the menorgs with complete directing authority), the result will be not only the perpetuation of the community but also the steady improvement of the community's members, generation succeeding generation.

Over time, presumably the community will also steadily take in from the outer world new recruits won over by the fetching success and happiness of the community, and one can also suppose that as the community grows, it will send out offshoots. Although Lawson says nothing about these matters, it is clear that somehow he expects a natural process of growth originating in his community-as-seed eventually to supplant entirely the present sorry state of humanity and to bring into universal application a new way of life made over on Lawsonomy principles. Paradoxically, the withdrawal of his community from the present corrupt world for purposes of planting the seed will result eventually in the transformation of the world.

Of course, even if all these glorious things could be expected to grow from the seed, several difficult problems remained in the way of planting it. Chief among them surely were the problems of paying the costs and populating the community with the right kind of residents. But on these two matters Lawson must have been aware of his enormous good fortune: he already had through the Direct Credits Society access to financial resources and also to large numbers of members ideally suited for the kind of community he wanted to build— persons who were blindly loyal to the person of Lawson, willing to give to him amply of their time and personal wealth, already disciplined "as a unit" through the hierarchical structure of DCS, and possessing a beginning knowledge of Lawsonomy. Certainly he could safely assume that the personal and financial support he had to have would be at hand when needed. All that was left for Lawson to do, then, was to settle on a specific plan of action. Once that was done, he could be on his way toward establishing "the self-perpetuating social body" and inaugurating the "new species." Perhaps the First Knowledgian could even hope that, before departing these scenes, he would no longer be the only Knowledgian.

Part Four

UTOPIA IN DES MOINES

By 1943, Lawson had determined a plan of action and begun its implementation. By his claim, he inspected the campuses of thirty defunct colleges or universities in the quest for a site for his new community. Whether he actually did carry out such an exhaustive search is not known, but it is certain that he had decided by then to locate his community on a campus of a former college or university. His thinking was not simply practical, based on the assumption that there he would find the kinds of buildings, grounds, and resources which would be useful for a new community. Rather, Lawson had decided that his community would also be a university.

He had already revealed in *The Almighty*, of course, that the study of Lawsonomy would be a central activity of the self-perpetuating social body; immersion by the residents in Lawsonomy was crucial to the development of the new species. However, promoting this end did not require that the community be organized as a university. Other communities have given high priority to inculcating doctrines without doing so. On the other hand, rarely had other communities had doctrines as multifaceted, complex, and prominent as Lawsonomy. Because Lawson was exceedingly proud of Lawsonomy, possibly he also wanted to turn the spotlight on it by making a curriculum of it. Certainly he thought of Lawsonomy as worthier of study than the usual university curriculum, for which he had vast contempt. Of course, his contempt for all things having to do with higher education makes puzzling and ironic his decision to adopt the form of a university for his community. In the end, perhaps one of his purposes was to set forth what a *real* university was—that is, unlike all the others, one which taught the Truth. At the same time, however, there could be no question that his university was also going to be a community—the self-perpetuating social body as the seed for the new species.

Whatever Lawson's reasons were for conceiving of his community as also a university, the result was something unique in the American communitarian tradition. Not before or since the Des Moines University of Lawsonomy has any other intentional community ever been as thoroughly organized as if it were also an institution devoted to the higher learning. Moreover, Lawson's imposition of the form of a university proved to have profound consequences for DMUL—for the activities of its residents, for the public's reaction to DMUL, for the clarity of Lawson's thinking about his purposes at DMUL, and, in general, for the life, health, and even the demise of DMUL as a community.

DMUL was Lawson's distinctive contribution to the American communitarian tradition, his last "remarkable achievement and creation," and the major vehicle of his final years as a reformer. Very quickly DMUL also became the storm center of the furious controversy and opposition which greeted the First Knowledgian's altruistic campaign to improve his fellows—a controversy and an opposition which raged until his death and the folding of the Des Moines University of Lawsonomy in 1954.

10

TOWARD

THE SELF-

PERPETUATING

SOCIAL

BODY

"So, balancing all things as a whole, this writer decided that the State of Iowa would be as favorable a spot as any from which to inaugurate the birth of a new species," Lawson proclaimed in a June, 1944, issue of *Benefactor*. Chief among the factors he cited as giving the edge to Iowa was the state's location: "The State of Iowa is situated in about the center of the most progressive nation on Earth." On this occasion he made no mention of the exhaustive investigation of thirty campus sites which he earlier had claimed. Instead, he hinted at providential help in finding the campus of the former Des Moines University: "As if the law of maneuverability upheld his past efforts in behalf of human improvement, Alfred Lawson was guided to an abandoned university within the city limits of that beautiful city of Des Moines, Iowa." Quickly recognizing that it was the perfect place for his new undertaking, he arranged the purchase in August, 1943. Surely it was no insignificant detail in this saga of the founding that this ideal site was also an extraordinarily good buy: fourteen acres of urban property and six large buildings for a price of $80,000. (The 1941 assessed valuation of the property was $106,110, but in 1943 Polk County had reduced the value for tax purposes to $34,850.) Lawson was quoted in the Des Moines press as finding the sale price "very satisfactory."

Situated at the corner of Second and Euclid avenues in the Highland Park district on the north side of Des Moines, the campus Lawson had bought occupied the equivalent of nearly four city blocks and was surrounded on two sides by residences and on the other two sides by a small neighborhood commercial area. The campus buildings included a gymnasium, heating plant, science and engineering buildings, and two dormitories capable of housing 240 and 150 students, respectively.

The weathered brick of the buildings, the many big shade trees, and the large, well-established lawns produced the serene and inviting park-like effect acquired by many an American college campus with the passage of much time, which in the case of this campus had been over fifty years. Originally laid out in 1889 as the campus of Highland Park University, in 1911 the property had passed into the control of a board of trustees affiliated with the Presbyterian Church and then in 1918 was purchased by the Baptist Church, which changed the institution's name to Des Moines University. In 1927, the property was again sold, this time to a fundamentalist religious group known as the Baptist Bible Union of North America. However, the new owners' tenure was very short-lived. Their attempts to impose a creedal test on faculty members and new restrictions on student activities stirred up great strife on campus, culminating in a violent student riot to which the trustees responded in September, 1929, by voting to discontinue the university.

The timing of the trustees' action could not have been worse. The arrival soon thereafter of the Great Depression, followed by World War II, dried up the market for university campuses, discouraging even buyers who might have had ideas for alternative uses for the Des Moines property. Incredible though it will seem in the light of today's high demand for well-situated urban properties having development potential, the Des Moines University campus went for fourteen years unoccupied, unused, and unable to attract a buyer until Lawson came along.

Although Lawson always claimed afterward to be the "donor" of the new institution, he spoke more candidly to a *Des Moines Register* reporter shortly after coming to Des Moines to take possession: he "isn't putting a nickel" of his own money into the purchase, he said on that occasion, but was using money raised by voluntary donations to the Humanity Benefactor Foundation.

Nearly two years later, the *Register* sent reporter George Mills to Detroit, capital city of Lawsonomy, to learn more about these "voluntary donations" and the financial relations between Lawson and his followers. Mills uncovered a Lawson circular dated February 16, 1944, which listed contributions totalling $84,219 for the purchase of DMUL. That is, within only six months of signing the purchase agreement, Lawson had been able to raise from his followers $4,000 more than the purchase price. Some former Lawson followers also told Mills that within another eight months, contributions for the DMUL project had reached $137,150. Clearly Lawson still had the magic touch when it came to fund-raising.

Within several weeks of the purchase, several officers of the Direct Credits Society arrived to begin the cleanup and repair of buildings and grounds, which had suffered greatly from fourteen years of vandalism and inattention. Lawson told a reporter that, although DMUL could not be in full operation for a year, he did hope to begin "agricultural courses" sooner. What he actually meant was that as soon as a considerable number of residents were on hand, they would begin to grow their own food. He had bought for this purpose approximately seventy-five acres of nearby fields and city lots, which were designated as "DMUL gardens." A former Lawson associate estimated that DCS members donated enough farm equipment "to farm 1,000 acres."

On December 3, 1943, Lawson filed articles of incorporation and an operation agreement with the recorder of Polk County. These documents identified Lawson as "donor" of DMUL and prescribed that a five-member, self-perpetuating board of trustees would receive the property in the name of DMUL. To DMUL Lawson granted a nonexclusive license to use and teach from his writings. The trustees were empowered to finance the University from the sale of Lawson's publications, from contributions and endowments, and from fees which could be assessed (but never were) against students. Three provisions made clear the realities of control at DMUL: Lawson retained the powers to appoint four additional board members and to remove any trustee (among the required five and the optional four) for any reason; Lawson had the power to veto any action by the trustees; and DMUL was empowered to teach only materials written by Lawson or authorized by him.

Although anyone in Des Moines bothering to read these documents would not have learned from them that Lawson's university was intended to be a community as well, they would have seen plainly that, as a university, DMUL had no chance to be other than a seminary for the teaching of ideas originating in or approved by a single mind. In written or public statements, however, Lawson seemed eager to give a different assurance. In *Benefactor*, for instance, he addressed the question of whether teaching Lawsonomy at DMUL would mean abandoning or neglecting all previous knowledge: "To which Lawson answers POSITIVELY NO. In his advanced lessons he intends to retain all knowledge that is provable according to constant laws. The provable formulas of physics, chemistry, astronomy, geology, biology, mathematics, mechanics, engineering, farming, invention, electricity, navigation, economics, transformation, transmigration, therapeutics, surgery, hygiene, art, music, aerology and photography will be taught in the Des Moines University of Lawsonomy."

Indeed, in his earliest statement—on August 20, 1943—to the press in Des Moines, Lawson actually claimed that DMUL would aim to become an accredited university, eventually offering B.S., B.A., and M.A. degrees. DMUL would start with only three or four "branches" of instruction, he said, but at the conclusion of World War II he planned to expand instruction to ten branches. DMUL would also "be 100% tolerant of the beliefs, opinions, and practices of the different peoples of the world" and would "stand for the freedoms of press, speech, assembly, and religion," "the freedom of race friendship," and "a free American government." In his depiction of an essentially conventional university, Lawson slipped in only one broad hint of what really lay ahead: "There are some principles which will be taught in the school which are needed. The old time college professor might not like some of it, just as some persons didn't like some of the ideas when I started in aircraft."

Lawson was obviously eager to cultivate good will in Des Moines, even to the extent of misrepresenting his views and goals. In Lawson's first interview with the Des Moines press, *Register* reporter Cliff Millen described Lawson as "friendly" and "pleasant." Because Millen had read Lawson's books and knew that Lawson's "underlying beliefs as to education are not according to the usual pattern," Millen thought it

DES MOINES UNIVERSITY OF LAWSONOMY

WILL ENROLL A LIMITED NUMBER OF APPLICANTS FOR
ITS HUMAN-CULTURE AND PLANT-CULTURE CLASSES
APPLICANTS MUST BE FREE FROM ALL PHYSICAL, MENTAL
AND MORAL DEFECTS, INCLUDING SUCH HABITS AS LIQUOR
DRINKING, TOBACCO SMOKING, GAMBLING, DANCING AND FACE-PAINTING

CHILDS HALL — will house 240 students

JOHNSON HALL — A restful home for about one hundred and fifty students

The object of the founder of the Des Moines University of Lawsonomy is to call the attention of progressive people everywhere to some advanced plans that he has arranged during the last half century according to Natural Laws that will, if put into general practice, improve the human race to a very large extent.

He fully realizes, however, that to improve mankind perceptibly in the work of many generations and he has arranged his plans for the gradual development of a new species through selection and instruction of only the most far seeing and unselfish beings with the highest natural intelligence, will-power, self-control and stability of character and purpose.

Therefore, he intends to begin with the training of optimistic, enthusiastic youth with free minds, strong bodies and clean morals who want to rise to a higher state of intelligence and usefulness through advanced knowledge.

As such a state cannot be acquired by sickly people who live contrary to natural laws, therefore, we can only accept for training such applicants who can meet our physical, mental and moral standards of excellence.

We do not hate nor want to harm anybody. Neither do we argue or quarrel with anybody about anything. We merely offer our knowledge to the people at large in our efforts to make the Earth a good place for all living creatures to live upon.

Written applications only will be considered as we give no personal interviews to anybody.

DES MOINES UNIVERSITY OF LAWSONOMY
Des Moines, Iowa

KNOWLEDGE HALL — where youthful minds will generate future KNOWLEGIANS

UNIVERSITY GYMNASIUM
Adjoining it is a 5 acre athletic field

GORGEOUS TREES with protecting means shade the CAMPUS and its velvet greens

65

An early promotional flier showed scenes of the campus and specified the kind of "students" wanted at Des Moines University of Lawsonomy. From Lawson, *100 Great Speeches.*

worthy of note that Lawson "said nothing [in the interview] to indicate that he is trying to start an educational revolution at the college." Knowing something about Lawson's Direct Credits doctrine as well, Millen was also surprised that Lawson's comments in the interview "did not contain denunciations of bankers and financiers." When pressed for his economic views, Lawson responded that "he does not regard himself as an enemy of capitalism. . . . The economics to be taught [at DMUL] will favor capitalism with improvements through the elimination of the interest system and similar steps"—in other words, the DCS doctrine. This from the man who was about to launch a new socialist utopia modeled on the life of the menorgs!

If Lawson can be charged with a fair amount of bamboozlement, it also seems likely that some of his statements were influenced by the excitement of the moment. For instance, his vision of the earth-shaking significance of DMUL probably underlay his announcement of grandiose plans for DMUL's physical development, to be carried out as soon as World War II had ended.

One of the first buildings to go up, Lawson proclaimed in *Benefactor*, would be Administration Hall, the ground floor of which would provide offices and classrooms. The second, third, and fourth floors would contain an auditorium to seat several thousand persons. A large swimming pool was to be located in the basement, with Turkish baths and dressing rooms placed at both ends. Leading from the second-floor auditorium entrance would be a huge platform, "large enough to accommodate One Thousand Musicians, who will furnish entertainment, free of charge, to the outside public during the warm summer evenings." The platform would also be designed to handle "occasional dramatic performances."

Opposite Administration Hall Lawson proposed to erect a nursery (that is, maternity ward) and kindergarten. Elsewhere on campus, classroom buildings would be built as the need for them arose. Later, when the university had "reached its full capacity," he projected the building of "one of the largest Stadiums on Earth." "Dotted here and there throughout the campus will be beautiful flower beds that send forth natural fragrance that help to develop man's superior qualities and furnish him with a real heaven here upon earth."

Lawson's grand talk of accredited degree programs, large enrollment projections, and multimillion-dollar building plans must have
given Des Moines residents reassurance about the value of DMUL to
the city. He was proposing to restore the campus to its full loveliness,
to put the property to productive use, and to provide cultural benefits to the city. True, a careful reading of his statements could have
prompted some questions. What were those curriculum elements
which the old-time professor wouldn't like? Why were a maternity
hospital and a kindergarten needed? But for the most part, Lawson
projected little in his public statements that went beyond familiar notions about what a university should be or do. Finally, the economic
advantages which would flow from having a university in their midst
could not have been missed by Des Moines residents generally and
Highland Park neighbors particularly. Officials of Polk County showed
their eagerness to cooperate by selling a small county-owned parcel
adjoining the campus to DMUL for the modest sum of $105.

Lawson's hope for continuing agreeable and frequent contacts between DMUL and its neighbors soon blew up, however. Surely this
was inescapable; Lawson had made too many statements about DMUL
goals and activities which he either couldn't realize or had no intention of pursuing. As DMUL's true purposes and character became
better known—or rather, as Des Moines residents became disabused
of their original expectations—DMUL began to excite outsiders' hos-
tility and fears. Soon complaints and grievances sprang up on both
sides of the campus gate. At first, the spats seemed minor enough, but
it didn't take long for a larger pattern of standing animosity toward
DMUL to set in among Des Moines residents. For their part, the Lawsonomists quickly became convinced that they were the victims of unfair treatment and a smear campaign by the press in Des Moines.

From the start, of course, there had been some in Des Moines who
were highly skeptical of Lawson, his claims, and his university. Certainly these included the Des Moines reporters who continued to
probe into Lawson's background. Soon the city solicitor joined the
ranks of the scoffers. In early June, 1944, DMUL submitted a petition
for the city's tax exemption available to nonprofit educational institutions. After looking into the matter, however, the city solicitor strongly

The Des Moines University of Lawsonomy campus, showing Knowledge Hall and the notorious fence erected in 1944. Photo courtesy of the State Historical Society of Iowa—Special Collections.

opposed granting the exemption. His written opinion characterized DMUL as a printing and bookselling establishment rather than an educational institution. The petition for exemption was denied then and in every year thereafter over the vehement protests of DMUL officials.

Later in that same month, DMUL officials asked a subcommittee of the Planning and Zoning Commission to approve vacation of a segment of Oxford Street which ran through the DMUL campus. The request provoked a petition of opposition signed by about forty neighbors, who cited their inconvenience if the street closing were granted. At a hearing several protestants complained that DMUL had already caused them enough trouble. Whereas they used to be able to walk diagonally across the campus, they no longer could do so, because the campus was now closed off by a fence and locked gate. Why had the fence been erected? they wanted to know.

"The fence" was to become one of the most frequently cited offenses in the neighborhood's bill of particulars against DMUL. The Lawsonomists claimed—probably truthfully—to have erected it purely for self-defensive reasons, in order to prevent continuing acts of vandalism against their property. About five feet in height, painted black, and made of wooden posts and narrow wooden pickets, the fence was far from unattractive; it served the purpose of blocking entrance without at the same time creating an opaque wall around the campus. In DMUL publicity materials Lawson claimed the fence was "similar in appearance to the fence around the U.S.A. White House at Washington, D.C." But his defense was of no avail in Des Moines. To Highland Park residents and Des Moines residents generally the DMUL fence became more than an inconvenience. It soon loomed large in their minds as a symbol of an alien presence in Des Moines and as an indication that menacing and unwholesome activities must be afoot within the DMUL campus.

In its petition for the street closing, DMUL had argued that "enlargement of the campus would increase the value of property in the district and bring more business to the merchants of the community." This prompted one complainant at the hearing to respond: "They haven't done the things they say they are going to do yet, and as for bringing business to the merchants, they [the Lawsonomists] don't eat meat and they grow their own vegetables."

The Planning and Zoning Commission deferred action and called another meeting one week later, in order to give DMUL a chance to have a spokesperson present. DMUL sent two officers, E. C. Schiesser, President, and Herbert Blum, Secretary.

Claiming that Oxford Street was badly needed for DMUL development, Schiesser described the street as presently "being used as a parking place in the dead, dismal, dark, wee hours of the night by men and women [whom he also characterized as "perverts"] under the influence of liquor for illicit purposes." He then loosed what a *Des Moines Register* reporter called an "implied threat": "Our plans are prepared for a tremendous expansion of this university and within the next 10 or 20 years, 10 or 15 million dollars worth of improvements and buildings will be made according to these plans, providing the people of the city of Des Moines will treat us fair."

However, DMUL was "not going to argue or quarrel with anybody for the privilege of spending" this much money. Other cities (unnamed), eager to have the University of Lawsonomy locate in their respective precincts, had made offers of property and tax benefits, Schiesser alleged. Although the University had already spent $200,000 (so he claimed) in Des Moines within the past nine months and had improved and beautified the campus, DMUL had in return, he reported, been subjected to continuing acts of vandalism, including attacks by "depraved maniacs" who drove cars through the University's flower beds.

Most of Secretary Blum's statement dealt with the virtues of Lawson and Lawsonomy. But in his concluding call to the committee to approve the street closing, he suggested that "as a reward for such a noble act you may someday see your own children and grandchildren graduated from the Des Moines University of Lawsonomy." Schiesser and Blum then abruptly left, refusing to answer questions.

In a statement made later in the hearing a protestant offered some new complaints against the Lawsonomists. They woke up each day, he said, to a bugle call. Also, he was disturbed to see young boys working on the grounds from sunup to late in the evening. He closed with another reference to the obnoxious fence: "They have put up the sort of fence that is put around institutions."

The Planning and Zoning Commission voted to deny the University's request but also agreed that DMUL officials should be "invited to return at some future date when they have more definite plans to present as a reason for the proposed vacation."

Several months later, in a September 19, 1944, meeting of the East Des Moines Club, the Club's president, Karl Wagner, voiced a new concern (in association with an old one) when he referred to "that mysterious school around which its owner built a high fence to keep people out and then tries to encourage our children to enter." Worries about children came up again later that same day at a meeting of the Des Moines school board. A board member wondered whether DMUL parents would be allowed to send children to classes at DMUL rather than to the public schools. (No, replied school superintendent N. D. McCombs.) Board president Thomas B. Couchman, Jr., then bespoke his additional concerns about children and the University: "All summer you've seen gangs of young boys working around the

buildings and in the gardens. This is just regimentation of persons.
How do they avoid the child labor laws?" Couchman added an unre-
lated complaint that no doubt represented the ire of many local businessmen: "They don't trade with merchants who don't advertise in the
Lawsonomy publication, *The Benefactor.*"

Violence against DMUL finally came on October 23, 1944. In view
of the neighborhood's concern about the menace of Lawsonomy to
their children, it was ironical that the attack on the DMUL property
was carried out entirely by an estimated seventy-five to one hundred
boys of junior high and high school age. The boys, coming in several
waves throughout the evening, smashed windows in the DMUL buildings and greenhouse, tore the tail light off Secretary Blum's car, and
threatened to overturn the car (Blum was in it at the time). The attacks began at 7 : 30 P.M.; the police finally dispersed the crowd around
11 : 00 P.M. The superintendent of the Playground and Recreation
Commission thought the cause of this incident had something to do
with the approach of Halloween. However, the School Board President speculated that anti-DMUL sentiments of parents, expressed in
front of their children, had been a factor in the incident.

In response to the mounting outside hostilities toward DMUL, sometime in 1944 an order came down from Lawson that no one should be
permitted to enter DMUL property without Lawson's authorization.
But because Lawson was often away and couldn't be reached easily
(few in his organizations ever knew where he was), important visitors
were sometimes left standing outside the gate, even when they were
public officers on official business. The first of these embarrassing
moments occurred in March, 1945, when city smoke inspectors, noticing apparent violations, succeeded in gaining entrance to DMUL only
on their third try. This scene was repeated many times in the future as
tax officials, boiler inspectors, and federal property officials were denied entrance. Each incident was good for sensational newspaper coverage giving further "proof" that DMUL was up to no good. In each
case, Lawson was eventually tracked down and the official visitors permitted to enter—on one occasion, however, not before several DMUL
officers were arrested, jailed, and fined for interfering with legitimate
public business.

To add to Lawson's accumulating woes in Des Moines, in the spring of 1945 an old enemy came into town for the sole purpose of "exposing" Lawson. Elias Cina, a Swiss alien, had been a Lawson associate in Lawson's ill-fated "super-airliner" project in the late 1920s and also in the New York–Washington bus service Lawson unsuccessfully attempted to initiate during the same time period. Cina harbored deep but unspecified resentments against Lawson. Now a chef in Los Angeles, somehow he had learned of Lawson's great project in Des Moines and took a leave of absence to go there to do something about it. At his own expense (about one thousand dollars, he claimed) he prepared disparaging materials about Lawson and rented a shop in Des Moines in which to make his anti-Lawson displays and information available to the public. The shop, open for the entire month of May and billed on its front window as the "Free Public Information Office about Mr. A. W. Lawson," was located at 114 Euclid Avenue, directly across the street from DMUL. Cina departed at the end of May to continue his anti-Lawson campaign in Detroit, the home base of Lawson's organizations. Although his stay in Des Moines was brief, it was well-timed to feed the fast-growing anti-Lawson sentiment there. George Mills, the *Des Moines Register* reporter, tagged Cina perfectly as a "disorg," a designation which Cina "cheerfully" accepted.

Several months later an incident occurred which, as reported in the *Register*, scuttled irreparably DMUL's sinking reputation in Des Moines. According to the newspaper, the facts were these: Edwin Baker, an electrician from Alexandria, Louisiana, and a widower, had entered a Veteran's Administration hospital for extended treatment. During his long absence he left his daughter, Margaret, age twelve, in Grand Rapids, Michigan, with Margaret's great aunt. The latter, a devotee of Lawsonomy, then enrolled Margaret in DMUL, to which Baker traced his daughter's whereabouts upon his return from the hospital. Forcing his way onto the campus, Baker was permitted to hug and kiss his daughter, then was surrounded and shown the door by six men.

Eventually released on a writ of habeas corpus, Margaret gave the *Register*'s reporter many details about an allegedly bizarre life within DMUL and claimed that attempts were made to persuade her to reject her father. Baker summed up his impression of DMUL in this statement to the court (reprinted in the *Register*): "When I got there, I saw the perfect picture of an insane asylum."

The Lawsonomists, of course, held a different version of the key facts, especially on the issues of who—father or aunt—had legal custody of Margaret and whether Margaret was an unwilling resident until subjected to suasion by her father. Unfortunately for the Lawsonomists, however, their views were not reported in the *Register*. Convinced by this time that the *Register* was committed to a vendetta against Lawson and DMUL, the residents of DMUL had long since become resigned to a bad press in Des Moines and did nothing now to try to place in the public prints their side of the Margaret Baker incident.

As if DMUL's strife with its neighbors in 1944 and 1945 were not sufficient trouble for Lawson, he also suddenly found himself confronting an organizational crisis. During these same years came a mass defection by DCS officers, including many having the highest ranks and longest records of service to the DCS cause. In an investigation—published June 2, 1945—of the organizational blowup, *Des Moines Register* reporter George Mills concluded that resignations reduced the number of officers in the ranks of general alone from twelve hundred to seven hundred in this two-year period. (Of course, even the larger of these two numbers indicated that the top officer ranks had already fallen off considerably by the early 1940s from much greater heights reached in the 1930s.) Disgruntled former DCS officers came forward to lodge with Mills various specific complaints against Lawson, but most had to do with what they believed was Lawson's authoritarian, exploitative treatment of his followers. Perhaps the most poignant statement was made by a former DCS major general, Mrs. John Romberger. Her testimony is especially worth noting for what it reveals about organizational relations between Lawson and his followers.

To Mills, Mrs. Romberger "told how she had to get written permission from headquarters before she could send a letter to her daughter, Violet, who still is working in a Los Angeles Lawsonomy information bureau." When Lawson ordered Violet to change her name from

Romberger to Romm, the mother finally had had enough of Lawson's demands. She prepared a legal affidavit from which Mills printed the following extract:

> Mr. Lawson influenced the young people in the organization to quit school and so our children, in following him, sacrificed their educations. Violet and Olga [another daughter] both quit in the eleventh grade and Emily [a third daughter] gave up college after 2 1/2 years at Wayne University after Mr. Lawson promised her that she would become a great teacher when direct credits comes into law. Emily devoted about six years full time without pay in promoting Mr. Lawson. In 1935 Violet started to work in Mr. Lawson's office, the Humanity Publishing Company, and worked there about four years. Then in 1939 Mr. Lawson sent Violet and three other women to California to organize. At that time he changed her name from Violet Romberger to Violet Romm, to which we objected but he said it was for the sake of the organization.

The affidavit claimed that Olga, too, worked without pay in Lawson's office in Detroit from 1939 to 1944 and submitted to the same name change that Lawson imposed on her sister.

In her statement Mrs. Romberger also detailed the dedicated labors by her and her husband on behalf of DCS. Naturalized citizens born in Hungary, the Rombergers "broke up our home in 1936," leaving Detroit in order to do organizing work among Hungarian-Americans in Ohio. There they translated issues of *Benefactor* into Hungarian, held organization meetings, and sold advertising in *Benefactor*, sending all money collected back to headquarters in Detroit. Unpaid for their DCS work, they survived on food and shelter contributed by other DCS members. How had they been persuaded to make such sacrifices? Mills found that "most of the former Lawsonites here [in Detroit] agree that the commander-in-chief seems to exercise some sort of a hypnotic influence over his followers," and the Rombergers had been among those succumbing to that influence. In Mrs. Romberger's words: "He looks you so strong in the eye." Her affidavit also described the high-pressure methods Lawson had used on his officers: "Mr. Lawson made us believe we were working for the good of humanity as his chosen missionaries. We believed Mr. Lawson when he often shouted at meetings, 'Officers, work harder than ever for the Direct Credits plan. Double your efforts in work and money contributions. The more you give, the sooner we will win.'"

But this was in the past; now disillusioned and disabused, the Rombergers wished to have nothing further to do with Lawson and DCS. Unfortunately, however, they were unable to sever connections completely, as Mrs. Romberger lamented at the close of her statement: "Since we are convinced that Mr. Lawson is not the humanitarian that he claimed, we have done all within our power to get our Violet to give up her work and to come home but are unable to budge her. While we are through with the organization, we are still forced to send money to Violet so that she has food, clothing, etc."

Of course, the key question in the case of Mrs. Romberger and in all the other cases Mills dug up is why, after making such great sacrifices for Lawson's cause and submitting compliantly to Lawson's extreme demands for so long, were they no longer willing to do so. An even more intriguing question is why the "hypnotic influence" ceased to exercise its hold precisely at this time not only for Mills' informants but also for many other DCS officers.

One factor figuring in the answers to these questions is readily suggested by an observation Mills made in his article: all of his informants claimed that "they still are strong for the Direct Credits idea." For them and many other officers ardently devoted to advancing the Direct Credits goals through political action, Lawson's shift of focus to a different kind of reform through Lawsonomy must have generated a personal crisis. However, awareness of the crisis and a determination to bolt from DCS would, in the usual case, probably have developed only slowly. Moreover, Lawson had handled his change of position very deftly, never abandoning the DCS doctrine even as he introduced and then steadily increased emphasis on Lawsonomy. A former major general with whom Mills talked identified the full nature of the problem which Lawson created for the Direct Credits militant: "If [Lawson] had stuck to [the Direct Credits program], he would have been all right. The trouble is, he switched us over so gradually to Lawsonomy we didn't realize what was happening."

But by the early 1940s many had at last come to realize what was happening, especially after Lawson began to talk more intently than ever before about the new species and made his move to Des Moines. It is not surprising, then, that a large-scale departure from the DCS ranks should have occurred at this time; for many who had given up so much for a cause viewed as almost holy, Lawson could at last be seen clearly as an apostate. Once reaching this realization, they would very likely also begin to reformulate their previous conception of Lawson as a great man and to see their past relations with him in a new light.

In his newspaper article, however, Mills ascribed the decimation of the DCS officer ranks to a different and quite surprising cause— namely, a row in the organization set off by Lawson's marriage, an event occurring at some undetermined time in the early 1940s. During the spring of 1944, Mills reported, Lawson's marital status was already an item of controversy discussed at several DCS meetings in Detroit. Then, on October 12, 1944, Lawson sent a mimeographed circular to all officers announcing that he and his wife had a son (who actually had been born nearly a year earlier). According to Mills, following this announcement came a "wholesale exodus of major generals." "Of the 250 to 275 major generals in the Detroit area, I would say that fully 50 percent are out," a former major general told Mills. He added that at least four of the seven district leaders in the Detroit area had also resigned. Presumably a ripple effect set in, soon bringing resignations in more far-flung districts.

Because Lawson was nearly seventy-five years old when he married and had been a bachelor all his life until then, it is understandable that his marriage would catch members by surprise. Because his bride was not quite thirty years old, some might also have found impropriety or unseemliness in the disparity of ages. If so, then their shock must have been greatly compounded by the announcement that Lawson's wife had delivered a child fathered by the septuagenarian. But neither the surprise of all nor the affront to the sensibilities of some over these unexpected events seems sufficient to explain the mass desertions from DCS.

Perhaps to many DCS members Lawson appeared to be a hypocrite, inasmuch as he had spoken and written harsh words against the contemporary institution of marriage. In fact, at the very time that the controversy over his marriage was raging, Lawson delivered the following opinions in his 1944 book *A New Species*: "It is about time that these disgraceful man-made marriage laws should be reconstructed for the sake of common decency among human beings. . . . Marriage, in most cases, is now treated as an affair of convenience, or for a money consideration. It is seldom undertaken strictly as a duty to GOD and humanity, as it should be done."

But it hardly requires a close reading of Lawson's words to see that he was only condemning current marriage practices, not marriage itself. What he objected to in particular was that "the average person does not give as much thought to an examination and selection of a prospective mate as one does in the choice of a new pair of boots." He also believed that much misery would be avoided if the marriage partners were "to sign between them a pre-marriage agreement stating the exact terms upon which they would conduct themselves."

Presumably in his own marriage Lawson complied with this latter dictum. As for his admonition to choose a mate carefully, in full recognition of one's "duty to GOD and humanity," Lawson had no doubt about his compliance. His wife not only was a long-time Direct Credits officer in Detroit but in his view also was ideally suited to be a mother. As Lawson wrote of her in his October 12, 1944, circular (as quoted by George Mills in the *Des Moines Register*), "If all mothers were to lead as natural a life as this 31-year-old mother does, physically, mentally, and morally, the world would soon be populated by a superior class of human beings that would eventually evolve into a marvelous new species that would be free from all the filthy vices bred into our present civilized creatures from which they do not even try to extricate themselves."

For her part, of course, there could be no question that, in marrying the First Knowledgian, Lawson's wife too had chosen a prospective mate responsibly and well. It should be noted, finally, that this union faithfully observed another of Lawson's major teachings—that is, that both parents should be at least thirty years old and have lived lives molded by the moral laws before producing offspring. In sum, if the defecting DCS officers thought they had found Lawson out in inconsistency between word and deed on the matter of marriage, they certainly had no valid basis for doing so.

Possibly many of the DCS officers believed that, by marrying and fathering a child, Lawson had reneged on his pledge to devote his energies exclusively to humanity's betterment—that is, to the Direct Credits cause. Certainly Lawson had trumpeted often his vow to devote the rest of his life only to selfless service to humanity. Many followers might very well have concluded that one professing to be The People's Coach and the Man of Destiny and extracting extraordinary sacrifices from his followers should be held to an extreme standard of conduct.

But was Lawson's conduct perfidious? The question moves the discussion back to the heart of the problem: although all of his long-time officers had been fetched by the Direct Credits doctrine, Lawson had moved beyond that doctrine to Lawsonomy. Certainly Lawson now believed that by marrying and having children (a daughter followed the son three years later), he was doing precisely what "duty to GOD and humanity" required of him. The very fact that, having gone so long without marrying, he was now resolved to undertake at a very advanced age a change of status as husband and father is itself evidence of Lawson's new conception of his duty. In fact, it was the best evidence possible of his newfound commitment to initiate the new species.

That he viewed his marriage exactly in this light was clearly revealed in Lawson's October 12, 1944, circular, in which he took account of his wife as exemplar and progenitor of the new species. Another small piece of evidence found there was Lawson's announcement of the first and middle names bestowed on his new son—John Convert, the name of the hero of *Born Again*. (However, the son [and later, the daughter, too] took the mother's last name in order to avoid "future confusion and jealousy" among organization officers, Lawson explained.) In the same circular Lawson also noted that the son was off to an excellent Lawsonomic start in life: "He has been taking several cold baths each day since birth and actually demands them at stated intervals. He has had no aches or pains since he was born." Here was abundant evidence that the campaign for the new species was off and running.

It is likely, then, that some of the DCS officers recognized in his marriage and the birth of his son how deadly serious Lawson was about pursuing a new path of reform at the expense of the Direct Credits program. Even so, it remains difficult to believe that, for most officers, these events were in any fundamental sense the cause of their departures from DCS. Much more likely, disgruntlements had long been simmering and private alarms growing over Lawson's steady shift of focus to Lawsonomy. Lawson's marriage and the arrival of little John Convert would then have provided convenient and sensational pretexts—or at the most, have been precipitating events—for the mass departures of officers who already were fairly far gone in disaffection from Lawson.

As Mills observed in his newspaper article, Lawson wasn't "idle while his one-time officers are speaking their minds about him." In a circular dated May 1, 1945, quoted by Mills, Lawson took account of his foes within his organization: "We frequently find that after spending several years of valuable time in making a nobody into a somebody, that he or she suddenly shows bad character by trying to harm the organization for some petty purpose by spreading lies about the commander-in-chief." Lawson also predicted dire consequences for all of those opposing him in the Direct Credits Society, in Des Moines, or elsewhere: "There is no law that will compel anybody to go along with Lawson. But there is a law that will punish anybody that tries to interfere with his plans for the people's benefit. It is the law of maneuverability, over which Lawson has no control whatsoever. That law is operated by God Almighty."

Whether or not the Law of Maneuverability had anything to do with it, Lawson was, in fact, able to survive the large-scale defection of DCS officers, because the loyalty of the many who remained was intense and assured. As reported by Mills, Lawson announced in his May 1, 1945, circular that "about 700 generals" had asked him to stay on as commander in chief and "not one general wrote in opposition to him." In other words, Lawson still had an ample membership base of generals and other officers needed to support his new undertaking in Des Moines. Their bond to him was still a strongly personal one, and they remained willing to follow wherever he might lead.

The external pressures impinging on Lawson in Des Moines eventually were contained, too. True enough, the downward-moving spiral of mutual antipathy in which both Des Moines and DMUL were caught never reversed direction and, in fact, hit rock bottom by the end of 1945. But this also meant that a point of stand-off was reached. DMUL could apparently do nothing to ameliorate its situation or placate the threats from its environment, and no legal process was available to Des Moines citizens by which they might rid the city of Lawson and his followers. Because DMUL had so starkly reduced its contacts with Des Moines, episodes of direct conflict also subsided. For the next six years—from 1946 through 1951—DMUL and Lawson actually managed to stay out of the Des Moines newspapers (except, of course, for the notices of DMUL's unsuccessful attempts each year to get a city tax exemption).

The years 1944 and 1945 had certainly brought much challenge for Lawson as he undertook to found the "self-perpetuating social body." Facing down the opposition arising both within DCS and in Des Moines and sticking resolutely to his vision, however, he succeeded in bringing into being his last great creation—the Des Moines University of Lawsonomy. As DMUL took on definite form as a community, Lawson must have felt gratified, and at some point late in this two-year period, he moved to DMUL with his family. By this time, of course, DMUL had become something like a beleaguered walled city. It nonetheless offered a precarious safety for Lawson's brave effort to institute new patterns of individual development and communal living. Probably some of the residents did not know fully what kind of life Lawson had in store for them. Yet most must certainly have known that they were engaged in the most important and exciting project in history: laying the Lawsonomic foundation for the generation of the new species.

11

ALMA
MATER
OF THE
NEW
SPECIES

The tax assessor of Des Moines, Bert Zuver, was perplexed. At the request of the Board of Assessment and Review he had come to the Des Moines University of Lawsonomy on May 27, 1948, to inspect the premises and form a judgment about the institution's eligibility for the tax exemption which had been requested every year since 1944. Assisted by two deputies, he made an inspection tour, during which, as he later wrote in his report, "we gave particular attention to the question of whether this organization had the normal characteristics which identify an educational institution." But no matter what they looked into, the inspection team "found no activities customary for colleges in this state." Moreover, some of the information which the team had requested (for instance, on student enrollments and DMUL finances) was not forthcoming. Noting "the secrecy and withholding of data" by DMUL officials, Zuver recorded his puzzlement: "This institution is in the position of claiming tax exemption, and refusing to furnish information on which such exemption could be based."

Much of Zuver's report was taken up with an account of what the inspectors did *not* find—for instance, classes in session, many persons "of apparent college age," "a faculty with scholastic training or degrees or qualified to teach college subjects," a board of trustees having genuine authority, a library, or evidence of accreditation or of association with an accreditation organization. Although the team found indications of use of portions of all buildings, they concluded the uses were "not necessarily educational." Only one building, equipped with "furniture, such as school desks, chairs, pianos, arranged in proper order for classes," fully met their expectations for a university building.

Zuver reported that several activities observed by the team "might be claimed as educational." However, he himself remained unpersuaded: "virtually all those activities involved maintaining of the grounds and buildings or the feeding and accommodation of the persons in residence there." He added this interesting observation: "An illustration of the emphasis placed on secrecy is the so-called classroom work in Law and Order, which involved day-and-night patrolling of the grounds. To our astonishment, we did discover that there are fifteen persons who had police permits furnished them by the City of Des Moines. I checked the records at the Municipal Building and found that Drake University, with all its buildings and large student body, does not have more than one police permit for their university."

In the light of the evidence he did and did not find, Zuver concluded that DMUL was "a university in name only," and he joined the 1944 recommendation of the city solicitor that DMUL not be given an education exemption. However, Zuver's characterization of DMUL veered away sharply from that of the city solicitor, who had insisted that DMUL was merely an establishment for the printing and selling of Lawson's books. Zuver's on-site inspection brought him to a much different conclusion: in his judgment, he reported, DMUL was best described as "a type of cooperative effort" and specifically, "a colony for a community within the community for the purpose of eulogizing Alfred Lawson."

It had taken four years to happen, but here at last someone in Des Moines had come close to an accurate understanding of DMUL. Led on by the "numerous words of praise, and extensive history pertaining to the works and speeches of one Alfred Lawson," Zuver went astray in concluding that eulogizing Lawson was DMUL's exclusive purpose. But the rest of his characterization was highly discerning and apt.

Just as Zuver noted, DMUL was "a type of cooperative effort"—

that is, an experimental community dedicated to forging a communal life based on new principles. The tax assessor's characterization of DMUL as "a colony for a community within the community" was also fitting. If this description conjured up the image of a boring from within of the larger society by the smaller community, this was not far off the mark of Lawson's long-range intentions. As Lawson saw it, DMUL was nothing less than the momentous first step toward someday winning over the larger society to a new way of life and at last achieving the new species.

If DMUL officials had been more forthcoming with information or if the tax assessor's mission had been a broader one, Zuver might have arrived at a more detailed understanding of Lawson's university-as-community (or community-as-university). It was sufficient for Zuver's purpose, however, simply to ascertain whether DMUL was a conventional university. Once satisfied that it was not, he had no reason to inquire further or to say more about DMUL's characteristics as a community. This is a pity, because Zuver and his colleagues had an opportunity which proved to be unique: they were the only outsiders on record ever permitted to enter DMUL for the purpose of inspecting every aspect of the community's activities and physical arrangements.

All other information about DMUL which is available today comes from Lawsonomic sources, and there is precious little of that—such things as occasional statements to the press by Lawson or disgruntled former residents of DMUL, legal testimony given in 1952 by Lawson and other DMUL officials, miscellaneous references to DMUL in Lawson's writings, and a few DMUL promotional documents. Over five hundred pages of materials in the FBI's file on Lawson cast no light on DMUL. If DMUL internal records still exist, they are not available today. Although an invaluable source of information lies in the recollections of several former residents of DMUL, many crucial details have blurred or receded as memories inevitably faded after the passage of forty years.

To one of the most obvious questions, however, a definite answer can be given: Lawson's claim to be running a university was not disingenuous, made cynically for the purpose of trying to secure a tax exemption. Every utopian community is, perforce, an educational system, but Lawson's community differed from virtually all others by putting forward as its most conspicuous feature its educational aspect. Organization around the formal, systematic study of a highly developed doctrine was the essential idea for this community. The perfection of individual lives and the attainment of an improved communal life could come only through the laborious study and increasing mastery of the most advanced learning of all—Lawsonomy.

The centrality of the university concept in Lawson's design for a new community was revealed in his applying in the communal setting many terms familiar in American higher education. Members were accepted into the community only upon submitting "written applications" and meeting prescribed "admission requirements," including a "qualifying exam" in Lawsonomy. Lawson always referred to the residents of this community as "Lawsonomy students." The fundamental arrangement of the community, by which members shared in all the work and had all their needs met by the community, Lawson sometimes described as a student aid arrangement, by which students worked in exchange for waiver of "tuition and fees" and "room and board charges." The imbibing of Lawsonomy was not left to be simply a result of participation in the life of the community but was also made a matter of formal study and attendance at "daily classes." The teaching done in those classes was provided by "faculty" organized by "departments." Lawson looked forward to the day, too, when DMUL residents would begin to take periodic "written examinations" to gauge their advance in the intellectual comprehension of Lawsonomy principles. At the happy point of complete mastery of Lawsonomy, the awarding of a distinctive "degree" awaited the dedicated Lawsonomist.

In his application of some of these conventional terms within the setting of a utopian community, however, Lawson imparted some unusual twists. Admission requirements, for instance, were highly unorthodox. Evidence of successful completion of a high school program of study was not among the requirements; instead, according to a DMUL promotional brochure, "one must be conversant with Lawsonomy Literature and pass a rigid examination concerning its principles." Consistent with the needs of a community of living, the remaining requirements emphasized "character and usefulness": "as we do not maintain a hospital or lunacy department for contagious diseases, all students must prove and retain a clean, healthy physical, mental and moral standard of personality to remain here." Both male and female students were welcome (at the start, at least), but Lawson's statement to prospective students made plain that gamblers, dancers, users of tobacco, liquor and cosmetics, and those who disliked physical work or "early to bed, early to rise" living need not apply. For evidence and assurances on these matters, including the applicant's basic knowledge of Lawsonomy, Lawson relied on screening and nomination of candidates by the district organizations of the Direct Credits Society.

Because DMUL officials had not told the tax assessor that DMUL was open to candidates of all ages and not just those emerging from high school at the conventional late-adolescent age, the assessor could not have known that his search at DMUL for persons of "apparent college age" was misguided. All residents—ranging from infants through young children, teenagers, and young adults, to the middle- and old-aged—were students. Presumably, the babies and young children had not taken the "rigid examination" in Lawsonomy. On the other hand, from Lawson's point of view, the unformed minds of minors surely made them good Lawsonomy prospects. Lawson never did establish his proposed maternity ward at DMUL, and it is unlikely that any offspring were ever born to couples during their stay at DMUL. Also, because DMUL had no state-certified schools, Lawson's purposes were thwarted by state school attendance laws requiring him to send children between the ages of seven and sixteen to the Des Moines public schools. Nonetheless, at least in the early years of DMUL, a large proportion of DMUL residents were minors and presumably Lawson could still hope that their crucial formative years would be molded decisively by Lawsonomy influences.

The academic degree which Lawson authorized DMUL to award was unusual, too. Called the degree of Knowledgian, it required thirty years to complete! Students would sit for interim exams at the end of ten years and twenty years and for a comprehensive exam after the full thirty years were completed. Lawsonomy was to be the *sole* subject matter of study and of these examinations. Because Lawsonomy was contained only in the writings of Alfred Lawson, and because all students had copies of these works, a library was not needed at DMUL. (Thus, one more of Zuver's objections was wide of the mark.) In fact, no works by other authors were permitted on the premises, since they would have a diluting effect on Lawsonomy's influence on the minds and lives of DMUL's residents.

According to a former DMUL resident, Lois Hans, Lawson carried his prohibition against non-Lawsonomy materials very far. Lois, twelve years old at the time, recalled for *Des Moines Register* reporter George Mills how angry Lawson allegedly got when a student brought in a basketball rule book. Lawson confiscated the book, Lois claimed in Mills' June 2, 1945, article, "because we were not supposed to read anything but his literature, not even a rule book." The allegation is perplexing, in view of Lawson's known enthusiasm for having his students engage in physical exercise and sports. Sounding more plausible was Lois' claim that Lawson made her turn in her dictionary, on grounds that it was not the one of which he approved. Lawson might very well have favored one dictionary—the 1912 National Press Association's *Webster's Dictionary Illustrated*, for which Lawson had been the aviation consultant. A final incident reported by Lois also has the ring of truth: "One of the boys had a murder mystery and he got caught with it. Lawson got awfully mad. He got awfully red in the face. Another girl had one and she got rid of it in a hurry."

At times Lawson suggested that it shouldn't be hard for a properly prepared and motivated mind to master Lawsonomy. This was not to say, however, that it could be done quickly, even by the most able student. For one thing, Lawsonomy's scope was vast; there was a lot to learn (and for that matter, for the older students, a lot of worthless previous learning to unlearn). And for another thing, one couldn't learn Lawsonomy through use of the mind only; Lawsonomy was a philosophy to be learned through living as well as through study. Both of these circumstances help to explain the unusually long time requirement for the Knowledgian degree. However, there was yet another circumstance, having to do with the method and objective of Lawsonomic learning, which guaranteed that knowledge of Lawsonomy couldn't be acquired in a hurry by the usual student.

In a 1952 United States Senate hearing, a DMUL student described the learning method favored at DMUL: "You study the books [that is, Lawson's books], read and recite from the books," to which another student added: "It is all in there. You got to go in there and find it." Aside from establishing the authority of Lawson's books, however, these statements do not make plain the essential feature of the study method at DMUL, and they might even falsely suggest that the student's job was to explicate and interpret the Lawsonomy texts. Nothing could be farther from the truth. The job of the student was to study, read, re-read, and recite from Lawson's books, *toward the end of memorizing them*. The goal of learning at DMUL was to put up in the student's mind the Lawsonomic truths precisely in the form in which Lawson had expressed them. By insisting that students stick to the exact letter of Lawsonomy, Lawson hoped to ward off the corruption of doctrine, doctrinal disputes, and schism which had led, in his view, to the perversion of the message of Jesus. But just as important, Lawson believed that through memorization the truths of Lawsonomy could be most firmly anchored in the mind.

The goal and method of education at DMUL exposed the rather restricted understanding there of the term "faculty member." DMUL had persons designated as faculty members, organized by "departments" of Lawsonomy, Management, Music, Oratory, Botany, and Theology. But in no sense did faculty members play an independent scholarly role or "profess" anything. Although Lawson was not a faculty member and did not teach classes, he was nonetheless recognized as THE teacher of Lawsonomy. The role of those very few persons called faculty members was merely to facilitate the learning (that is, memorization) of Lawsonomy by the students. They were not even Knowledgians; so far, Lawson was the sole possessor of that degree. Faculty members were nothing more than Lawsonomy's advanced students, who had been given short-term appointments to help along the less advanced students. They were put in charge of the several daily one-hour classes in which all—faculty no less than the other students— tested their advancing prowess in reciting from memory whole pages of the Lawsonomy texts.

At the time of his purchase of DMUL, Lawson assured a Des Moines reporter there would be no lack of students at DMUL. The organizations which he led could easily supply one thousand from their own ranks, he claimed. Although certainly DMUL never accommodated that many, how many were there at any time is impossible to determine precisely; enrollment records (if they ever were kept) are unavailable today. However, fragmentary information pieced together from several sources suggests that the number of residents at DMUL rose rapidly to a very respectable level during the first several years.

Lois Hans told *Register* reporter George Mills that, when she was at DMUL for three months in 1944 (the opening year), the student body consisted of seven girls and ten or eleven boys, ranging from little children to teenagers. In the next year occurred the sensational Margaret Baker incident, in which Margaret's father went to court to secure the release of his daughter from DMUL. After exiting via a writ of habeus corpus, Margaret reported a greatly increased DMUL enrollment of twenty-nine girls and twenty-seven boys; the oldest, she said, was seventeen years, and the youngest was four months. Both Lois and Margaret were twelve-year-olds, a fact which obviously shaped their judgment about whom to count as students; if adults had been included in the student lists, as they should have been, the total enrollment figures reported by each girl would have been much higher.

That membership of the DMUL community did reach a substantial level by 1945 was confirmed by a witness who was an adult resident there throughout that year. This person reported in 1980 that "when things were at their peak [in 1945] there was between seventy-five and one hundred people there daily." Although all of these lived, worked, studied, and took meals at DMUL, some were there only temporarily; there was frequent coming and going: "People would come to visit . . . write in for permission, come in for a week or two weeks and go home, and then maybe some of the regular people would have to go home for awhile and look after their property or whatever, and maybe not return at all. There were all different sorts of situations." Nonetheless, there were, in this witness's estimate, "not less than fifty people, probably more like sixty people" who could be considered more or less permanent residents of DMUL in 1945.

In his last interview, given several weeks before his death in November, 1954, Lawson claimed that enrollment had reached a high of two hundred in 1948. This claim does not square, however, with the tax assessor's impression of a low residence figure at DMUL in that same year. In his report, Zuver wrote that "never at any time did we observe more than fifteen people in connection with the institution." Other evidence suggests that, in fact, by 1948 the number of DMUL residents was already on a downward trend.

Probably closer to the truth was a Lawson statement made in 1952 in a United States Senate hearing that enrollment once (date not given) had reached one hundred persons. An undated DMUL promotional flier published sometime in the second half of the decade of the 1940s contains a photograph purporting to show DMUL residents in the dining hall, and one can indeed count about one hundred persons, the greatest number of them apparently in their teens. This may have been a staged photograph, of course; nonetheless, Lawson's claim to have once had one hundred residents at DMUL seems entirely reasonable. If one hundred is taken as DMUL's highest level of enrollment, then the time parameters imposed by the few scraps of information available would seem to suggest that this enrollment peak was reached sometime between 1945 and 1947, probably closer to 1945.

Of course, even in the palmiest days of DMUL's communal life, in several important respects DMUL actually remained more like a conventional university than a self-directing community. The residents at DMUL neither collectively owned the property nor collectively made the community's important policy decisions; the Humanity Benefactor Foundation owned and Lawson controlled. Also, the "self-perpetuating social body" never was or could be a fully self-sufficient community. Residents provided much for themselves—most of their food, laundry service, upkeep of buildings and grounds, and entertainments, for instance—but property taxes needed to be paid, and some goods and services, such as medical and dental care, electricity, water, and coal, had to be purchased by the community from others. Because residents did not hold outside jobs, made no products which could be sold to outsiders, and earned only modest amounts from the sale of Lawsonomy books and of advertising space in *Benefactor*, they relied on continuing contributions from fellow Lawsonomists living elsewhere to supply the "foreign exchange" needed for essential transactions outside the community.

Within these limitations, however, Lawson sought to promote a communal life characterized by classlessness, simplicity, sharing of all work, cooperation, and selfless devotion by individual members to the interests of the whole. These were the values implicit in the conduct of the menorgs and were also the lessons taught by Lawsonomy. To make the values regnant and the lessons effective, one thing above all was needed—the abolition of money among the DMUL residents (even while DMUL continued, of course, to raise and use money for external dealings). "We want to live a life without money," Lawson explained in a statement made in the 1952 Senate hearing, adding that humanity had "had too much trouble already with money."

Prospective students were told to bring no money or property with them to DMUL. All their needs would be supplied by the University. (Although it was widely believed in Des Moines that students were required to turn over all of their property to Lawson's organizations, there is no evidence that this ever was a condition for enrolling.) In return, students would be expected to participate fully in the work needed to sustain the community. But this was not really a quid pro quo, "work-study" arrangement, as Lawson sometimes claimed and as was found in the typical university. In the community eschewing money, the work done without salary was an essential part of the instruction offered. One learned some useful subjects in a way far excelling mere book-learning—for instance, botany, from growing one's own food; management, from doing any number of tasks requiring planning and supervision; law and order or police methods, from patrolling the grounds in security watches; pedagogy, from leading classes in the memorization of Lawsonomy; salesmanship, from selling advertisements in *Benefactor* to local merchants or going door to door with Lawsonomy books (both of which were done only in the first several years of DMUL, however).

In the absence of money, all DMUL residents would be equal, and all work activities needed for support of the community would be recognized as being of equal standing. At the same time that the valuable contribution made by each member to the community became more apparent, each member, having no money in hand, would be made thoroughly dependent upon the community for economic sustenance. The member would be made dependent on the community, too, for the fulfillment of all social and cultural needs.

Contrary to the impression conveyed by the *Des Moines Register*, DMUL residents (at least the adults) were not locked in and forbidden to leave the campus. Social pressures may have acted powerfully to discourage "unaccountable" walking away, but probably most residents had little incentive or inclination to leave anyway. In any event, without money in their pockets, they could not have gone far or done much. Thus, the ban on money and property did more than promote the cooperative, egalitarian spirit which Lawson sought. It also reduced the threat of outside influences—for instance, movies, other public entertainments, books, magazines, newspapers, radios—contaminating the shaping power of a purely Lawsonomic culture.

The Lawsonomists' day began with a bugle call summoning them from their beds at 6:00 A.M. and ended with all in their rooms at 10:00 P.M. and lights out at 11:00 P.M. Although only several hours were spent each day in classes, students were expected to find other time during the day for individual study. Of course, much of the day was necessarily spent in work; there was so much that had to be done— planting, hoeing, harvesting, and canning crops, preparing and serving meals, washing dishes, doing laundry and making up the beds, cleaning and dusting, renovating and maintaining buildings, keeping up the grounds and flower gardens, shoveling coal and hauling ashes, patrolling the property, selling books and advertising space. Precisely how the right talents and numbers of persons got assigned to the work crews is not clear, but presumably Lawson had little problem getting the necessary cooperation from his followers.

The *Des Moines Register* once reported a claim made by a former (disgruntled) DMUL resident that Lawson had fired an early DMUL president for buying a basketball for the students in defiance of Lawson's express command against the purchase. Whether or not this allegation and the one made by Lois Hans concerning the basketball rule book were true, Lawson—an enthusiast for physical fitness—

directed that several hours each day be spent in physical exercise. Margaret Baker acknowledged that she spent two hours in the gym every day. Two other former students, asked in 1980 to recall their experiences at DMUL, made similar reports about the place of physical exercise at DMUL. One, who was a teenager at the time of residence, claimed to have played baseball regularly at DMUL's field. The other, who was an adult while at DMUL, gave the following interesting account:

> Lawson was a great advocate of sports. He even formulated an indoor baseball league that was in operation during the winter months over there in the gymnasium, and it was comprised of boys and girls, men and women . . . I happened to be a participant in it. There were people of all ages there. I never laughed so much in my life. It was so much fun, you know, to see women of all ages running and playing and, you know, had their heart right in it. And Lawson taught them the fundamentals of baseball. He wanted them to get down and stop a ball if it was rolling across, you know. He wanted them to be agile, and he wanted them to be baseball players.

Perhaps the statements published in the *Des Moines Register* indicated nothing more than a preference by Lawson for baseball over basketball.

In addition to proper exercise, Lawson had other prescriptions for personal cleanliness and sound physical health. First published in *Manlife* and then added to over the years, they included, for instance, sleeping in the nude, a daily change of the bed sheets, two daily cold showers (even in the winter), fifty chews of each bite before swallowing, and drinking a glass of water during each waking hour. One of his most intriguing prescriptions called for two daily dunks of the head in a basin of cold water, upon which the eyes were then to be opened and revolved several times. According to the testimony of a former DMUL student, none of these practices was mandatory at DMUL; they were encouraged but doing them was a matter "entirely of the student's own volition." Still, what this witness had to say about cold showers suggests that "encouragement" may really have been more like "expectation."

Vegetarian diet was one Lawsonomic health practice definitely required at DMUL. Lawson had made the moral case for vegetarianism
in *Born Again*, and in *Manlife* he advanced the argument on behalf of
its beneficial consequences for health. Although on both grounds
many persons have since joined Lawson in favoring a meatless diet, in
the 1940s vegetarianism was for most Americans an exotic doctrine.
Add to this that Lawson recommended some peculiar practices—for
example, eating the cores of fruit and sprinkling fresh-cut grass on
salads. The result was that the vegetarianism of the Lawsonomists
contributed to their reputation in Des Moines as weird and alien.
Speaking ruefully in 1980 about this reputation, a former DMUL
resident acknowledged that the Lawsonomists were popularly viewed
as a group which "is locked in and eats grass."

As usual, a *Des Moines Register* story helped along the image of the
Lawsonomists' oddness. In her account emphasizing a bizarre life at
DMUL, Margaret Baker briefly discussed for a *Register* reporter the
food served there. She described a typical breakfast as consisting of
uncooked oatmeal, toast ("but it was so darn dry"), and a small chip of
butter. Lunch and dinner, she claimed, were built around bread and
potatoes ("sometimes mashed and sometimes they were regular potatoes, with the skins on"). Most vegetables, she said, were eaten raw;
"you had to eat the ends of celery, and the greens of radishes and
onions." Once she had strawberry shortcake, but ice cream, gum, or
candy were forbidden. Milk and water were the only beverages served.

But surely much was left out of Margaret's account; described so
sparsely, and with an emphasis on a few peculiarities, the food served
at DMUL was made to sound much drearier than it probably was.
Any outsider who has eaten meals at a Lawsonomy gathering would
have to testify that, while it is plain and features no prize-winning
vegetarian delicacies, the food is ample, varied, attractive, and whole-
some. In sum, the Lawsonomists at DMUL were, for the most part,
probably practicing an ordinary vegetarianism, which in a later age
would hardly have been deemed worthy of newspaper comment.

In basic living arrangements, the DMUL community was staunchly
conservative and conventional; the values emphasized were privacy
(at least among the adults) and propriety. Children at DMUL without
their parents lived in the DMUL dormitories, segregated by sex.

236 UTOPIA IN DES MOINES

Housing for unmarried adults was provided on the same pattern in
the dormitories. Although a child might share a room with one or several others of the same sex, unmarried adults had private rooms.
Childless married couples had their own quarters in the dormitories,
and married couples with children had private quarters in nearby
houses owned by DMUL.

Those readers eagerly waiting to learn whether Lawson's quest for
the new species led him to introduce unorthodox sexual practices at
DMUL will be disappointed. DMUL pursued none of the novel measures—for example, "polyfidelity," "free love," "complex marriage"—
found in some other utopian communities. The conventional values
of premarital chastity and customary sexual relations in monogamous
marriage prevailed at DMUL.

Lawson did preach a novel eugenics view, however: the species
would improve if parents would bring forth children only after each
parent had reached the age of "maturity." In Lawson's view, that age
was thirty years. (Lawson's mother and father had been thirty-two and
forty-two, respectively, at the time of his birth.) But to produce great
strides forward, more was needed than simply guaranteeing parents
of the proper age. Only parents whose lives had been shaped during
their first thirty years by Lawsonomic practices and values could produce the superior offspring needed to generate the new species. Lawson's argument wasn't merely that such parents would provide the
best cultural influence on their growing children or that they would
produce healthier children. His was a Lamarckian view holding that
much of the parents' perfection of mind and character, acquired
through Lawsonomy, would be transmitted genetically to the next
generation—and even that the parents' strong desire to strive for
moral, mental, and physical improvement would be passed on.

In a sense, then, the entire system of life and learning at DMUL
could be considered a eugenics program—or certainly the most important feature of a eugenics campaign to initiate the new species. Beyond this, Lawson apparently didn't go; he had no formal program
for securing the most desirable marriages among his followers or for
preventing undesirable marriages or the births of children to parents
under thirty.

However, he allegedly took a very strong informal interest in these matters. According to an informant who was there in DMUL's early years, Lawson lectured the young people frequently on the desirability of parenthood only after the age of thirty. He engineered no marriages but was ready to give advice on a proposed marriage, if consulted: "Now he might tell a person I wouldn't marry that person, but he wouldn't say I would marry that person." Were followers likely to heed his advice? "That would depend on the person, you know. But there probably were a few cases of that sort." Finally, in order to make his followers conscious of their responsibilities for initiating the new species, Lawson encouraged them to develop "pedigrees" and passed out charts for this purpose.

Contrasting with the emphasis on privacy found in rooming arrangements was the sense of community promoted three times a day when all residents met for common meals in the DMUL dining hall. Of course, taking meals in common was also efficient and assured the proper vegetarian diet for DMUL's residents. But the meals in common sometimes had an importance extending far beyond these values. Early in DMUL's existence, according to the testimony given in 1980 by a former student, Lawson had noticed that some students left the table immediately after eating. Convinced that working or moving about before digestion had been completed was an unhealthy practice, Lawson soon imposed a requirement that all remain at the table for twenty to twenty-five minutes after each meal. This became a pleasurably anticipated period of relaxation, conversation, and fellowship, in effect whether or not Lawson was present. When he was there, however, the post-meal rest period was characterized by especially good cheer and joviality, because, in the words of this former student, "Lawson had the talent to get everybody laughing in just minutes and seconds."

Concerned about being misunderstood, however, this witness continued: "I don't mean to say it was all joking—oh no. Lawson also used that period for educational purposes and particularly in the morning, he would say things that he seemed to know were timely." Although Lawson allegedly encouraged others to participate in the discussion with him, "everybody was always hanging on wanting Lawson to talk because they valued his words so much." In fact, since Lawson taught no classes, "the largest part of [personal] instruction" gotten from him occurred at these end-of-the-meal sessions. Thus, their occurrences were highly valued by students; they were prized moments in the life at DMUL.

The Lawsonomists at DMUL necessarily provided all of their own amusements, and as with sports, gardening, and the after-dinner discussions, all the other recreations permitted or encouraged at DMUL were ones having some larger communal or instructional value consistent with Lawsonomic teachings. For instance, dramatic productions at DMUL ran to the hortatory and inspirational, as in *Truth At Last*, a four-act reprise of the Direct Credits doctrine, and in *The Childhood Days of Alfred Lawson*. Because the latter play called for a very large cast of both adults and children, it was a particularly good choice for presentation at DMUL. One former resident recalled more than thirty-five years later how proud he had felt to be chosen to play the boy Lawson in a major DMUL production of *Childhood Days*.

Another field of recreational activity of particular importance was music. The immense repertoire of Direct Credits and Lawsonomy songs got a real workout at DMUL, often informally in the evening around the piano. Also, every Sunday evening a formal program of group singing, instrumental performances, and memorized Lawsonomy recitations attracted all the residents. Residents (both young and old) who took piano lessons from some of the accomplished pianists at DMUL occasionally performed in recital. Finally, in the early days of DMUL, when residents were numerous, DMUL enjoyed band concerts. A photograph published in an issue of *Benefactor* showed the band members resplendent in uniforms and hats.

Following his 1948 inspection tour, the tax assessor reported that there was no chapel at DMUL. In fact, however, Zuver's conclusion was wrong, since from the earliest days space had been set aside and used for church services. Moreover, in 1948, sometime after Zuver's visit, this space was made more recognizable as a chapel when an appropriate entrance was built and a large sign reading "Have Faith in God" was put across the front. The upgrading of the chapel coincided with Lawson's incorporation of Lawsonian Religion in 1948.

A promotional flier from the late 1940s depicted a uniformed band at DMUL.

Lawsonian Religion was the last development in Lawsonomy but not its dénouement. Lawsonian Religion neither perfected, nor added anything to, nor transformed Lawsonomy. Lawsonomy remained a highly rationalistic philosophy, purporting to rest on a scientific base. However, it was permeated by references to God, souls, and the moral law and also by endorsements of traditional Judeo-Christian values (even as its specific articles of faith were quite antithetical to this tradition). While never claiming to be divine, Lawson had also never hesitated to aver in the Lawsonomy treatises that the hand of God could be found in Lawson's discovery of God's scientific and moral laws. Lawsonian Religion simply highlighted these religious and moral elements of Lawsonomy, changing the status of Lawsonomy not at all.

To Lawson's mind, Lawsonian Religion was merely an alternate form of expression of Lawsonomy. But even though Lawsonomy retained its primacy, Lawson doubtless saw Lawsonian Religion as Lawsonomy's useful assistant, and, in fact, he came increasingly to count on it to further the Lawsonomic cause. It provided one more way to

CHAPEL OF GOD
DES MOINES UNIVERSITY OF LAWSONOMY

For several years past, the Students of the Des Moines University of Lawsonomy have been holding their Theological Services in this Chapel every Sunday morning and thereby have been receiving first class training as Sermoneers and Missionaries for the Lawsonian Churches.

"Have Faith in God" graced the front wall of Lawsonian Religion's first church, built at DMUL in 1948. From *Benefactor* 4, no. 20 (1950).

impart the teachings of Lawsonomy. It ensured that the religious yearnings of followers were satisfied with a religious philosophy— faith is not quite the right word—consistent with Lawsonomy. Most immediately, however, it was a response to the urgings of many of Lawson's followers for a doctrine and a ritual which could be embodied in regular, formalized church services.

The chapel at DMUL was the first Lawsonian church built; by the mid-1950s seven others had followed, scattered throughout the United States. Today, perhaps three or four Lawsonian churches survive. In form, their services are similar to the services of other churches—with one main exception: Lawsonian services do not include prayer. The omission of prayer is understandable, since the God of Lawsonomy,

ALMA MATER OF THE NEW SPECIES

not a personal God, does not intervene directly in human affairs, acts only through immutable laws discoverable by reason and science, and leaves it to the operation of the Law of Maneuverability to mete out justice. In most other respects, Lawsonomy services incorporate the elements of other churches' services—sermon, responsive reading, offering, hymns.

Of course, the contents of the forms (except for the offering) are greatly altered. Responsive readings are drawn from the Lawsonomy texts. Sermons feature some writing, statement, or activity of Lawson; in fact, Lawson wrote many sermons (published in 1948 as *Lawson's Mighty Sermons*) which may be memorized and used by Lawsonian ministers. (All of Lawson's sermons conclude with "THUS SAYETH ALFRED LAWSON.") The hymns allow the congregation to sing about the truths of Lawsonomy and their eventual triumph in the world. Lawsonomy churches use a very attractive standard hymnal, *Songs of Lawsonomy*, containing responsive readings and well over a hundred songs, many of them employing familiar melodies but having new lyrics written by various Lawsonomy students. The flavor of the musical ministry of Lawsonian Religion is conveyed in the titles of some sample hymns found in the hymnal—"My Story" (to the music of "Blessed Assurance"), "Be a Knowledgian," "Lawsonomy Will Envelop the Earth," "Mighty Menorgs," and "We Give Thanks for Lawsonomy."

According to one who was there in the earliest days of DMUL, the religious activity arising from Lawsonomy was intended to supply for the students "a part of their education but not a focal part." Students could attend services or not, as they wished. But were students really free to ignore the Lawsonian services? And were they free to omit them in favor, say, of services at the Methodist church? "Yes, they were free, but I'm not so sure that they would be—what do I want to say?—accepted by the other students there because they would feel that if they wanted to go to a Methodist church [for example], that's all well and good, but they had no right to avail themselves at somebody else's expense of the accommodations there [that is, at DMUL]."

This statement suggests that, at the least, a strong expectation of members' participation in Lawsonian religious services operated at

DMUL—an expectation which must have become even stronger once Lawsonian Religion was officially established in the fall of 1948. On the other hand, Lawson had no wish to undermine the advance of Lawsonomy by raising religious squabbles. At the outset of DMUL, at least, his solution was to schedule Sunday *afternoon* services, thus leaving his adherents free to attend the services of other denominations on Sunday morning. According to the witness cited immediately above, Lawson viewed Lawsonian Religion as like a "post-graduate course," appropriate for the highest "grade of consciousness;" as their consciousnesses became steadily upgraded by instruction in Lawsonomy, adherents would eventually find Lawsonian religious services sufficient and cease attending the other services.

As the brief account given here should make apparent, this new way of life was not one likely to appeal to many. In what Lawson sometimes called "the age of extreme falsity," only a tiny fraction of unselfish ones were likely to see the merits of the Lawsonomic life or to accept its demands and rigors. Even at DMUL there were backsliders who soon left, and, in the words of one early DMUL resident, "from time to time Lawson put people out of that organization [i.e., DMUL] because they did foolish things, they didn't follow his direction and so forth. . . . It was a very straitlaced organization. You had to be serious about the thing if you lived there. You couldn't be there to just talk idly and, you know, play and be in the way."

One can easily imagine that the expectations and patterns of daily life at DMUL collided most frequently with the inclinations of minors in late childhood and early adolescence. None, presumably, had chosen to be there, and all might have been content to talk idly, play, and be in the way. In the judgment of one twelve-year-old, Lois Hans, "about all she did while in the university was work in the kitchen." Concluding that "she was just a servant," Lois' mother removed Lois from DMUL. For her part, the twelve-year-old Margaret Baker complained that the children "never [had] any time for play." She described to the *Register* reporter her typical day at DMUL: about two hours of doing dishes and cleaning up after every meal, a morning class in which "we would learn a whole page of a Lawson book by heart, so we could stand up and say it out loud," about two hours of exercise in the gym in the afternoon, and then, "in the evening, we would work in the parlor. We'd dust, and shake rugs, and clean up the rooms and make the beds."

In one of her most vivid statements, Margaret recalled that DMUL was full of "generals" (that is, DCS officers) who were always whispering to one another. Apparently the initiation of the new species required that the children at DMUL be monitored closely by the generals, a conclusion suggested by Margaret's reaction to her first DMUL reading assignment, Lawson's *Manlife*: "I was so sick of it, I didn't go on any more." It is hard to imagine any other child of Margaret's age reacting differently.

However, another former DMUL student, entering DMUL in the fall of 1943 at the age of sixteen, in 1980 recalled happier days at DMUL than the younger Lois and Margaret had ever reported. This student found great satisfaction in participating in baseball and dramatics and acquired valuable skills as manager of the book sales department, a position of seemingly very large responsibility for one so young. Even so, the experience at DMUL had not been totally satisfactory. In fact, eventually unable to cope with the "pressures of responsibilities imposed by adults" and with frustrations arising from "confused lines of authority and command" (Lawson changed presidents frequently in those years), this student left DMUL after nearly two years there. Looking back in 1980, however, the former DMUL student was inclined, on balance, to rate the DMUL experience very positively, citing as especially valuable the lessons learned there in "practical experience, human relations, and moral values."

The adults at DMUL were doubtless the ones most likely to find the way of life there consistently satisfying. All of the adults, at least, had voluntarily accepted Lawsonomy as a total life philosophy and thereby had the strongest motivations to master that philosophy and live their lives in conformity with the regimen imposed at DMUL. To outsiders, the communal life organized totally around Lawsonomy in near-total seclusion from the outer world will doubtless seem constraining and uninviting. To devoted Lawsonomists, however, such a life, based as it was on correct principles and values, was more likely to seem liberating and fulfilling. Moreover, DMUL could be viewed not so much as constricting its members' lives as shielding its members from the slings and arrows of "the age of extreme falsity." This allowed the residents to get on with the exciting business of perfecting Lawsonomic solutions to humanity's age-old problems of social living.

How profound the satisfactions and gratifications of life at DMUL could be, at least for the adults there, was nicely conveyed in testimony given in 1980 by a former student who had been thirty-seven years old upon arrival at DMUL in its earliest days. Until leaving to accept a Lawsonomy assignment elsewhere several years later, this student enjoyed at DMUL a way of life which seemed to be "pursuing the ideals of the book *Born Again* and putting them into action." The result was a "classless society":

> You'd see the president down washing dishes after a meal, you'd see the vice president there, or anybody, no matter what their office or their capacity there. They all participated in the actual work. If the buyer went out and bought a supply of fruits and they wanted to do some canning . . . why, you'd see the vice president helping to prepare them along with everyone else. It was just totally classless. The ideal was that all work is important work, that you're not too good—no, that's the wrong way to say it—but it's just as honorable to be a floor scrubber as it is to be the top man, and although each one took their posts, yet in a situation such as dish washing time or food preparation or food canning . . . why, they'd all turn in and help. That was what I thought was the beautiful part of it.

This former DMUL student also obtained great satisfaction from the time spent studying Lawsonomy ("I went there because I wanted to know more, I wanted to know as much about those teachings as I could absorb because I recognized their greatness") and found great relief in DMUL's isolation from the outer world: "And another thing that I enjoyed about being there: I heard no radio and I saw no newspaper. I could have in the office. I could have gone any time and picked up the morning paper . . . and read it. But I was so happy to be away from that part of life."

Secure behind DMUL's fence, immersed in the study of Lawson-

omy, and participating in the development of a moneyless, classless
society, this student could conclude that "I felt right with myself, and I
was never really happy before." In fact, the experience was a powerful, transforming one: "I became a totally different person"—allegedly, one whose health improved, who gained a new self-confidence,
who overcame snobbish attitudes of class-consciousness, and who
found a permanent, positive, unselfish orientation to life in the moral
teachings of Lawsonomy.

Taken by itself, this testimony of a single person proves nothing,
but at the least, it makes a valuable addition to the other accounts
of DMUL already on record. It presents an insider's view of DMUL
strikingly different from the unfavorable appraisals made at the time
by persons viewing and judging DMUL from the outside. Moreover,
the former student's testimony and the other material presented in
this chapter, when taken together, suggest that much in the outsiders'
appraisals was mistaken.

The city solicitor, for instance, had pegged DMUL as merely a distribution and promotion center for the sale of Lawson's books, but the
evidence shows clearly that DMUL was far more complex than that.
Within that complexity, too, was a shared, purposeful, coordinated
life which made of DMUL not at all the insane asylum which Edwin
Baker had suggested it was.

Only the tax assessor had seen that DMUL was, in fact, a community, but where he fell down was in identifying the community's purpose merely as the eulogizing of Alfred Lawson. Finally, there was the
problem of the image of DMUL conveyed by successive stories in the
Des Moines newspapers. The Lawsonomists were convinced, of course,
that the papers were out to smear Lawson and DMUL; on the side of
the newspapers, however, it must be said that the Lawsonomists were
not very good at making their purposes clear or at supplying information. In the absence of other sources of information, the papers understandably relied heavily on information from renegades or from reporters' quick readings of Lawson's writings, which could readily be
made to sound ridiculous. The almost inevitable results were stories
which must have seemed to confirm for many readers the view that
DMUL's residents were either sinister or loony.

The material presented in this chapter should dispel the view, doubt-less held by many in Des Moines, that DMUL was a center for hatch-ing fiendish misdeeds (for instance, entrapping and brainwashing the children of Des Moines). Far from being sinister, the residents of DMUL were exemplary in conduct; law-abiding, patriotic, intense, se-rious, they were as ready as, even readier than, most to comport with the conventional ethical norms given lip service by many Americans. True enough, the record shows that they held a number of specific beliefs at which most outsiders will scoff and pursued some practices in which outsiders will see no meaning or sense. But did such beliefs and practices necessarily imply that their adherents were loony? If so, then theirs was a familiar kind of looniness found in countless other groups, before and since, who have taken their basic commitments se-riously and withdrawn in order to construct an improved social order consistent with those commitments.

In time, of course, many of those reviled and ridiculed groups gained a widespread acceptance, and what was once thought to be looniness on their part was eventually accounted instead as valuable and admirable elements of American pluralism. Alas, however, this was never to be the case for the earnest folks at the Des Moines Uni-versity of Lawsonomy. The outside world never did come to under-stand, and certainly never warmed up to, their brave effort to plant the seed for the new species.

12

COLLAPSING

EQUAEVER-

POISE

On several occasions in the early 1950s Lawson professed to be pleased with the way things were going at DMUL. He had long since ceased to reside there. Removing his family to Columbus, Ohio, sometime in the mid-1940s, Lawson had returned to the road in his familiar pattern of incessant wandering. However, in testimony before a United States Senate subcommittee in 1952, he disclosed that he still came to the Des Moines campus for short visits every month or so to make sure that "the boys" he had left in charge were doing their jobs properly. "They haven't done anything wrong as far as I can see," he concluded. Evidence of his continuing interest and pride in DMUL was his oft-stated determination to open more universities, including one for women only.

But if all was well, why had Lawson and two DMUL colleagues been subpoenaed to testify in a Senate hearing? Since 1945, the residents at DMUL had been left more or less free from outside interference. What was portended, then, by this resumed interest in DMUL by outsiders—this time, not merely neighbors or city officials, but officials of the federal government?

The circumstances leading up to the investigation of DMUL by the Senate revealed Lawson's continuing knack for finding and exploiting opportunities. Once again, he had shown, in Vincent Burnelli's words, "a positive genius" for "latching onto a new trend"—in this instance, acquiring from the federal government valuable surplus machines at huge discount prices after World War II. But Lawson had then multiplied his good fortune by selling most of the machines at a very substantial markup over the ridiculously low purchase price. To be more specific: the sale had yielded for DMUL close to a 3,000 percent profit. When this astonishing bit of entrepreneurial derring-do became known, DMUL and Lawson were suddenly thrust into the spotlight again.

In the background of Lawson's new difficulties were these facts: in 1946–1947 the War Assets Administration (WAA) had made surplus production machinery available to educational institutions which held a tax-exempt status with the Bureau of Internal Revenue (BIR) and swore that the machines were needed and would be used for educational purposes. The terms offered were extremely generous; when all the calculations were made, the cost ran to 5 percent or less of the current market value. Many institutions fell in line to take advantage of this deal. Among them was DMUL, which bought sixty-two machines, valued at $204,000, at a cost of about $4,400. DMUL's purchase included such items as production milling machines, production automatic lathes, grinders, gear shapers, drilling and tapping machines, turret lathes, precision boring machines, and thread mills.

But then came the Korean War, and suddenly machine tools of the kind sold by WAA a few years earlier were in short supply for use in war industries. What had happened to the government's machines? Why hadn't they been stored? Were they recoverable? These were questions of keen interest to various government agencies. Included among the interested ones was the United States Senate's Committee on Small Business, which empowered Senator Blair Moody (Democrat–Michigan) as a one-man subcommittee to find the answers. To this end, Moody subpoenaed officials from a number of businesses and educational institutions, including DMUL.

There were several things Moody wanted to know about DMUL's involvement with government machine tools. First, how had DMUL ever qualified for them in the first place? That is, was DMUL a legitimate educational institution? True, DMUL had a BIR tax exemption, first granted in 1946. But early in 1952 the *Des Moines Register* published a story revealing that ever since 1948 the Des Moines city

A portion of the production machines which DMUL bought from the federal government, shown in Machine Hall. From a DMUL promotional flier from the late 1940s.

assessor, Bert Zuver, and an Iowa congressman, Paul Cunningham, had been pressuring BIR to withdraw the exemption on the grounds that DMUL was a university in name only. BIR had let the matter drift for over three years but promised a ruling shortly. Lawson's most potent argument in his numerous unsuccessful attempts to get a city tax exemption had been his federal tax exemption; it now looked likely that his failure to get a city exemption might become the basis for a reconsideration and removal of his federal exemption. Moody hoped to determine for himself what kind of an educational institution the Des Moines University of Lawsonomy really was.

Four more major questions which Moody wanted to ask were: What educational uses had DMUL made of the machinery? Why had DMUL sold forty-five of the sixty-two machines purchased from WAA (as had just been revealed in a *Des Moines Register* story)? Was DMUL legally able to sell the machines? What had happened to the profit from the sale? The preliminary evidence, as published in the *Des Moines Register*, indicated a profit in the vicinity of $120,000.

Moody's office prepared a subpoena for Lawson on March 7, 1952, but then faced the problem of finding him (his whereabouts were usually a mystery) in order to serve it. Getting information that Lawson had been in Des Moines earlier in the week but was then in Detroit and scheduled to arrive next in Columbus, Ohio, Moody's staff sought the help of the Columbus police department, which assigned two squad cars and a pair of detectives to the task of tailing Lawson until the subpoena arrived. As the *Des Moines Register* reported, "a 21-hour shadowing operation in the best who-dun-it manner enabled Columbus, Ohio, police [on March 8] to finally serve a congressional subpoena" on Lawson.

This faintly melodramatic operation may have succeeded in getting Lawson to the Senate subcommittee's hearing on March 10, but his presence proved to yield very little information helpful for answering Moody's questions. Lawson was nearly eighty-three years old at the time and professed to have a hard time hearing or understanding the questions. One also finds in the hearing record his claim to another disability of age: "I have written 50 books already in the last 20 years, and that wears on your memory." Who were the members of the board of trustees? "Boy, if you want me to tell you all these things, you will wreck my mind. I can't think of all these little things." What was the first name of DMUL President Hayter? "I have had probably 2 million names float through my brain the last 20 years, and it is getting stagnated with names."

Lawson's main defense in the hearing was that he was only the "donor" of the University and had left its day-to-day care in other hands. His mind remained in the more ethereal regions of Lawsonomy. But didn't he have some idea how much money had been realized on the sale of the machines? "I never go into figures at all. I am thinking of great philosophical thoughts for the benefit of mankind that will come after me. I don't go into these little details of dollars and cents at all." Once, in response to another question involving "these little details," he told Senator Moody he was more "interested in where your soul goes to after you die." The helpless Moody replied, "So am I," but stuck doggedly to his valiant effort to squeeze out of Lawson information pertinent to the investigation.

Although he didn't know the details of the machine deal, Lawson claimed, he was sure "the boys" had done nothing wrong. DMUL had gotten no more favorable terms in the machinery purchase than any other institution, and the machines had been used for educational purposes. Did the University of Lawsonomy teach mechanics? "They teach the biggest and greatest mechanics the world has ever known; they teach Lawsonomy principles." Then, had Lawson actually seen the machines in operation? "I have been there when they have been sawing up one thing or another." But for the most part, Lawson admitted, DMUL instruction was not in the operation of machines but rather in "the reasons and uses to be made out of them" and also in "the different parts of the different machines as they stood there."

Still, there was a war on, the machines were needed elsewhere for production, and DMUL didn't need all its machines for the kind of instruction it was offering. Lawson admitted he had concurred in the decision to sell some of the machines but defended that decision as grounded in patriotism. He vigorously denied that the sale was illegal. DMUL had not sold within the three-year period specified in the original sales contract. As for the amount and uses of the sale profit, Lawson denied there had been any profit. When moving and storage costs and the costs of renovating Machine Hall were taken into account, he claimed, DMUL had lost money on the whole deal!

After questioning Lawson for about an hour, Senator Moody gave up the effort to get any detailed information from him. He asked Lawson to return a week hence with President Cecil Hayter, Secretary George Sorensen, and the University's machine purchase and resale records. As he rose to leave, Lawson sputtered, "The damnedest thing I ever heard of in all my life." This brought a response from Senator Moody: "I do not know whether we are talking about the same thing, but I am inclined to agree with you."

Moody made much more headway in the second hearing, held on March 17, 1952. Obviously fascinated by DMUL and Lawsonomy, Moody often strayed away from his main questions to learn more about the exotic goings-on in Des Moines. However, by the end of the hearing he had established that DMUL had never made genuine educational use of the machines (most had never been taken off their

EDUCATION

Zigzag & Swirl

People in Des Moines have been wondering for years about the mysterious school that took over the old Des Moines University* campus in 1943. A silvery-haired, 82-year-old gentleman named Alfred William Lawson had bought the grounds and announced a new school: the Des Moines University of Lawsonomy. From time to time, a few students of varying ages were seen through the high picket fence, but there seemed to be no faculty. Founder Lawson, a pioneer aviation man who claims that he built the first double-decker airliner and got the U.S. started on its aircraft industry, kept out of sight. As far as Des Moines could tell,

International
LAWSONOMY'S LAWSON
"Damnedest thing I've ever heard . . ."

no one ever graduated with a degree in Lawsonomy.

Des Moines newspapers got interested in the strange school and started asking questions. School officials were reluctant to talk, but Lawson's newspaper described the founder enthusiastically as the kind of teacher who comes along "about every 2,000 years." Reporters found that Lawsonomy was sweepingly billed as "the study of everything," based on 47 principles set forth in the dozens of books of which Lawson is the author. All life, according to Lawsonomy, operates according to the laws of "maneuverability, penetrability, and zigzag-and-swirl."

No Tuition. Lawsonites said it would take a student 30 years to earn the degree of "Knowlegian" in Lawsonomy, but that 20 full-time students are working away at it. The school charges no tuition, they

* A liberal arts college which shut down in 1929 when its owners, the Baptist Bible Union of North America, ran into financial troubles.

said, and it pays no salaries to its teachers. Students (men only) are accepted only on a ten-year basis, and the curriculum consists largely of memorizing Lawson's books. No other reading is permitted; on one occasion, it was even forbidden to refer to a basketball rulebook.

Des Moines's 1950 records show $12,000 paid in taxes on land held by the college. Lawson's books are peddled around town for as much as $5 a copy and contributions seem to pour into the university's coffers. In Detroit a Ford worker said he had donated $8,000 to the school; a postman said he gave close to $5,000. Yet Founder Lawson insists that he is a poor man, frequently turns his pockets inside out at meetings, and lives in seclusion away from the school.

No Figures. Last week Lawsonomy-Founder Lawson was called out of seclusion and summoned to Washington to appear before the Senate Small Business Committee. The Senators wanted to know why his university, claiming to be a tax-exempt institution, had paid $4,480 for 62 war-surplus machine tools "for educational purposes" in 1947, and resold 45 of them for $120,000. The committee also wanted to know if the University of Lawsonomy is a bona fide college. If not, it had no legal right to the machines.

Alfred Lawson fixed the committee with a steady gaze and nimbly dodged a barrage of questions from Michigan's Senator Blair Moody. How much had the machines been sold for? "I don't know, I never go in for figures at all." Had Lawson made any profit on the deal? "Profit? Why no. What profit could I get out of it?" What courses were taught at the school? "Well, they teach Lawsonomy." And that deals with mechanics? "[It teaches] the knowledge of life and everything pertaining thereto, and that takes in mechanics." Finally Lawson got exasperated. "God, boy," he cried at 50-year-old Senator Moody, "if you want me to tell you all these things, you will wreck my mind . . . I'm thinking great philosophical thoughts for the benefit of mankind."

The Senators kept at it for almost two hours but never managed to pin Lawson down. Finally they let him go with an order to come back later with his account books. Educator Lawson hopped out of his chair and headed for the door. "The damnedest thing I've ever heard of in all my life," he snorted. Said Senator Moody: "I don't know whether we're talking about the same thing, but I'm inclined to agree with you."

Goodbye, Shakespeare

The world's No. 1 rare book dealer and one of its most avid collectors is Philadelphia's Dr. Abraham S. W. Rosenbach. Last week Rosenbach announced that he had sold his famous collection of Shakespeares—73 prized folios and quartos of plays and sonnets, many of them first editions in excellent condition. The buyer: Europe's outstanding collector, Dr.

In its issue of March 24, 1952 (the date of Lawson's eighty-third birthday), the news magazine *Time* published a story on DMUL's machine sale problems and Lawson's encounter with Senator Moody. Lawson may not have appreciated this birthday gift, but it did bring him to national attention again.

skids or had their drive shafts connected); although DMUL did not sell within the three-year period, it had not gotten the required agency permission to sell; DMUL grossed a profit of $150,000 on the sale (not $120,000 as originally supposed); DMUL paid most of its operating expenses for 1949, 1950, and 1951 from this profit; and DMUL had never paid federal income taxes on the profit.

At one point in the hearing Lawson interrupted the discussion to say, "I wish you had in the government as honest people as we had at the university." Moody acknowledged that if the government could handle its finances as well as the University did, "we wouldn't have any deficits." At the conclusion of the hearing, Lawson thanked the senator from Michigan for being "real fair to the boys" and then added pointedly, "I've got a million friends in Michigan." Lathering Moody in soft soap got Lawson nowhere, however. One week later, the senator called on BIR to reexamine the tax status and affairs of "that weird institution."

DMUL's problems ballooned within the next several months. The Federal Security Administration (FSA), which in early February, 1952, had released the first report on DMUL's machinery dealings, completed its investigation in April and sent its findings to the Justice Department for possible criminal prosecution. The FSA also recommended civil action to obtain whatever was left of DMUL's machine sale profits and to repossess the seventeen unsold machines. Then, in early May, the BIR announced it was revoking DMUL's tax exemption. Later in May, the Justice Department notified the United States district attorney of the southern district of Iowa to prepare to seize the property of the University in order to recover the remaining machinery and the value of the funds received from the resold machines. By year's end, another federal agency had entered the picture. The Office of Price Stabilization (OPS) filed suit for treble damages to recover profit earned on a machine sold over the legal price ceiling. OPS indicated more treble damage suits were being prepared. Finally, ever sensitive to a good issue, other members of Congress began to exploit DMUL's problems for their own respective political ends.

Formal DMUL resistances to these governmental actions temporarily slowed the federal onslaught. In late March, 1954, however, the

Lawson responded in *Benefactor* to the charges piling up against DMUL. On an inside page he warns all "plotters who try to harm Lawson" that the Law of Maneuverability will protect him. From *Benefactor* 4, no. 25 (1952).

BIR added a devastating blow to the attack by bringing suit for over $80,000 against DMUL for nonpayment of corporation taxes in 1949, 1950, and 1951. (Also, earlier that same month, the University had been "sold" in a local tax sale for failure to pay 1952 and 1953 county property taxes totaling $19,280. DMUL had until the end of December, 1956, to redeem the property by paying the back taxes, penalty, and interest.)

DMUL filed a court petition seeking to resist the BIR suit for back taxes and to regain tax-exempt status as an educational institution. However, doubtless feeling cornered at last, Lawson decided to sell the University. Plans for the sale were announced in early August, 1954, but a contesting claim from other would-be buyers held up the sale. On November 18, the *Des Moines Register* reported that the way had finally been cleared for the purchase of the property for $250,000 by F. A. DePuydt, a Des Moines businessman.

After the transaction was completed, the purchase money was put
in escrow until federal tax liens and county tax claims had been satisfied. From the proceeds nearly $30,000 in back taxes eventually were
paid to Polk County, and in July, 1955, the federal government accepted $89,000 and the return of the remaining machines in settle-
ment of all its claims against DMUL. Because these payments still left
a balance from the sale of about $130,000, the Humanity Benefactor
Foundation apparently emerged rather handsomely from Lawson's
legal problems. The greatly scaled down amount for which the federal government finally settled reflected the conclusion of federal officials that fraud was not involved—or at least that fraud would be
nearly impossible to prove.

A few days before the sale was concluded, Lawson consented to give
an interview in his DMUL office. It was the first time news reporters
and photographers had ever managed to get into the University.
There they found a thin, silver-haired old man—nearly eighty-six
years old—who was still prepared, after all his tribulations in Des
Moines, to say (as reported in a November 16, 1954, *Des Moines Tribune* story) that "most of our neighbors have been real friendly," even
though a few had been troublesome. Also, Lawson explained, there
had not been any deliberate policy of secrecy at the University. The
notorious fence was only a wooden picket fence. "You'd think it was
made of iron the way people talked." It had gone up simply to keep
people from "cutting through our flower beds and leaving debris on
the lawn."

After covering a number of other nostalgic topics and also a few
having to do with his current tax problems, Lawson looked to the future, proclaiming that the "University isn't done." Although he wasn't
yet sure where it would move, he promised that "it'll keep going,
whether we go ten or a thousand miles for a new location."

Anyone familiar with Lawson's lifetime of heroic projects and indefatigable enterprise would probably have been inclined to take his
statements about the future at face value. Even his advanced age, it
seemed, would not necessarily be an obstacle to his pursuit of ambitious new Lawsonian projects. He had always appeared to be in
good health, and possibly some had even come to believe he might

Lawson leaving the DMUL campus in November, 1954. Two weeks later he was dead, and within a year the DMUL buildings were razed. Photo courtesy of the *Des Moines Register.*

live to reach the two hundred–year age which he said was possible if all the prescriptions in *Manlife* were followed. It must have caught most by surprise, then, when just two weeks later—on November 29, 1954—Lawson died in a San Antonio, Texas, hotel room.

The death certificate listed Lawson's occupation as "writer," an identification correct so far as it went but hardly doing full justice to the man who was the First Knowledgian. It also identified "coronary occlusion" as the cause of death. Understood in conventional medical terms, doubtless this was so. However, those more discerning persons schooled in Lawsonomy could recognize the true cause of Lawson's death: his body's equaeverpoise had finally collapsed. As Lawson himself had taught, it was simply a matter of external suction and pressure at last getting the upper hand over internal suction and pressure.

If Lawson's untimely death had not ended all prospects for further Lawsonian enterprises, it is by no means certain what he would have done next. True, there was his assurance to newspaper reporters that DMUL would continue elsewhere. However, two Lawsonomists of very long standing have independently attested that Lawson had pretty well settled on a quite different notion. According to these informants, Lawson's new scheme would have had his followers move en masse to a single neighborhood in California, where all would buy their own homes and provide for their own livelihoods but maintain some facilities—social, religious, educational—in common. A condominium arrangement of this sort would, of course, have marked a radical departure from the ideals of the self-perpetuating social body and life without money once aimed at in Des Moines. If it had gone through, however, the California condo scheme would not really have done as much violence to DMUL's ideals as it may seem, because DMUL had already long since thrown over those ideals.

DMUL had, in fact, been losing equaeverpoise as a community for a number of years before its liquidation in 1954. Whereas in 1945, and perhaps for the following year or so, the number of residents of DMUL hovered around one hundred, in 1952 Lawson acknowledged in his Senate testimony that the number was then at merely twenty. Nothing can be determined precisely today about the pattern of declining enrollments during this time period, but the city assessor's observation of only fifteen persons at DMUL in 1948 suggests that the falloff was early, sudden, and precipitous, leaving DMUL in its final seven years as only a ghost of its former self.

But there were actually many more DMUL students than the twenty currently enrolled ones, the three DMUL officials insisted in the Senate hearings. They were scattered over the United States, said Secretary Sorensen: "Sometimes they are there at the University two weeks, two years. They come for different periods. They come and go continuously." In an interview given in the same month in 1952, Lawson spoke of two thousand part-time students "who come in occasionally for a week's training—some of them four weeks' training." However, by the time of Lawson's last interview, given late in 1954, even the part-timers had apparently fallen substantially in number. A recent survey, Lawson claimed on that occasion, showed "361 students studying at home now." But fundamentally, of course, it hardly mattered what the number of such students was, because, in and of itself, the new emphasis on part-time enrollment, short-term training, and home study of Lawsonomy showed how far DMUL had gotten off its original track.

Why had DMUL come down to this? Lawson suggested in his 1952 Senate testimony that student enrollments at DMUL had been devastated by the students' military service obligations. "So far we have lost about four hundred of our students in war," he claimed. He did not make clear whether he meant that they were killed in action or simply were removed from Lawsonomy ranks by military service. No one asked him why, eight years after the end of the mass conscription of World War II, DMUL's enrollment had not been able to recover from the alleged wartime attrition. Certainly the Korean War could not have had much to do with the enrollment problem, because DMUL enrollments had already fallen drastically before that war began.

Neither the rigorous life Lawson imposed on members nor the intense opposition DMUL faced in Des Moines seems likely to have been a major source of DMUL's decline. Neither of these prevented the community from growing in vitality, morale, commitment, and numbers in the earliest years, and each may, in fact, have contributed to that growth. Nor was there any evidence at DMUL of schism and leadership rivalry, strife among the residents, rising opposition to Lawson's total domination, or any of the other divisive factors which have disrupted many another utopian community.

If internal conflicts or conflicts with neighbors did not sink DMUL, then was it brought down by burdens deriving from its location in a city? Taxes on DMUL were probably higher than they would have been in most rural or small-town jurisdictions. Also, DMUL's location on a relatively small property in the heart of Des Moines, as well as DMUL's refusal to develop commercial relations with the outer world, meant that DMUL could never become self-supporting. In the time period under consideration, however, neither this latter defect nor any shortage of funds for taxes or other expenses caused the decline of the community. Continuing contributions from Lawson's followers, plus the proceeds from the sale of government surplus machines, gave DMUL funds adequate to its needs. Acute money problems arose only in 1954, when it became clear that DMUL would have to pay a large settlement to the federal government. But by then the community had already disintegrated.

Several specific developments and events at DMUL clearly contributing to DMUL's disintegration can be identified, but the most interesting fact about them is that all can be plausibly traced back to a common origin: Lawson's conceptualization of his community as a university. That is, the main problem Lawson's community faced may have been his insistence on imposing on it the organization, the activities, even the name of a university. This peculiarity of his communitarianism appears to have clouded his vision and made it difficult for him to keep steadily in mind that it was primarily a community which he had set out to establish. In the end, his commitment to DMUL as a community very likely was subverted by his commitment to DMUL as a university (so-called).

Lawson's determination to apply in the communal setting terms and practices familiar in American higher education reveals a blurred focus which did not interfere with the building of a genuine community at DMUL during the first several years but which increasingly led Lawson to make decisions detrimental to the community. The first truly harmful blow to the community came in 1945 following the sensational incident in which Edwin Baker went to court to obtain the release of his daughter Margaret from DMUL. Apparently without thinking of the full implications for his community, Lawson announced that henceforth girls would not be admitted to DMUL. They caused too many problems, he said, and distracted boys from an exclusive attention to Lawsonomy. But by the late 1940s, boys and women, too, had apparently been excluded, for an announcement published at that time claimed that DMUL wanted only "men with mature minds who realize that it is the last half of their lives in which they are capable of doing their best work for GOD and humanity." Evidently Lawson had made important decisions about community membership as if he were only making decisions about the composition of a student body. In his quest for the right student body he undermined the very promising start he had made in establishing the "self-perpetuating social body."

Other evidence reveals that Lawson came increasingly to view Lawsonomy as a doctrine more to be learned by students than to be lived by a community. For instance, his creation of the Knowledgian degree—which one former DMUL resident claims was not a feature of DMUL at its inception—worked powerfully to move the emphasis at DMUL away from the life in common toward the formal study and intellectual mastery of Lawsonomy. But a thirty-year degree program requiring memorization of all of Lawson's books was not likely to be nearly as enticing as the prospect of participation in a new communal life. Even if one wished to memorize all of Lawsonomy, a thirty-year residence at DMUL was hardly necessary for the purpose. Possibly in recognition of this fact—or perhaps simply in response to the reality of an ever-diminishing number of residents at DMUL—by the early 1950s Lawson was emphasizing the home study of Lawsonomy.

Because Lawson's capacity to elicit devotion, élan, cooperation, and sacrifices from his followers was profound, the importance of his presence on the campus during DMUL's earlier, palmier days cannot be overestimated. But then, probably not long after 1945, he removed his family to Columbus, Ohio, and took to the road, interrupting his travels by only brief stops at DMUL every month or so. This change to a sharply limited and intermittent personal involvement must have been a serious blow to the life of the community at DMUL. Why had he pulled out? Although the exact purpose of his many trips during these last years of his life is not known, probably they had to do with maintaining contacts with his still-numerous followers. But, as already suggested, his action may have been determined on a more fundamental level by a personality quirk making it difficult for him to stay put for long in any place (even at home with wife and children, whom he also saw on only short visits every month).

(In the first 1952 Senate hearing, insisting that he had no address, Lawson finally gave DMUL as his mailing address but refused to identify his family's address in Columbus. He explained: "I got a couple of children I am sure they have been trying to kidnap." Who "they" were he didn't reveal. Perhaps here was a reason for his removal of family from DMUL, and perhaps, too, Lawson's own removal and constant wandering were efforts to thwart imagined kidnappers of Lawson himself.)

If Lawson had left matters as they were in 1944 and 1945, he might have been able to keep the DMUL community in relatively good shape, at least until the time of DMUL's closing and his death in 1954. However, when he changed his "admission policy," placed a new emphasis on the Knowledgian degree and the formal study of Lawsonomy, and concluded that his books could fill his place, Lawson made decisions which mortally wounded the community—a result he almost certainly had not intended. Soon DMUL had meaning mainly as a center for brief retreats and training sessions, as the distant institutional expression of the thirty-year study program which most Lawsonomists pursued at home, and as a formal organization which someday would bestow Knowledgian degrees. Possibly Lawson convinced himself that the far-flung Lawsonomy students were the "self-perpetuating social body." If so, this conception was certainly a comedown from the social body in the literal sense.

It is impossible to escape the conclusion that Lawson himself had undone his last great project. But of course, this was not the first time this had happened; the pattern was by now a thoroughly familiar one. The same striking knack for faltering when success hove into view, for burdening his efforts disastrously with unwise decisions, or for losing focus and making quirky changes of direction in mid-course was seen in his endeavors in big-league baseball, in air passenger service, and, to some extent, in depression-era agitation. Now community building could be added to the list of fields in which Lawson had undermined his own aspirations.

At the same time that Lawson drifted into the habit of thinking of DMUL exclusively as an educational institution rather than as a community, he began to speak grandly of new educational roles for DMUL and of the good works which could be expected someday from DMUL's alumni. Ignoring the fact that the enrollment at DMUL was now negligible, he spoke of these alumni as future "missionaries" of Lawsonomy and contemplated the need for more Lawsonomy universities in order to expand the missionary force. But in order to have more students qualified for study at Lawsonomy universities, more teachers of Lawsonomy were needed at the pre-college levels, Lawson concluded. Here, then, was a principal missionary task for future Knowledgians, and here also was revealed a new purpose for DMUL and additional Lawsonomy universities. Lawson "must first teach the teachers [in order] to teach the people at large," he explained in a full-page advertisement published in a 1948 issue of *Benefactor* (vol. 4, no. 15).

Addressing his advertisement to "teachers of all grade schools, including principals and superintendents," Lawson went at them in a manner smacking of the come-ons for career upgrading in locksmithing and taxidermy found in the back pages of pulp magazines: "Are you satisfied to remain on the lowest rung of the educational ladder? Or would you prefer to rise to the top rung within the next few years of your lives by obtaining the necessary knowledge now?" "Great opportunities for progressive educators" were at hand, he claimed, because it was "necessary to establish preparatory schools in all parts of America and the world as soon as possible to prepare capable students for entry to Lawsonomy universities." Teachers not wishing to spend their lives "studying and teaching ancient gossip" would be well advised to enroll at DMUL now, inasmuch as "preparatory schools will be opened all over the world as soon as capable operating forces and instructors can qualify to operate them."

A similar diffusion of the attention originally given to establishing the unique community in Des Moines was found in Lawson's effort, beginning in 1949, to promote Lawsonian Religion out in the hinterland. A story in a 1950 issue of *Benefactor* (vol. 4, no. 20) proclaimed: "Thousand Churches to Be Built by Alfred Lawson." It was only hype, of course; the churches of Lawsonian Religion have never numbered more than eight. Nonetheless, the ballyhoo reflected accurately a shift of Lawson's focus from community building to proselytizing on a grand scale.

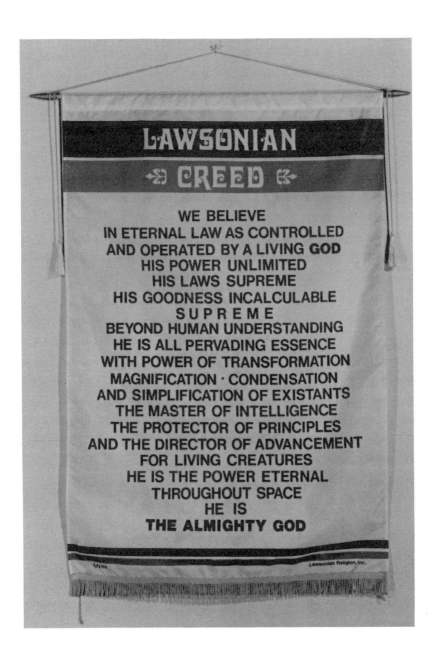

A banner used in Lawsonian Religion churches, which have never numbered more than eight. Photo by the author.

The shift had another implication for DMUL, too. Now Lawson referred to DMUL as an "ecclesiastical college" and looked to it for the
production of Knowledgians to carry the banner of Lawsonian Religion. "Therefore Professors of Lawsonomy for Lawsonian ecclesiastical colleges and teachers for Lawsonian Parochial Schools,
Church Managers, Secretarial Forces, Pulpit Sermonizers, Foreign
Missionaries and various higher dignitaries will all have to be educated at the University of Lawsonomy in large numbers as quickly as
possible."

"As quickly as possible" would not be very quickly, however, thanks
to the thirty-year study requirement for the Knowledgian degree.
The same impediment awaited those teachers whom he challenged
"to rise to the top rung within the next few years" of their lives. In his
enthusiasm for expanded activities in the educational and religious
fields, Lawson had overlooked this stumbling block to his plans, just as
he had ignored the alarming anemic condition into which DMUL had
slumped in the late 1940s. Although the anemia could be traced in
largest part to Lawson's shift away from DMUL's original communitarian mission, Lawson now proposed to go even further in that direction. In a new expansionary phase of Lawsonomy, DMUL was to
play a critical role, yet the very lines of policy which had sapped
DMUL's vitality were now expected to give DMUL increased vigor
and even lead to the creation of offshoot universities.

A major factor in Lawson's muddled thinking and increasing loss of
touch with reality in his final years was doubtless his advanced age.
When DMUL began to fall apart in the late 1940s, Lawson was, after
all, nearing the age of eighty years. He wrote frequently in *Benefactor*
about his achievement in reaching this august age while at the same
time retaining a remarkable vitality. Moreover, he promised, greater
Lawsonian prodigies than he had so far achieved lay ahead. He offered his life as Exhibit A for his conviction that it was possible to re-
tard aging and even to improve one's powers with age, so that one's
best work would come in the latter half of a very long life. All the
brave talk could not cover over the reality, however: while he may
have been in better shape, physically and mentally, than most octo-
genarians, his powers were failing.

Near the end of his life, Lawson counted on the advance of Lawsonian Religion to bring the final triumph of Lawsonomy by the end of this century. From Lawson, *Lawsonian Religion*.

His performance in the Senate hearings gave clear evidence of the fact of his physical and mental decline, and even Lawson acknowledged there that he was beset by loss of memory and other infirmities of old age. Claiming that he had been working too hard, he got Senator Moody to defer the second DMUL hearing for a week. Although both he and DMUL were in serious legal trouble, Lawson then took time off for rest and recuperation in southern Florida before returning for the second round with the Senator.

The books Lawson published in the last dozen years of his life also generally showed a falling off of his creative powers. An obvious exception, however, was the next book to appear after the Lawsonomy trilogy. This curious book—*Gardening* (1943)—was subtitled "Text Book for Des Moines University," and slightly over half of its pages consisted of short articles by other Lawsonomists giving practical gardening advice. Filling the remaining half was a treatise by Lawson on the application of Lawsonomic science to agriculture. Although Lawson's contribution relied heavily on excerpts from previous writings, it contained some fascinating new material, too—for instance, his proof that plant and animal life first appeared at the earth's poles, and his observation that "animals that subsist entirely upon the flesh of other animals are squatty by nature and grow upon the horizontal plan, while animals that subsist exclusively upon the substances emanating from plants are more upright and intelligent by nature and are built upon the perpendicular plan."

A major burden of Lawson's essay in *Gardening* was to denounce the fertilizing of crops with manure: "Some old time gardeners say that animal manure is necessary for good gardening as the Earth must have it to raise plants. That is pure nonsense not borne out by the facts. For, if that was so, then how did nature produce plants before there were any animals to make manure?" So strong was Lawson's antipathy to manure that he called on humanity to stop breeding the "lower animals," which are not needed in "the machine age" and which "spread their filthy waste matter over the soil of the Earth." He looked forward to the day "when man becomes economic enough to utilize everything without the loss of anything" and thereby can assume complete control of nature, because on that happy day "nature will then have no further use for the millions of other species of animals who partake of the food produced by nature and . . . cultivated by man."

In the history of ideas, a very infrequent thing is the totally new idea—that is, an idea having no precedent whatsoever or at least a hint of a connection to something said or written before. Among the rare exceptions, however, must be Lawson's enthusiastic call for the abolition of all the animals; had any thinker ever come close to that one before? Be it noted, too, that this was Lawson's second go-round with the fantastic idea. In *Born Again* he had projected the disappearance of animals as humans improved morally, because increasingly fewer animal bodies and more human bodies would be needed to house the finite number of souls in the world. Now, in *Gardening*, humans are authorized to take a hand in the eradication of the animals, a project legitimized by the fact that animals (but apparently not humans!) befoul the earth. Moreover, animals are no longer needed for work, they are an undesirable source of food, and they eat the vegetable food which humans cultivate for their own use. Humans in the future will recognize that the presence of animals violates the fundamental axiom of natural economics: "the utilization of everything without the loss of anything."

Although *Gardening* thus offered some fresh and arresting material, this was not so for Lawson's subsequent books. Failing even to mention the idea of the self-perpetuating social body, *A New Species*, appearing in 1944, was not the full-scale discussion of the concept of the new species which it should have been. Aside from a few comments on marriage, parenthood, and pedigrees, the book offered little not already covered in the Lawsonomy trilogy. The same charge can be levied against *Lawsonian Religion* (1949), a book which did little more than restate the major tenets of Lawsonomy, encrusting them, perhaps, with a few more references to God than were found in the earlier books.

Also marring these books was Lawson's frequent verbatim excerpting of whole chapters from previous books. He had done quite a bit of this in those earlier books, too, but indulged the habit so far in *A New Species* and *Lawsonian Religion* as to make the reality starkly clear: in his old age, he had nothing new to say. *Lawson's Proverbs*, published in 1945, did not even purport to be other than a compilation of witticisms, humorous definitions, and pithy profundities, most culled from earlier writings. As for *Aircraft History* (1952), a book which Lawson had proposed to write ever since his days as an aviation journalist, it turned out to be yet another vehicle for the celebration of Lawson's aircraft work. Its publication coincided with the formation at DMUL of an Aircraft History Museum, which had much the same purpose.

Inasmuch as *A New Species* appeared in the same year (1944) in which Lawson claimed to be founding the self-perpetuating social body at DMUL, his failure to discuss either the concept or the project in this book is truly perplexing. But perhaps it was an indication that he had already started to lose his focus at DMUL. In place of discussion of any plan for "planting the seed" for the new species, Lawson merely expressed a hope that "from the thousands of splendid Lawsonomy Scholars now on Earth, and from the millions of newcomers that are on their way, there will arise a sufficient number of intelligent human beings with unselfish traits of character and extreme stability of purpose to stand solidly together . . . to carry forward the advanced superlative lessons" of Lawsonomy.

Lawson's hope for—and expectation of—the continued spread of Lawsonomy was only one of "three future hopes" or "three paramount desires" which he specified in *A New Species*. His second hope was that before his mind and body "weaken from age . . . GOD ALMIGHTY will recall his soul from this human formation while it is still at its strongest point of physical, mental, and moral development." Then there was his third hope: "During this coming transformation from one physical body to another he reverently hopes that GOD ALMIGHTY will grant him a special audience in which HE will say—ALFRED LAWSON, YOUR WORK HAS BEEN WELL DONE." If Lawson's first hope reflected an addling of mental capacity in old age, his final two hopes made plain that he nonetheless recognized that his work was essentially completed and that the end of his life was imminent.

By the time (1949) *Lawsonian Religion* was published, the world had become acutely aware of the awful destructiveness of nuclear weapons. Lawson modified his indictment of contemporary civilization accordingly; now he opined that the Law of Maneuverability might "permit the whole people of Earth to commit suicide by stabbing and shooting each other to death, as they have been doing, and then blowing the earth to bits as they are now in danger of doing themselves." Even if humans did not engineer their own demise, a "disappointed" God might choose to, letting the Law of Maneuverability run full blast in order "to obliterate the entire human Species and start all over again with an entire new breed."

The rapid spread of Lawsonomy could counteract the forces leading to human extinction, of course, but Lawson here revealed a very grave problem: "Scientists have claimed it would require a million years for people of earth to attain the high grade of consciousness that Alfred Lawson demonstrated within the pages of his fifty educational books." Here was discouraging news; for sure, humanity would face much danger, probably even extinction, while waiting out a process of transformation taking this long. "But, in this case, that is unnecessary," Lawson now trumpeted joyfully in *Lawsonian Religion*, "because GOD sent to earth a Soul that governed the physical mind of Alfred Lawson with knowledge, truth and power, to ward off a greater danger [that is, nuclear annihilation or God's wrath] than waiting a million years for such development in man's progress." A few pages later Lawson confirmed the significance of his presence during humanity's hour of critical need: "Now, people of Earth, you have been stampeding to nowhere, and it is the life work of Alfred Lawson to head you off and get you upon the right track of improvement . . . so that you will arrive somewhere within GOD's domain eventually."

Lawson's message only seemed to add another loose end to the others already characterizing his thinking in his declining years, however. How could his presence on earth provide the means to "ward off" the danger of nuclear annihilation—that is, to short-circuit the slow-moving process otherwise required for humanity to absorb the Lawsonomic wisdom needed to avert disaster? And how could he expect to get a world which was ready to blow itself up to accept his leadership?

Very likely Lawson was counting on Lawsonian Religion to make the rapid headway which Lawsonomy as a philosophical and scientific system could not. As a religious prophet, he probably believed, he would be more readily accepted as humanity's leader than he would be as a moral and natural philosopher. This would explain why he shifted so much emphasis at the time to church building and the promulgation of Lawsonian Religion. It also helps explain why the concept of DMUL as a community continued to recede from Lawson's mind; now DMUL was needed urgently as a seminary for the preparation of toilers in the vineyards of Lawsonian Religion.

In principle, Lawson's decision to try to hasten the spread of Lawsonomy by making a religion of it was probably sound enough, but grave problems still lay in the way of the rapid advance of the new religion. For one thing, as already noted, Lawson had no fully certified Knowledgians to help him promote the cause and would not have for quite a while longer, thanks to the thirty-year degree requirement which he continued to impose. But even more important, Lawsonian Religion was still Lawsonomy, an austere and highly intellectualized creed. Not only were its sacred texts the full shelf of Lawson's numerous challenging treatises, but adherents to Lawsonian Religion were expected to keep grinding away at the thirty-year program of mastery. Moreover, at the same time that it made tough mental demands on the adherent, it offered none of the usual solaces of religion. Would-be converts seeking a warm personal relationship with God would certainly not find it in Lawsonian Religion.

Initiating the new species at DMUL and launching the New Dispensation of Lawsonian Religion—here were two projects of such enormous difficulty, one would think, as to demand Lawson's exclusive attention for his remaining dozen years. Lawson said as much in *A New Species*:

> Alfred Lawson realized, early in life, that he was born to improve the mental machinery of mankind, as well as to show how man could construct great physical machines. . . .
>
> From man-made machines to GOD-made machines, is what Alfred Lawson finally decided to give all of his time to accomplish during the remainder of his natural life. His program now is to

show everybody how a [human] machine can be made to think, strictly according to provable Eternal Laws.

Lawson's pronouncement was amusingly worded but not accurate, however. Even as he bent his efforts to the intellectual and moral reform of "GOD-made machines," his interest in "man-made machines" remained as avid as it had been in his younger years; the pages of *Benefactor* in the 1940s and 1950s bear witness to that. His continuing dalliance with technological marvels was another evidence of Lawson's inability during this critical period to maintain a sustained and clear focus in his activities.

In this instance, however, Lawson's shortcoming can be excused: he probably couldn't help it. Ever since writing *Born Again* and his aviation editorials, he had taken great pride in his standing as a dreamer, and probably no one had ever dreamed more imaginatively of technological innovations. In *A New Species* he recalled some of his drum beatings in the past for improvements and "a better way to do things"— for instance, a plan he had offered in 1900 for cooling all houses in Philadelphia by use of a "central cooling plant," his promotion at about the same time of the ideas of "coagulating Sunlight, controlling the weather, building cities under one roof, transporting sound without the use of wires, the introduction of man-made cosmic animals [this idea actually came much later]," and, of course, his later demonstration of the practicality of air transportation. He still had more to say about some of these marvels, too, and also had new marvels to disclose, yet he was aware that his time was running out. Hence, his continuing attention to thinking about "man-made machines" was perfectly understandable.

Because Lawson had been obsessed all of his life with the movement or transporting of things and people, it was not surprising that one of the innovations he wrote about most frequently in *Benefactor* was the greatest transportation project of all time—interplanetary travel. This was a prospect he had enthusiastically foretold in *Born Again* and his aviation editorials. Now the time was at hand to undertake to do it; Lawson especially recommended learning about "our neighbors . . . who live upon the different planets of our own Solar Sphere" as a constructive alternative to "the destructive study of blowing ourselves to bits by the utilization of the microscopic explosives obtainable through the pop-gun Lucifers of the Atomic Sphere."

Of course, there was still the question of how (but not whether) interplanetary travel could be done. Here Lawson was a bit vague, only asserting that he had a plan for doing it:

> Another great project Alfred Lawson would like to put into operation, that will also require the backing of the entire nation, is his plan of SOLAR TRANSPORTATION which will lead to regular PLANETARY TRAVEL for human beings of the future.
>
> "It will be no harder to get this plan into practical operation," says Lawson, "than it was for me to introduce during the year of 1908, the plan of AIRCRAFT INDUSTRY and PASSENGER AIRLINERS flying everywhere throughout Earth's atmosphere."

But it would be as difficult for Lawson to describe his plan as it would be for Ordinary Mortals to grasp it: "To be able to understand the Lawson Plan for Solar Transportation one would require such advanced knowledge as can only be found with LAWSONOMY literature and more particularly within the movable methods of PENE-TRABILITY." The closest he ever came to specifying the space ship he envisioned were his observations that it "would have to be of such size that it could withstand the bombardment of floating debris that it would encounter out in the Cosmic regions" and must be "able to hitch up with, or disentangle itself from, the various solar currents that it will utilize to some extent for power purposes."

During this period Lawson also became interested in applications of atomic energy; in 1952 the *Des Moines Register* uncovered a letter which the assistant secretary of DMUL had written in 1948 to the War Assets Administration asking for "atomic machinery" as well as "radar-sending equipment." Of course, DMUL never got the highly restricted equipment requested, but what Lawson would have done with it if it had been obtained is a mystery. The letter, as excerpted in the March 6, 1952, *Register* story, only hinted that something impressive could be expected: "This university hopes to lead the world in future development of machinery, at present unknown to man. . . . It is our main purpose to do our best to furnish America with the latest and greatest of all inventions."

There is much irony in the letter's assertion that DMUL was "making good use" of the equipment already obtained from the War Assets Administration. But DMUL's request for atomic equipment was itself ironical, inasmuch as Lawson had long held that there was not enough "force" (he couldn't use the word "energy"!) within an atom "to move a hair on a flea's back." The explosion of atomic bombs seemed to suggest otherwise, however. Quickly regaining his balance, Lawson ably explained away the apparent discrepancy. The atomic explosions had, in fact, been caused "by the squeezing together [of] untold numbers of atoms." The consequent friction produced a "microscopic spark" which set off a particularly far-reaching explosive process in which "the substance HEAT, acting by Pressure as the male gender, is forced and drawn toward the substance COLD, acting by Suction, as the female gender." The Law of Penetrability, he calmly asserted, could still provide a better explanation of what happened at Hiroshima and Nagasaki than could the physicists' wild theories of a supposed vast energy residing in the atom.

The presence in the world of atomic bombs figured in Lawson's quest in his final years for two other remarkable inventions often discussed in *Benefactor*—the "solar coagulator" and the "solar engulferator." The first of these was an objective of very long standing, first discussed by him in *Born Again*. The basic idea was this: because light is a substance, it should be possible to collect and "coagulate" the "particles" of which sunlight is composed. Then, as in Sageland, the concentrated substance could be mixed with a medium and, like paint, applied to the interior walls of buildings, thus producing interior lighting. Lawson stressed the special merit of this in the atomic age: "The atomic bomb could not harm people living in cities built under the crust of the earth and furnished with artificial oxygen and coagulated sunlight."

Although Lawson came up with the idea of the solar engulferator in 1940, he saw that it had even more urgent purpose in the atomic age. According to Lawson, it was a defensive weapon that "would be able to swallow up all offensive instruments of warfare, such as ATOMIC BOMB carriers and other murderous devices and make them turn upon and annihilate those who were sent to operate them." In Lawsonomic terms, its operating principle was "the penetration of lower

spherical particles of combustible ingredients, broadcasted from a
central pressure station to an Enemy's receptive suction position, that
would have set fire to and exploded any number of airplanes, rockets,
etc., at such distances as the mechanism of the broadcasters were arranged for." Lawson believed that a defensive system of engulferators
for the United States "will take considerable time to make ready and
will require a large number of our most progressive thinkers to do the
detail designing and engineering and supervising under the direction
of the natural mechanic who understands the plans." However, the
payoff would be enormous: the solar engulferator will "be the means
that will eventually abolish war entirely."

In his final interview in Des Moines as reported in the November 18, 1954, *Des Moines Tribune*, Lawson confided that he was "working on an invention that will do away with all wheels, all autos." Someday "we'll travel a new way," thanks to this invention, he proclaimed;
he also opined that the automobile companies would not be pleased.
Two weeks later, however, Lawson's death ended the chance for the
world ever to learn more about his revolutionary thinking about
wheeless transportation. In this last interview, the reporter instead
pressed Lawson for more information about another of his inventions—the celebrated "smoke evaporator." Unlike Lawson's other
inventions, the smoke evaporator appeared to have been reduced to
practice at DMUL, and tantalized Des Moines residents were eager to
learn how or whether the device worked as Lawson claimed.

Apparently it was Lawson's original scuffle with city smoke inspectors which got him thinking about the smoke evaporator. A new
method for handling smoke was needed which would eliminate smoke,
and therefore neighbors' complaints about smoke, and therefore city
inspections of DMUL's central heating plant and smoke stack. Lawson
applied Lawsonomy principles to the problem and soon had a solution. The essence of the solution was to put the smoke in the ground.

In 1946 DMUL residents began to build a three hundred–foot–
long, seven-foot-square, cement-lined tunnel leading from the furnace. The next step came in the summer of 1953, when the fifty-foot
steel smoke stack came down and the concrete chimney base was
capped. Finally, a new stoker was installed beneath the heating plant

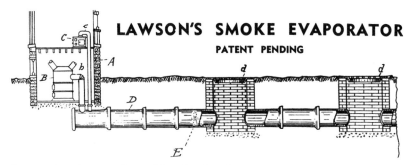

LAWSON'S SMOKE EVAPORATOR
PATENT PENDING

Depiction in Lawson's patent application of the celebrated "smoke evaporator." From Lawson, *100 Great Speeches.*

boiler. The smoke evaporator was ready to go. DMUL continued to order and burn coal at the usual rate—about one hundred and fifty tons during the winter, 1953–1954, and fall, 1954, heating seasons— but there was never again a trace of smoke.

Understandably, the smoke evaporator stirred up great interest in Des Moines. Shortly after the removal of the smokestack, the *Des Moines Register* published a story headlined "Hint Lawson Really Does Bury Smoke." Reporting that DMUL was apparently continuing to burn coal, the story noted that "there were a lot of laughs at his expense when [Lawson] said he was going to put smoke into the ground. Among the gigglers were city smoke inspectors." But now, the *Register* reporter claimed, it may be Lawson who "has the last laugh."

Continuing to insist that it was impossible to "bury" smoke, the city smoke inspector speculated that Lawson's method must have employed a suction fan and filters. In a 1953 issue of *Benefactor* (vol. 4, no. 19), Lawson published a drawing showing several brick-lined pits intersecting the tunnel but, other than in the most general of Lawsonomic terms, provided no explanation of how the evaporator system worked. When the reporter conducting Lawson's final interview asked for an explanation, a chuckling Lawson declined to say more. "Everyone wants to know about it," he acknowledged. But "I'm not letting go of it now until I get it patented." Also, he noted, his contract with the purchaser of DMUL specified that he could take the smoke evaporator with him (the tunnel, of course, remained).

Although Lawson did, in fact, apply for a patent on the smoke evaporator, a patent never was issued. Possibly Lawson's death caused the abandonment of the application. Or perhaps the patent examiner found it was impossible to allow claims expressed in Lawsonomic terms. Or just possibly the examiner discovered a flaw in the claims. Many years later a story in the *Des Moines Register* (January 22, 1984) described what the purchaser of DMUL subsequently discovered about the smoke evaporator: "But when the school was razed, construction workers found 300-foot tunnels leading from the underground boiler room to eight-foot-tall risers. The risers led to vents, which were covered by shrubbery. A fan in the boiler room blew the smoke into the tunnels, through the risers and out the vents." Apparently the city smoke inspector had been right: Lawson did not "evaporate" or bury smoke.

From one point of view, Lawson's singular lack of success with his inventions in these last years of his life does suggest that he might better have concentrated his attention exclusively on fostering the growth of either Lawsonian Religion or the community at DMUL. On the other hand, who can say for certain that Lawson's final foray into the field of invention was in vain? Anticipating some of the urgent needs and dreams of our time, he may someday be seen as a pathbreaker, just as he clearly was with his airliner.

If, after a lifetime of thinking about it, Lawson was unable to achieve interior lighting by coagulated particles of sunlight, it seems unlikely anyone else ever will do so, at least in the manner proposed by Lawson. Nonetheless, he clearly was on the path to the solar energy collectors which are likely to be of increasing importance in the future. Solar vehicles, of course, are already a reality, and perhaps someday Lawson's dream of scheduled, frequent flights among some of the planets of the solar system will be, too. And who knows? A world now having passed the acceptable limits of atmospheric pollution and beset by the "greenhouse effect" may be driven in desperation to find some way to bury smoke. Finally, Lawson's idea of the solar engulferator is already very much alive in Ronald Reagan's beloved Strategic Defense Initiative. Although this is the name the former president insisted upon, one can readily believe that Lawson would have preferred the more colorful and dramatic term "Star Wars." However, their minds are as one in believing that this colossal technology is the key to perpetual peace. Perhaps someday, when the definitive history of these times is written, those who have wondered where President Reagan got the far-out idea may even find that he got it from the First Knowledgian!

Part
Five

LAWSONIAN

LEGACIES

"New-as-tomorrow" was how the advertisements whooped up the Park Fair Shopping
Center at its gala opening in Des Moines in
November, 1957. As it happened, the ballyhoo was right on the mark. The Park
Fair, the first enclosed shopping mall to go
up in Iowa, really did give a clear foretaste
of a coming transformation of the face of
America. Air-conditioned and fluorescent-
lit throughout, the prototypal shopping
center brought together under one canopy
"the world's largest drug store" and twenty-
five other businesses. It really was a shame
that Lawson wasn't still around to see this
forward-looking development. An early
prophet of roofed cities and central cooling stations and ever a fan of new ways to
organize people "as a unit," the First Knowledgian might have thought the Park Fair
almost smacked of the Lawsonesque.

Progress always exacts its price, however. To make way for the "most glam-
ourous" and modern shopping center in
Iowa, six large buildings, some stately and
handsome, had been pulled down. Ancient, overarching trees, broad lawns, and
flower beds had once surrounded the de-
molished buildings, but these, too, had had
to yield—to an asphalt lot offering "acres
of free parking." Sun glare, noisy getting
and spending, and auto traffic now filled
the space of the serene and shade-cooled
urban oasis which had had the misfortune
to stand athwart the path of Progress. If
the price of progress seemed high in this
instance, most residents of Des Moines—

especially of the Highland Park district—probably were still eager to pay it. The Park Fair's displacement of the Des Moines University of Lawsonomy was, in a sense, the definitive final act in the long-sought exorcism of Lawsonomy from Des Moines.

Of course, vivid recollections of Lawson and his community must have remained for quite a few years after Des Moines was finally shut of both; the tornado of fustian and rant stirred up while Lawson and DMUL were still on the scene would have assured that. But during the more than three decades which have passed since Lawson's death and the subsequent razing of DMUL, tempers have cooled and memories have dimmed. Probably most of today's residents of Des Moines are not even aware that the First Knowledgian once was there, convulsing the city with unbridled claims for the greatness of both his mysterious university and himself. Thus Lawsonomy's sojourn in Des Moines is by way of fast becoming a forgotten episode in the history of Des Moines, memorialized only in musty newspaper files.

But, alas, this is the fate of Lawsonomy elsewhere, too. The flattening of Lawson's university in Des Moines and the crumbling there of all memories of the man are merely tokens of the larger and sadder truth: both the First Knowledgian and his crusade to upgrade humanity have faded everywhere from the world's ken. So soon after his death, Lawson is already a prophet dishonored not only by the world's outright rejection but also by the cruelest form of dismissal imaginable—that is, by being completely forgotten.

Well, not *completely* forgotten. If taken literally, the conclusion goes too far. More than thirty-five years after Lawson's death, a remnant of his once-large following lingers on. This still-loyal band—Lawson's most obvious and definite legacy—comprises one small sector, at least, in which he has not been forgotten.

More than simply remembered, of course, Lawson continues to be venerated by his remaining followers in the exact terms he had commanded—as "God's great eternal gift to man." However, the chance of this official line ever catching on outside the ranks of Lawsonomy has long since fallen to zero. If, after the last foot soldier of Lawsonomy is gone, the keeping alive of Lawson's memory depends on others coming forth to champion Lawson on his own stipulated terms, then he is doomed to fade even farther into the unlighted recesses of the past.

But to reject the claims to greatness of the First Knowledgian is one thing, and to fail to find Alfred Lawson worthy of note and remembrance is another thing altogether. The former action does not necessitate or justify the latter. Indeed, so remarkable was Lawson's life that it cries out for attention and an effort at understanding and assessment. How can his astounding life be accounted for? What was its relation to his time and place? Did it make any lasting difference to the world? These are the intriguing questions to which the mere recounting of Lawson's zig-zag-and-swirl necessarily gives rise.

13

THE

LAST

KNOWLEDGIANS

Every day thousands of travelers on U.S. Highway 94, passing just outside of Sturtevant, Wisconsin (near Racine), notice a large, long billboard proclaiming "The University of Lawsonomy." An occasional traveler, finding curiosity piqued, leaves the highway at the next exit and drives back a short distance on a frontage road in order to take a closer look. He or she reaches what appears to be a farmyard; however, the label on the mailbox reads "Wisconsin University of Lawsonomy."

Pressing the inquiry further, the traveler will discover that three of the four buildings in this scene are not the farm buildings they appear to be; they contain dormitories, a chapel, a kitchen, and a large dining hall. Upon entering the dining hall, the visitor will find its walls covered with framed photographs of groups of men and women wearing unusual white uniforms; telltale details indicate that the photographs are many decades old. At the far end of the room are a fireplace, a couch and some easy chairs (but also a barber's chair!), and a bookcase containing only books by a single author—Alfred W. Lawson. Above the fireplace hangs a framed large color photograph of an old man, whose suit and bow tie look slightly outsized on the sitter's thin, frail-looking body. On the mantel, next to the portrait, stands a metal urn inscribed "Alfred William Lawson / 1869–1954 / The First Knowledgian." Therein reside the ashes of the man depicted in the painting, the visitor will learn.

Many other things seen at this site will also intrigue the inquirer. For instance, in the anteroom of the chapel he or she will find displayed in glass cases more urns containing the remains of former students of this mysterious university. Suspended over the tables in the dining hall are models of five different airplanes of early vintage, all of which bear the name Lawson. Beyond the university's buildings is a 1,600-foot dirt airplane runway. The huge whirling contraption in the front yard, the visitor will learn, is a wind generator, still under construction but expected someday to supply most of the university's power needs.

But few persons are about; where are the professors and the students? The inquirer will be told that this is not a university designed on the standard model. All instruction is obtained from the study of the books of Alfred Lawson. No one is a professor, all are students of a doctrine called Lawsonomy. For many years, however, only three or four students have lived on campus. They are also the university's officers and caretakers. None receives a salary. Their simple, frugal life is supported by the food which they grow in the garden and by money contributed by other students who live off campus. These other students (number not specified) study Lawsonomy by correspondence, although those living close by are able to attend classes held on campus on the last Wednesday of every month. Also, at least once a year, usually on the long weekend of Independence Day or Labor Day, as many as one hundred of those off-campus students get together on the campus. On these occasions, students come from as far away as California and Florida.

All of this will doubtless be perplexing to the unprepared traveler, but anyone knowing the history of the Lawsonomy movement will certainly find no mysteries or surprises here. For most of the more than thirty-five years which have elapsed since the closing of DMUL, the Wisconsin University of Lawsonomy (WUL) has rigidly stuck to all the routines of DMUL in the last years of DMUL's existence.

As noted earlier, after the collapse of DMUL, Lawson's mind may actually have been tending away from the university concept and toward a condo arrangement in California. However, the Humanity Benefactor Foundation already owned the Wisconsin farm, and re-

The chapel and dormitory of the University of Lawsonomy, which lives on in a new incarnation on a farm along U.S. Highway 94 near Sturtevant, Wisconsin. Photo courtesy of George A. Hardie, Jr.

locating DMUL there was indeed a possibility which had been mentioned by Lawson. In any case, reestablishing the University of Lawsonomy at the farm in 1956 was the easiest path for Lawson's survivors in the Lawsonomy movement to follow. Keeping all existing Lawsonomic activities on course and as close as possible to the forms they had taken in Lawson's final years probably was also nearly a necessity for persons who were well trained to follow but had suddenly lost their leader. Lawson's other organizations—the Direct Credits Society, the Humanity Benefactor Foundation, and Lawsonian Religion—also continue, unchanged in any essential respect.

Of course, not everything has remained unchanged. Gone are Lawsonomy's battles with the outer world. For more than three decades the residents at the Wisconsin University of Lawsonomy have been left alone, granted security and tranquility by their remoteness from neighbors. Their experience in this respect suggests that, had Lawson established his community here or in a similar location, he might have spared DMUL the strife it was almost certain to stir up by its presence in an old, established neighborhood in Des Moines.

A wind generator in the yard of the Wisconsin University of Lawsonomy draws in many intrigued passers-by. Photo by the author.

If WUL's bucolic setting has prevented the bad relations with out-siders which DMUL experienced, its location on a busy interstate highway has caused it to arouse curiosity among at least as many out-siders as ever took notice of DMUL. Also, in recent years, some ac-counts of WUL have appeared in newspapers in the region—but never as news stories. In all cases the stories have originated in the search by reporters for an interesting feature. In another significant change, Lawsonomists have overcome enough of their suspicions of newspapers to talk with the reporters. Further evidences of the Law-sonomists' new openness to outsiders are the absence of a fence sur-rounding the property and the presence of a sign inviting inquiries. Even the attention drawn by the wind generator in the yard is wel-comed by the residents.

The passing years have produced another noteworthy change: the First Knowledgian is no longer the only Knowledgian. At the annual meeting of Lawsonomy students held at WUL during the 1979 Labor Day weekend, Knowledgian diplomas were for the first time bestowed on some very happy old-timers in Lawsonomy. The majority of the nine candidates were in their eighties and nineties; two had been studying Lawsonomy for over forty-five years. In subsequent years, more sheepskins have been awarded, so that now most Lawsonomy students over the age of sixty are Knowledgians.

Before graduating these students, however, the officers of WUL had first to solve a problem. Only Knowledgians were qualified to certify a student's eligibility for award of the Knowledgian degree. But there was only one Knowledgian, and he was dead. The solution adopted was to waive the examination requirement, while continuing to require presentation of evidence of sincere, good-faith study of Lawsonomy for a minimum of thirty years. But younger Lawsonomy students were admonished that this was a one-time-only procedure; when their times came, they would have to sit for the examinations administered by the Knowledgians.

The number of candidates likely to come forward in the future for the Knowledgian degree is not great, however. The years since Lawson's death have brought very few additions to the ranks of Lawsonomy, mostly ones born into Lawsonomy families. These additions have been more than offset by the deaths of old-timers. Today, the Lawsonomists are a much smaller group than they were at the time of Lawson's death; fewer than three hundred remain, their average age skewed toward the golden years.

These days, the most important events occurring in the Lawsonomy movement are the annual brief get-togethers of Lawsonomy students each summer. Some organizational business is attended to at these meetings, but in largest part they are social events, fittingly called reunions. At them friendships of long standing are renewed and common memories of the exciting early days of DCS and DMUL are recalled and enjoyed. And, of course, reunions are occasions for collectively recalling Lawson's greatness and expressing fealty to the one whom the gathering Lawsonomists still refer to as "Commander." Sad to say, Lawsonomy is today a movement very considerably frozen in the past and living on memories.

How much more exciting and full of promise things had seemed in DMUL's early years! Even in the final moribund years of DMUL, when Lawson's judgment was wobbling badly, at least his presence had continued to infuse his still-numerous followers with confidence and optimism about a glorious Lawsonomic future. But with Lawson's death came the removal of the movement's mainspring. Also abetting the winding down of the movement was Lawson's failure to provide for a successor, one of the most critical of his several failures in the last decade of his life.

During that time period, several Lawsonomist informants have recently claimed, Lawson did survey his generals for their views about who should succeed him. The unanimous consensus was that a committee, not a single person, should take over when the Commander was gone. But this result was perfectly predictable, and Lawson doubtless had counted on it when he made his survey. Who, after all, could fill the shoes of the Commander? And who would have the presumption to put his name forward—or even wish to have it mentioned in this connection by anyone but the Commander? However, the Commander had no intention of anointing anyone.

On the matter of leadership succession, Lawson had already tipped his hand in the DCS *General Orders*. There he had specified that, at the end of his "presence in mortal life," the board of trustees would take over. Perhaps the main purpose of this provision was to scotch factional turmoil and challenges to his authority, but Lawson may also have sought to minimize the chances that the Absolute Truths he had laid down in his writings might be altered or lose their grip on organizational policy. If this was still a risk when matters were left in the hands of a committee, at least it was less a risk than if some one person presumed to fill the role of Commander.

Lawson's insistence on obedience to him as Commander and on strict conformity to the letter of his teachings has insured a continuing vacuum of leadership since his death. No Lawsonomist has assumed Lawson's leadership role or even had the temerity to try to do so. The Lawsonomists' continuing fealty to a man dead for over thirty-five years and their refusal to budge from the policies and routines instituted by the Commander (except for their decision about awarding Knowledgian degrees) have undermined the viability of the movement. However, one senses that the Commander would nonetheless approve their conduct.

In place of instituting a system of effective decision making and strong leadership needed in the post-Lawson years, the surviving Lawsonomists appear to an outsider's eye to have fallen into an informal system of close monitoring of one another to prevent any heresies or departures from routine from occurring. But thanks to another leadership failure of Lawson, the burden of this informal system is even greater than it might otherwise have been. That is to say, Lawson can be particularly faulted for his failure to clarify in the mature Lawsonomy movement the relationship between the DCS doctrine of reformed capitalism and Lawsonomy's utopian ideal of a socialist "life without money." In result, Lawsonomists striving to follow Lawson's teachings and to insure adherence of all Lawsonomists to those teachings have found two different sets of teachings (and two different organizations) in contention for dominance in the movement today.

Lawson's presence had made it unnecessary to address this ideological conflict, and indeed, as noted earlier, he probably judged it the wiser course not to address it. DCS had been overwhelmingly the source of his following, and too strong an effort to repudiate or downgrade the DCS doctrine would undoubtedly have cost him many more followers than he already had lost when he shifted his emphasis to Lawsonomy.

Even while Lawson lived, however, the ideological bifurcation may have had a cost, because it meant that there were some DMUL residents who never did grasp fully what Lawson was trying to do at DMUL and who were proof against the inculcation of the new communitarian values. Going through the motions of the routines instituted there but probably unaware of how thoroughly Lawson had changed ideological direction, they continued to give their true allegiance to the DCS doctrine and program. But with Lawson no longer at hand to cover over the divergent ideological tendencies among his followers, those different tendencies have come more clearly to the fore. They don't seem to have generated overt bickering, yet the factional division among the Lawsonomists today must be as apparent to most of them as it is to an outside observer. At the very least, the two ideological tracks on which the Lawsonomists have continued to move have assured a blurred focus for the moment. By far the larger number of Lawsonomists gives priority to the economic program of DCS (these might be called the "economists"), while a minority (the "utopians") favors the more spiritual content and the utopian goals expressed both in *Born Again* and in Lawson's last books.

Although the position of the economists in the Lawsonomy movement may appear to be the more realistic, it probably is not so. The DCS doctrine is not likely to be a very saleable item today. Its demands for an enormous expansion of the money supply and extension of free credit to all were attractive goods in depression days but will not have as much appeal in an age when inflation is widely perceived to be the greatest economic evil. If the DCS program and accompanying diatribes against the financiers were modified to zero in on the problems of today's high interest rates, federal budget deficits, and staggering national debt, possibly DCS could pick up new customers. But, of course, making modifications is inconceivable. Instead, the Direct Credits enthusiasts in the Lawsonomy movement doggedly push the pure doctrine by distributing reprints of *Benefactor* containing Lawson's articles from the 1930s. Whenever they make public presentations, they do so by reciting memorized Lawson speeches from the same long-gone era. Thus, the prospects for DCS making much headway seem slim.

The minority insisting that Lawsonomy must be a crusade for humanity's spiritual renewal and a movement for radical reform of human nature and institutions is truer to the position Lawson reached near the end of his life. No less than the economists, however, the utopians face an uphill struggle today. In the first place, some elements of Lawsonomy are likely to scare off some who might otherwise be good enlistment prospects. Talk of the new species, for instance, may trigger in some minds disturbing notions of the Nietzschean "Overman," the Hitlerian "master race," and odious eugenic practices; perhaps suspicions along these lines figured in the negative response Lawson received when he heralded the new species during America's crusade against Nazi Germany. The "huge cosmic animal"—telepathically coordinated by officers under the command of one benevolent mastermind—will suggest to some an appalling regimentation and mind control. Probably most who learn of Lawson's gleeful pro-

jection of the eventual extirpation of animals will consider it one of
the most wrongheaded and preposterous goals of all time. On its scientific side, too, Lawsonomy will probably not carry conviction to most
seekers of truth. Even among the large portion of the public which is
scientifically unsavvy, many will hesitate to accept the claim that Lawson's scientific work replaces the work of Copernicus, Galileo, and
Newton. Most, in fact, may simply find the heavy scientific overlay of
Lawsonomy too tedious to bear.

This indicates the other problem for the utopians: Lawsonomy is a
difficult doctrine of wide range demanding years of head-scratching
study by its adherents and imposing numerous stern requirements on
their conduct. Here is one respect, in fact, in which the economists
certainly do have the advantage over the utopians. The DCS doctrine
is much more limited in scope, far easier to master, and better calculated to elicit and accommodate the cupidity of potential recruits than
is Lawsonomy.

On the other hand, too much must not be made of these impediments to Lawsonomy's appeal and progress. Many other systems of
thought containing at least as many elements susceptible to unflatter-
ing interpretation, or as many challenges to orthodoxy, or as many
tough demands on the intellects and conduct of adherents have nonetheless won a large following. In fact, the United States seems never to
have enough of such creeds, and almost daily one hears of the fabulous success of new ones.

Moreover, Lawsonomy is a far more rational and benign creed than
some others on which large movements have been successfully based.
Stripped of its more exotic doctrinal elements and boiled down to the
elements most relevant to everyday living, Lawsonomy teaches an un-
exceptionable standard of conduct for its adherents and gives a special prominence to such values as unselfishness, economic and social
justice, healthful living, and homage to God. One recent commen-
tator has, in fact, characterized Lawson's religious views as "little more
than a misty blend of transmigration, Lawsonomy [that is, Lawsonomic
science], and Christianity without Christ."[1] The apparent linkages of
Lawsonomy, whether considered as a philosophy or a religion, to the
Judeo-Christian mainstream definitely help to counterbalance its more
startling and novel scientific, social, and religious teachings.

But some of the other, more novel features of Lawsonomy may have their own appeal, too. Adroitly, Lawson produced a doctrine which simultaneously claims to be a science, a secular moral philosophy, and a religious creed. An obvious strength of this skillfully wrought construction is its claim to be of a piece, harmonizing all knowledge, speaking to all areas of human concern, surmounting the alleged gap between the realms of fact and of value, and linking an orientation toward a this-worldly future with some traditional moral and religious teachings.

Lawsonomy is, in fact, a modern gospel, speaking to those who, finding that older faiths no longer seem relevant or adequate in a scientific age, confront a spiritual void. Like some other new gospels of our time (for example, Scientology and some of the theologies centered on flying saucers and ancient astronauts), Lawsonomy unites much that is old with much that is new and in many instances, dresses what is old in new clothing. Thus, salvation and damnation are still provided for, but through reincarnation and the inexorable operation of scientific laws; the struggle between good and evil is made more dramatic as cosmic warfare between menorgs and disorgs; the unregenerate and the elect are recast more appealingly for modern minds as backward Apeman and enlightened Sageman; and those yearning to be "saved" or "born again" can become so by submitting to the discipline of the Lawsonomic life and dedicating themselves to bringing about the new species. In the new cosmic scenario, hell is the reprehensible here-and-now and heaven is an earthly utopia of the future.

Gratifyingly optimistic and suitably scientific for modern tastes, Lawson's doctrine trots out in new guise the familiar heresies of progress and human perfectibility. But more wonderful yet, the doctrine attaches to tenets reeking of secular humanism a spiritual penumbra, which makes the observance of the tenets seem a matter not of hubris or heresy but of religious duty. In signing on with Lawson's humanity-centered creed, the Lawsonomist is assured of submitting only to the dictates of God. Here, indeed, is an anxiety-relieving gospel for our time.

It seems clear, then, that Lawsonomy does have some assets for acquiring a larger following today. There is no necessary reason, stemming either from the content or the difficulty of the doctrine or from the rigorous demands it imposes on adherents, why it must fail to pick up new adherents. The main problem probably has not been the marketability of Lawsonomy but the feebleness of recent efforts to market it. That feebleness of promotion of doctrinal wares is both an indicator and a consequence of the general wanness of the Lawsonomy movement today.

In an attempt to act meaningfully in the yawning Lawsonomic void, the few remaining utopians, and the economists as well, seek to perfect their individual lives in accordance with Lawsonomy and otherwise stolidly go about their independent, small-scale promotional efforts, bearing individual witness to the truths of Lawsonomy. In this, of course, they follow in the steps of John Convert. However, in spite of their street-corner evangelistic efforts, the movement continues to wind down, a fact of which they must be aware. The only solace possible in this situation must come from a conviction that the intrinsic worth of the truths they preach guarantees that someday those truths will triumph.

In the last years of his life, perhaps even Lawson had come to share this conviction. Bedazzled by the power and truth of his ideas, he may not have thought it necessary to give detailed attention to the organizational requisites for the vigorous promotion of his movement and his ideas once he was gone. If so, however, this negligence appeared only at the very end of his life. Not much earlier, he had seen the indispensability of organization, clearly specified the character of the organization needed, and actually created the foundations of that organization. The needed organization was "the self-perpetuating social body."

Thinking of the self-perpetuating social body also as a university, however, he soon lost sight of his original perception that it was to be foremost a community. Thus Lawson let slip through his hands the very promising beginnings of the one kind of organization which could give substance to his final ideals of social life and which might have been able to provide the Lawsonomy movement with point and direction following his death. In shifting the attention of his followers away from the community concept and towards the university concept, Lawson also undercut the position of those among his fol-lowers—the utopians—who have remained most faithful to his final utopian vision. Certainly the empty and distracting shell of the Wis-consin University of Lawsonomy has not prevented the economist ma-jority from keeping the Direct Credits doctrine at the forefront today.

Thus has Lawson's final message to humanity continued to be dis-torted and feebly served in the time since his death, thanks in great part to his missteps in his last years. Once again, he proved to be a major factor in the undoing of his own great projects—this time, of his efforts to secure the advancement of Lawsonomy during the post-mortem phase of his leadership. A movement programmed for early extinction—this was the major but unintended legacy of Lawson's campaign for the redemption of humanity through the inauguration of the new species.

Far-flung and dwindling in number, Lawson's followers today none-theless have cause never to forget the First Knowledgian. So long as enough remain to hold reunions, they will surely go on hymning their praise for "God's great eternal gift to man," memorizing his inspired writings, and testifying to how profoundly their lives were touched by the one they consider the best and wisest man they ever knew. But just as certainly, too, the time is not far off when none will be left to lift the hosannahs, and the books of Lawsonomy will then gather dust on the shelves, disturbed only by the occasional aficionado of curiosa. More than anyone else, the First Knowledgian himself was responsible for the fact that the present handful of Knowledgians will almost cer-tainly be the last Knowledgians.

14

LAWSON
AND
AMERICA

"I have worked like hell for the United States, and I am going to as long as I live," an impassioned Lawson told Senator Moody in 1952. But was this the same Alfred Lawson who had already logged so many years claiming to be the benefactor and servant of all of humanity? The pronouncements and reform goals served up by the First Knowledgian had always been global, even cosmic in scope, certainly not directed to the well-being of a single nation only. Lawson's expression of special solicitude for the United States might therefore have struck an observer as uncharacteristically parochial.

Of course, at that moment Lawson was also under fire for selling machines purchased from the federal government. Might his patriotic professions have been nothing more than a grasping for protective red, white, and blue coloration? In the circumstances, one could easily believe that Lawson might seek to wrap himself in the flag.

Despite any hints of inconsistency or expediency, however, Lawson's patriotic utterances were unquestionably sincere. Having lived nearly all of his years in the United States, he was inextricably entangled in American life and culture. In spite of his pretensions to a world-class standing, he remained thoroughly a provincial, never going farther afield than the United States in his quest for power and fame.

Lawson knew very well, too, that time and again, he had made great exertions and sacrifices on behalf of his country and its citizens. As he spoke at the hearing, doubtless foremost in his mind were his efforts to boost American aviation in its infancy and to introduce a national air transportation system in the United States. On that occasion certainly he also recalled his valiant campaign in the 1930s to free the American people from the stranglehold of the financiers. Possibly he even dredged up from distant memory his work as a builder of baseball teams and leagues for many small towns and cities in the United States. But these were only the most visible entries in a long record of patriotic services; his zeal to do good for his fellow Americans had spun off many other benefactions throughout his entire adult life.

At the outset, his good deeds typically were aimed at enhancing the amenities and comforts of the lives of his compatriots. A good example was his plan, devised while Lawson was still a very young man, for cooling all houses in Philadelphia by use of a central cooling station. Also, in 1908 he had written to the presidents of leading American colleges and universities offering to teach, free of charge, a correspondence course in aeronautics. Both proposals were spurned by the intended beneficiaries—sad to say, a frequent response to Lawson's charitable gestures. One can hope, however, that at least the baseball games which he staged at night in the early years of electric lighting brought an appreciative roar from the fans.

In later years, Lawson's altruistic impulses usually issued in efforts to improve Americans physically, morally, intellectually, or spiritually. For example, he once approached many magazine and newspaper editors with a proposal to write a series of articles advocating a federal law making it illegal to manufacture or sell cigarettes in the United States. When no publisher was willing to risk the loss of advertising income from the cigarette companies, Lawson carried on the fight alone. In speeches, books, and *Benefactor* articles, he blasted away at the smoking habit, accurately observing that "one may hunt the world over but can find no other animal strutting around with a lighted pipe or cigarette stuck in its face and using its mouth to suck in and blow out smoke, using at times the nostrils as human smokestacks."

To cigarette smoking Lawson attributed rising rates in the United States of crime and feeblemindedness as well as sickliness. His worries about the degeneration of the American population in these respects also led him to advocate a law requiring parents to be at least twenty years old before having children. Finally, Lawson was concerned to counteract a falloff in religious observances among Americans. One of his reasons for founding Lawsonian Religion, he claimed, was to offer a spiritual alternative which would appeal to the many American citizens who were unchurched.

One can also find throughout Lawson's life many direct expressions of patriotic fervor. During the 1930s, for instance, even while claiming that American party politics, elections, and civil liberties had been rendered meaningless by the manipulations of the financiers, Lawson often wrote glowingly in *Benefactor* about American democracy, contrasting it favorably with the dictatorships of Europe. And in 1916, his fears for the fate of American democracy in a world menaced by despotism led him to champion the cause of American entry into World War I against Germany.

Lawson's call to arms against Germany took the form of an allegorical tale, "The Death of Liberty," published in October, 1916. Highly flavored by Social Darwinist arguments concerning the inevitability and benefits of conflict in the lives of organisms and nations, the tale treated the struggle between Democracy and Despot, characters standing for antagonistic principles contending in international politics. Other characters in the tale included Wealth and Peace, who insidiously encouraged Democracy in indolence and soft living. Coaxed by them into physical and moral flabbiness, Democracy fell to the power of Despot, dragging down Liberty in the process. Both the tale and its obvious moral were very familiar ones in Lawson's writings, of course. As was always the case in Lawson's universe, good and evil were locked in titanic struggle, and the outlook for the triumph of good was bleak. On this occasion, however, the forces of good and evil were political principles embodied by the United States and Germany respectively, rather than the soul and the mind, good thoughts and bad thoughts, the menorgs and the disorgs, or the producers and the financiers.

When Lawson reprinted "The Death of Liberty" during World War II, he added a preface claiming that the tale had "made a profound

impression upon the President of the United States at that time. Previously he was a pronounced pacifist and it was publicly promulgated
that he was 'too proud to fight.' But after he had pondered over the
story . . . for a few months, he changed his mind completely and then
in 1917 he issued his never-to-be-forgotten words—'THE WORLD
MUST BE MADE SAFE FOR DEMOCRACY.'" Although Lawson
never bothered to document his claim of having had such extraordinary influence on President Wilson, plainly he believed his cautionary
tale—"The Outstanding Tale of All Time," he subsequently subtitled
it—was one of his greatest services to the United States.

It was in times of actual war, however, that Lawson's nationalistic
fervor was put most fully on display. Recall his patriotic actions during World War I—for instance, his campaign to awaken Congress to
the need for air power to overwhelm the Kaiser, his hinted willingness
to serve as the American "air generalissimo," and his offer to implement the Transoceanic Float System. And it was during World War II
that he first proposed to make the solar engulferator operational for
the defense of the United States, if the federal government would
only give him the needed R&D support. Finally, it was Lawson's patriotism during the Korean War which caused him to sell the machines purchased from the federal government and subsequently to
be summoned to Senator Moody's hearings. As Lawson told the story,
the decision to sell was made largely in response to the importunings
of machinery dealers, who stressed that the machines were urgently
needed for war production.

Although all this evidence backed up Lawson's claim of deep devotion to the United States, his unusual activities and writings were
bound to stir up the apprehensions of some Americans (and not just
Des Moines residents) during the jittery years of the Great Depression, World War II, and the early cold war. From the early 1930s
to the mid-1950s, letters expressing anger or alarm about Lawson
poured in to the FBI; to these, J. Edgar Hoover, the FBI director,
always responded by thanking the tipsters for their vigilance against
subversive activities and encouraging further reports of anything
deemed suspicious.

In 1939, the Direct Credits Society was identified as a "borderline

organization" on a list of subversive organizations coming into the
hands of the FBI. This, of course, called for an FBI investigation, con-
ducted in 1940. Although the investigation found no DCS connection
with any "Communist, Fascist, or Christian Front organization" or
with Coughlin's Social Justice movement, the FBI continued thereafter to be wary of Lawson and his organizations. As late as 1954,
when one of Lawson's followers sent Hoover a copy of *Lawsonian Religion*, the FBI chief agreed with his advisers that "it is not deemed ad-
visable to acknowledge the letter . . . or the book."

A lot of FBI hours were also spent after 1940 preparing and sending intra-agency reports on Lawson. However, the successive reports
did little more than summarize "findings" from earlier reports, and
these "findings" consisted of little more than accumulated hearsay
and information culled from Lawson's books. In other words, after
having built a large file on Lawson over a twenty-five-year period,
even the FBI was hard put to find anything subversive or "un-Ameri-
can" in the words or deeds of Alfred Lawson. From the start, of
course, the agency's suspicions had been absurd and outrageous.

There is no reason whatsoever, then, to question either the sincerity
or the validity of Lawson's contention that—after his own fashion, at
least—he had "worked like hell for the United States." However, the
many benefactions which Lawson sought to bestow on the American
people were not only frequently exotic and usually transparently
linked to his self-promoting ambitions; they were always pursued, too,
in an inimitable Lawsonian manner. The result was a truly distinctive
life, seeming almost to verge on the sui generis. If Lawson were placed
among all American go-getters of his generation (or any other), he
would clearly stand out by virtue of many unique attributes, aspirations, and activities. Playing these wild cards frequently in his quest
for the jackpot of power and fame, he inevitably ended more unlike
than like the run-of-the-mill entrepreneur of his day.

Certainly Lawson's low regard for money as a goal of entrepreneurship contributed much to distinguishing him from the largest
portion of his fellow upward-strivers. Conventional wisdom has always held that the prospect of financial reward is the main spur to
economic activity, and the actual attainment of personal wealth was

often taken in Lawson's day as a sign of having successfully served the general good. Having no truck with those views, however, at the very outset of his entrepreneurial career Lawson denounced the life given over to money getting as a morally unworthy one. Explicitly rejecting in *Born Again* the self-serving success ethic popular at the time, he purported instead to opt for an altruistic ethic of direct service to the collective interest. Although these youthful convictions didn't inhibit Lawson's intense pursuit of self-advancement, they did foreshadow the indifference to money which increasingly characterized his conduct and also the perfervid disavowals of self-interested motives which always accompanied his actions.

As the foregoing pages have documented, not wealth, but power and fame, were the objects of Lawson's entrepreneurial striving. Most persons would undoubtedly have assumed that the acquisition of personal wealth was a useful step toward the attainment of power and fame. But this assumption calls attention to another respect in which Lawson differed from most of his contemporaries: the power and fame at which he aimed were actually not of the same character as those pursued by others. Neither the servants nor the by-products of money grubbing, his power and fame would arise inexorably, he believed, out of his many heroic and selfless services to the people and their grateful recognition that he alone could be trusted to act always in their interest. In effect, the power and the fame which Lawson craved were to be the objectification in the world of the exalted perception of personal greatness which resided in his mind. Their realization would also constitute a recognition and a confirmation by the world of the truth of that perception.

When Lawson rejected great wealth as the bench mark of success and set out in quest of power and fame commensurate with his self-imagined greatness, he put in motion an entrepreneurial career destined to depart from the norm. Never held back by petty financial concerns about the "bottom line" and always certain that all things were possible in his hands, he assailed many difficult and risky projects which would have daunted Ordinary Mortals—or which Ordinary Mortals would never even have thought of. But Lawson's singular brand of entrepreneurship not only opened to him a wider latitude of action than was available to the usual entrepreneur; it also permitted a greater freedom to roam among disparate fields of activity.

In spite of Lawson's many departures from the norm, however, there remains a limit—albeit a very broad one—to how far one should go in pushing the notion of his uniqueness. For instance, even though the objects of his ambitious strivings may have differed considerably from those of hordes of other Americans on the make, his easy identification of his quest for personal advancement with the serving of the public interest made him a representative specimen of his time, place, and circumstances.

Lawson's was, after all, an age which venerated the norm of self-help ("God helps those who help themselves"), admired the adjoining ideal of the self-made man, and could confidently believe Alexander Pope's assurance that

. . . God and Nature planned the general frame
And bade self-love and social be the same.

The desire and the effort to get ahead, so long as they stayed within the boundaries of the laws and conventional morality, were widely approbated as, respectively, the surest engine of social progress and the best means to secure the general good. Lawson's avid pursuit of personal advancement and his convenient conflation of his private interest and the public interest were therefore hardly out of the ordinary. At least in this respect, then, Lawson can be regarded as an authentic instance of the very large subclass of white American males of his generation who had been inoculated with the success ethic and took their bearings from the ideal of the "self-made man"—and this despite Lawson's alleged rejection of these prominent American cultural norms.

Even the pronounced utopian strain running through Lawson's career was a telltale sign that, despite all its peculiarities, his life remained a true flower of American culture. Indeed, his longstanding dalliance with utopia was one of the most "American" things about Lawson, linking his life in manifold ways to the rich utopian tradition which has adorned the social and cultural history of the United States. Earlier chapters recounted four distinct episodes in Lawson's journey to utopia: accompanying his entrepreneurial quests in baseball and aviation were two phases of utopian rhapsodizing (*Born Again*, his air-craft magazine editorials), which subsequently gave way to two phases of strenuous full-time effort at utopian reform (Direct Credits, Des Moines University of Lawsonomy). In all four phases, Lawson was snugly ensconced in modes of utopian thought or practice well established in the United States.

Of course, if Lawson's hankering after utopia was far from being out of place in the United States, the multiplicity of his successive conceptions of what utopia was and how it should be attained was unusual. And positively novel was the way in which his utopian views shifted with the changing prospects of his entrepreneurial career. Thus, when things were going well for Lawson in his early days in aviation, he was quickly able to overcome his earlier position in *Born Again* that utopia waited on humanity's change of heart; now, he found, utopia would eventually come through technological advancement, especially in aviation. But when things soured for Lawson in the aircraft industry, he turned to a new conception of utopia, which legitimated his taking up a political role as the People's Coach and the Man of Destiny. Aided and abetted by the arrival of the Great Depression, he now went after the financiers, whose removal would bring utopia under capitalism. However, the dynamism of the Direct Credits crusade eventually began to falter, and in any event, the movement limited too greatly the outreach of the man who sought greater recognition for his aviation accomplishments and all of his other material and intellectual benefactions. What was left for Lawson, then, was once again to redefine utopia and the means to its attainment and, in the course of doing so, to stake out new and greater claims for his personal role as the First Knowledgian.

In sum, not only was Lawson's thinking about utopia hinged to the ups and downs of his career but he eventually attempted to use utopian reform as a means of overcoming and accommodating his failure in aviation. Indeed, he employed utopian reform as one more field of entrepreneurial endeavor in his all-out pursuit of power and fame. In all these respects, Lawson's utopian involvements certainly were distinguishable from those of most persons in the United States who have been fetched by utopia.

Alas, Lawson's assault on greatness through utopian reform was no more successful than his earlier efforts had been along more conventional entrepreneurial lines. In every phase of his career the same pattern always appeared: successful in getting the public's attention at the outset, he invariably found that his celebrity (or increasingly, his notoriety) was short-lived, and soon the public's memory of his activities was lost altogether. It was a terrible fate for one who thirsted so for fame and who knew that his greatness outshone that of all others.

The attainment of power—Lawson's other obsession—always eluded his grasp, too, but the evanescence of Lawson's fame was simply the flip side of his inability to convert opportunities into success or to carry through with the projects he essayed. His failures can be chalked up to various factors. Among them, certainly, were bad luck (for instance, the rain-out of his projected major baseball league and the plowing of the farmer's field across the path of the Midnight Liner) and the vagaries of timing (for instance, the ending of World War I before he could get his first aircraft company firmly established and the prematurity of his effort to found an airline service, further complicated by the emergence of a major business recession in 1920–1921). And, at least from Lawson's point of view, he also had often been thwarted by the lack of vision of Ordinary Mortals (for instance, in his failure to get backing in 1913 for a solo flight across the Atlantic Ocean, or to win acceptance during World War I for his vision of an enormous American aerial fleet under the command of an air generalissimo, or to obtain the money he needed to make Milwaukee the Detroit of the aircraft industry).

As earlier pages have amply disclosed, however, the obstacles to Lawson's success welled up from within Lawson at least as often as they obtruded from the external world. Was there ever another man who so regularly acted in ways well calibrated to undermine his quest for lasting fame and power? Always ready to pop up and to mar his projects in every phase of his career were some familiar and distinctive Lawsonian attributes. These included a sometimes disastrously bad judgment, an arrogance born of a conviction of omnicompetence, a propensity for surmounting or masking problems through press agentry, and a lack of realism in setting his goals and pursuing his course.

All too often, too, Lawson seemed unable to shepherd his energies and maintain his focus. The instances of this last failing were as flabbergasting as they were numerous. Illustrating the point, for instance, were Lawson's return to baseball management in 1915–1916 in the midst of his struggle to get a foothold in the aircraft industry; his allocation of precious time and energy to self-celebrating autobiographical writing in the very years (1920–1921) of his greatest opportunity—and stiffest challenges—in aviation; his attempt to found an intercity bus service in the late 1920s, even while trying to regain his position in the airline business; the increasing diversion of his attention during the 1930s from Direct Credits to Lawsonomy; and his astonishing inability to keep clearly in mind what he was trying to do at DMUL.

Poor Lawson! Probably no one else had ever tried so hard, along so many lines of endeavor, to make a deep impression on the world and to secure the world's acclaim, and yet every time, it seemed, personal shortcomings, sometimes deriving from a glaring hubris, had unfailingly shoved him along toward failure and oblivion. The recounting of Lawson's doomed enterprises—especially in aviation—can't help but stir up in the observer the most acute feelings of sympathy for the man. Strong whiffs of classic Greek tragedy are undeniably in his story.

Perhaps no more than whiffs, however; anyone lingering for long over the life of Lawson may conclude that his poignant story is less evocative of tragic scenes from the theater of ancient Athens than of rollicking moments on the plains of La Mancha, where the great Don Quixote once performed his remarkable feats. Who could miss, for instance, Lawson's Quixote-like determination to impose his private construction of reality on the world and then to sally forth in singular adventures finding significance and meaning mainly within the context of his private vision? It was a vision in which all personal weaknesses were transformed into strengths, no failures were conceivable, airplanes flew by means of suction and pressure, and the redoubtable Lawson single-handedly established the aircraft industry, reformulated all scientific knowledge, and routed the financiers. Indeed, Lawson was even more thoroughgoing in these respects than was the Don, who concluded on his deathbed that the exploits of the Knight of the Sorrowful Countenance had been a series of self-delusions. In contrast, to the end of its final chapter, Lawson held fast to his view of his life as a steady unfolding of triumphs and greatness.

But if it is easier to see Lawson as a modern Don Quixote than as a tragic hero, that characterization, too, doesn't begin to capture the man fully or fairly. For one thing, not until the last phase of his life was it certain that he was totally enwrapped in a private vision of reality; until that point, he usually had at least one foot planted firmly in the real world and sometimes was engaged in rationally calculated pursuits of quite sane, even estimable, and certainly not quixotic objectives. And for another thing, despite his larger failures, he had many smaller successes along the way—enough of them to make plain that he was capable of acting very effectively. For examples, one has only to recall his early baseball expeditions to Cuba, his profitable career as a builder of minor baseball leagues, his two successful ventures into aviation journalism, and—greatest achievement of all—his construction of the first airliner. Convinced though he was that heavier-than-air flight was a matter of suction, pressure, and penetrability, he nonetheless always got his planes off the ground, and indeed, his airliners—both the one which he flew and the one which he crashed—were praiseworthy efforts in the early history of American aviation.

Lawson's success in building airplanes was highly dependent, of course, on the contributions of some exceptionally talented persons whom he had brought together in his employ. But this fact points to another of Lawson's assets for making his way in the world: he had a definite gift for persuading, organizing, and leading people. When he had finally reached the point of touting himself as the Man of Destiny and the First Knowledgian, the range of his appeal and his effectiveness among the generality of humankind obviously narrowed. Up to that point, however, a wide spectrum of quite sober people from the workaday world—small-town baseball boosters, subscribers to his magazines, newspaper editors looking for authoritative commentary on aviation developments, officials of the Post Office and War Department, numerous small investors in Milwaukee, city council members and mayors along the route of the flight of his first airliner, employees of his aircraft companies—all were ready to take him seriously, buy into his enterprises and his dreams, and follow his lead.

And even after Lawson had gone off the deep end of utopianism, first with Direct Credits and subsequently with Lawsonomy and his pursuit of the new species, he still had in tow minions by the thousands passionately devoted to him and his causes. Hardly Sancho Panzas, they wholeheartedly embraced Lawson's world view and enthusiastically took their assigned places behind him in his successive assaults on the New Jerusalem. Of course, under Lawson's direction, those assaults began soon enough to lose focus and effectiveness. Nonetheless, in view of his ability to arouse a large following prepared to share his private visions and to stick with him through every zig-zag-and-swirl of his utopian quests, one must still adjudge Lawson to have been a utopian leader of the first water.

Tragic hero, comic tilter at windmills, daring and effective entrepreneur, chronic failure, utopian visionary and charismatic leader, busted seer—if none of these characterizations captures Lawson fully, each applies in part and must be provided for in any summing up of the man. But can a rubric be found which will cover and account for these amazingly diverse features of the man and his life? Is there a single pigeonhole of explanation into which Lawson can be shoved? The foregoing pages have presented Lawson's life as an unrelieved, supercharged quest for fame and power commensurate with his exalted conception of his personal greatness. This may be as close as one can come to finding a formulation supple enough to depict Lawson in the round. But the puzzle persists: *why* was Lawson as he was? How could anyone ever have essayed a life so extraordinary and full of zig-zag-and-swirl?

Lawson had a ready answer, of course: all that he was or did could be fully explained by his unique goodness and his inspired genius; he truly was the greatest of God's special agents. Unable to swallow that, however, anyone not a Lawsonomist will insist that Lawson's explanation is the very thing which needs to be explained. How or why did he come to hold and act on such exalted views of himself?

At this point will doubtless arise a powerful urge to search for the source of Lawson's self-assessments and conduct within his personality—that is, just as Lawson did, to look to the man for the wellsprings of his thought and action, albeit employing a framework of analysis quite different from Lawson's. One such framework is supplied in the American Psychiatric Association's *Diagnostic and Statistical Manual of Mental Disorders*, particularly in the discussion there of the so-called Narcissistic Personality Disorder, defined as "a pervasive pattern of grandiosity (in fantasy or behavior), lack of empathy, and hypersensitivity to the evaluation of others, beginning by early adulthood and presented in a variety of contexts as indicated by at least *five*" of nine listed indicia. And among the indicia are these five: "is interpersonally exploitative: takes advantage of others to achieve his own ends . . . has a grandiose sense of self-importance . . . is preoccupied with fantasies of unlimited success, power, brilliance, beauty, or ideal love . . . has a sense of entitlement: unreasonable expectation of especially favorable treatment . . . requires constant attention and admiration."[1] (Without benefit of psychiatric guidance, the FBI, too, appeared to arrive at something like the conclusion that Lawson was in the grip of the Narcissistic Personality Disorder; "overwhelmed by egotism" was how successive FBI reports described him.)

Beyond the straightforward evidence suggestive of a narcissistic personality lay other materials in Lawson's life bound to strike the observer's eye and pique interest in Lawson's psychological make-up. Items coming quickly to mind include his curious pattern of always starting well but then fizzling out or faltering at the brink of success; his manner of handling failure both by denying its reality and by attributing it to the machinations of the financiers; his off-base conviction that the financiers were working day and night to thwart the success of the Direct Credits Society; his poignant claim (stated so often) that he wanted nothing more for himself than the "love and respect" of the American people; his anti-intellectual foamings at the stupidities and charlatanries of the professors and orthodox scientists; the authoritarianism manifested in his fondness for hierarchy; and his delusion that an unspecified "they" wanted to get at him by kidnapping his children.

Another striking psychological fact about Lawson is worthy of separate comment: throughout most of his life he pursued a course which insured that he would be not simply a loner but also virtually an outsider to the fields in which he worked. Thus, most of the teams and leagues he created lay beyond the domain of organized baseball. After World War I, when he began to pursue his dream of a national air passenger service, he struck out on a solitary path which brought him in the late 1920s to the hapless superliner project, far from the mainstream in which aviation industry was then flowing. Certainly his scientific studies put him completely beyond the community of the orthodox scientists. In the 1930s his Direct Credits crusade had no tie-in with other financial reform movements of that time or little connection with American politics generally. And by the time he came to Des Moines, he obviously was caught up in a quest lying beyond the comprehension of both the humanity he proposed to redeem and many of his followers.

True enough, during his earliest years in aviation, he was a very important insider, tightly entwined in the nascent community of the partisans of flight and, indeed, an important agent in the formation of that community. However, by virtue of such things as his more flamboyant magazine editorials, his speculations about the alti-man, and his lobbying on behalf of an extreme view of American needs for air power in World War I, Lawson probably came rather quickly to be viewed by his peers as "different"—or as Vincent Burnelli put it charitably, as a "visionary." When, by the start of the decade of the 1920s, he had begun to construe flight in terms of Lawsonomy principles, there was no longer even a shared universe of discourse between him and others in the field of aviation—and thus, even had Lawson wanted it, little possibility of common action or communication with others (except on Lawson's own terms, of course). In result, others remained generally indifferent to or unaware of his most important aviation work after World War I, just as organized baseball apparently did not feel threatened by his projected new major league, and just as politicians and other financial reformers ignored the Direct Credits crusade. Moreover, in all these instances, Lawson's self-determined outsider status clearly contributed to the swiftness with which he passed from the memory of humanity, unable until recently even to secure a footnote in the monographs of historians. Here was the supreme irony for one who yearned so for lasting recognition.

Other evidence—or in some instances, absence of evidence—buttresses the case for Lawson's standing as the quintessential outsider. Seldom throughout his long life did Lawson own any property other than the clothes on his back and other personal effects, and not until his eighth decade did he have any family ties or responsibilities. Even then, he continued his lifetime's pattern of staying constantly on the road; for Lawson, there was no such place as "home," as understood in the psychological and emotional senses in which most people use the word. Nowhere, too, in all of Lawson's writings or published collections of documents does one find any expressions of indebtedness to other writers, very many telltale signs that he even read the books of other writers, any evidence that he shared his dreams or projects with intimates, or even any evidence that he had any close friends. "Associates" Lawson had, of course, either as employees or DCS members, but his relations to them were as superior to subordinates. Such bonds, founded on the hierarchical principle so beloved of Lawson but eventually characterized by charismatic ecstasy, constituted the only kind of community discernible in Lawson's life. In sum, Lawson was the ultimate rootless person, unanchored in any place, family or property relationships, political alliances, civic associations, hobbies, professional groups, or major interests shared and cultivated with others (except in circumstances in which he could define those interests and be in charge).

Thus the Lawsonian record is strewn with eye-catching data of a sort which make it impossible to ignore the impact of an unusual personality in accounting for an unusual life. Anyone interested in the etiology of Lawson's adult personality could have a field day, too, rummaging about in his writings about his childhood (especially in *Childhood Days of Alfred Lawson*), in which are disclosed revealing tales of youthful emotional turmoil, sibling rivalries, struggles with parents, and uncertainties about parental love. Clearly Lawson left much for the psychohistorian to chew on.

By itself, however, neither a descent into the murky waters of a dubious psychoanalytic account nor any other exhumation of Lawson's attributes of personality will bring a complete understanding of the unfolding of his life. The strong temptation to account for Lawson's unusual life solely by reference to his pronounced personality quirks must be rejected, along with Lawson's contention that his life was exclusively the product of an unalloyed genius and goodness bestowed by God. Both views miss the fact that Lawson actually was an unusual variant of the American self-made man and an atypical devotee of the American success ethic—that is, that the key to understanding Lawson's life, or any other life, will be found in the interplay of personality, social order, and culture.

Even then, a full accounting for Lawson's life will be forever unobtainable. Probably the greatest mysteries lying beyond the possibility of explanation today center on his "born again" experience in his twenty-eighth year. Here was the first of two major turning points in his life, revealing in its emotional intensity, transformative impact, and some of its effects the earmarks of a familiar American religious conversion experience. What happened? Why did it happen then? Why did an experience essentially religious in character have as its main consequence a newfound secular ambition of such extraordinary magnitude?

Although these questions can't be answered, it is clear that this episode not only marked the takeoff of Lawson's pursuit of fame and power but also set him up for a crisis when his remarkable exploits in aviation didn't pan out. His aviation failures hit him very hard—an understandable consequence, when seen in the light of the exalted self-concept and the lofty goals which had taken possession of Lawson's mind. What followed was a second great turning point in his life, producing denials of failure, ever more grandiose projects, and steadily escalating claims for his greatness. If these post-aviation phases of Lawson's life also present flabbergasting features difficult to account for fully, at least one can see that they flowed, almost inexorably, out of that original mystery—the "born again" episode of his young adulthood.

Another truth concerning the aftermath of this second turning point in Lawson's life is self-evident: when viewed against the backdrop of his intensified assault on power and fame, the failure and rapid fading from the limelight of the First Knowledgian have got to be reckoned an even worse setback for Lawson than was his fall from one-time eminence in aviation. The Lawson saga, it may seem, comes down to a poignant story of steadily pumped-up efforts to achieve greatness, followed by ever higher magnitudes of failure. But is there no other wise in which this remarkable man can lay claim to the attention he craved from posterity? Did he leave no legacies other than a string of failures and a slowly disintegrating small band of adulators?

Certainly Lawson's strongest claim to lasting recognition arises from his activities in the early years of American aviation. Although he overbilled himself as *the* father of the American aviation industry and as *the* inventor of the airliner, his self-proclaimed accolades were far from being completely unfounded. Only in recent years has Lawson begun to get, in several articles and in brief sections of aviation histories, some of the notice to which he is entitled. The two chapters herein give the fullest account yet of the complete range of his aviation exploits, but a much more detailed examination is warranted in order to pin down precisely all that he did and the nature and extent of his contribution to American aviation.[2]

Lawson is also entitled to a place of notice in the rich American communitarian tradition. His versatility of activities and talents puts him among such notable American utopian jacks-of-all-trades as Josiah Warren—musician, printer, inventor, and founder of communities— and King Gillette, the blue-blade razor man; at the same time, Lawson is entitled to high standing among such better known communitarian champions of scientific unorthodoxy as Cyrus Reed Teed, leader of the hollow-earth devotees of Koreshanity, and Wilbur Glenn Voliva, dictator of the flat-earthers of Zion City, Illinois. Lawson's conceptions of the utopian community as the "self-perpetuating social body" and as the "seed" of a new species of improved humanity were not original ideas. However, Lawsonomic embellishments made his uses of these notions distinctive—and in his vision of his community as a university, he unquestionably delivered a genuinely novel contribution. His struggle to make a go of the community-as-university suggested that the notion was internally contradictory and self-defeating, but the DMUL episode nonetheless added a colorful chapter, worthy of remembrance, to the annals of utopian communities in America.

In the realm of utopian speculation, Lawson's call for the development of a new species of humanity was not unprecedented, but his several formulations of the concept were. Surely the alti-man will stand forever as the most bizarre product of that species of extreme optimism known as "technological utopianism." But Sageman, the quite different conception of the new species which Lawson finally settled on, also provided some novel twists. These were evidenced in Lawson's plan for creating Sageman through a thirty-year program of indoctrination in Lawsonomy, his determination to organize the new species of Sageman "as a unit," like the menorgs, and his vision of the "huge cosmic animal," composed of individual Sagemen as cells subject to the direction of a single controlling intellect through telepathy.

If the specter of a global totalitarianism seems to rise out of Lawson's vision of the new species, it was certainly unintended by him. He sincerely sought a worldwide regime of reason and virtue in which the common interests of humanity had at last been recognized, all strife and injustice had ended, and cooperation had become the norm. Here was the ineluctable next evolutionary step, the stage to which the evolutionary process, under the guidance of the menorgs, had been driving all along. But it also was a step to be taken and achieved by human agency; from this point onward, humanity would relieve the menorgs of further responsibility for human development and for management of the universe. In other words, an expanded human consciousness had been the goal of evolution, and eventually human consciousness, organized globally, would become the main directing agent in all remaining evolutionary chapters.

With these views, Lawson seems to have anticipated—in his own inimitable way—several key ideas given prominence today by so-called New Age writers. Several other themes found among the contemporary New Agers are also evocative of Lawson's thinking—for example, the New Agers' call for a scientific "paradigm shift" needed to accommodate the alleged continuity between the realms of mind and matter and of fact and value; their view of the earth as a living organism ("Gaia"); their boundless optimism about a human future built on an emergent collective consciousness of humanity, in control of advanced technology (including "psychotechnologies"); and an enthusiasm for the exploration and colonization of space as the necessary next phases in humanity's destiny. Too, when many of the lesser New

Age gurus, such as Shirley MacLaine, loose their fluttery thoughts about such "higher realities" as reincarnation, astral projection, telepathy, and psychokinesis, they cross into territory also occupied by Lawson. It would certainly be unfair to both Lawson and the New Age thinkers to shove the former into the latter's camp; there are too many differences between them to justify that. Nonetheless, the considerable overlap of shared concerns does give a prophetic quality to some of Lawson's views and has assured that they stay alive in the present time.

On several other matters, too, Lawson's was a prophetic voice, heralding ideas whose time has come. Although it reposed in limbo for over forty years, the strategic defense concept implicit in Lawson's solar engulferator has at last made it onto the American policy agenda, where it seems destined to be lodged for many years to come. And an age in which joggers clog the streets, the anti-smoking campaign has become a juggernaut, and two of every three persons are obsessed with dietary concerns is an age which certainly ought to recognize a soul mate in Lawson. Many decades before the movement had gained its present head of steam, Lawson already was there, proclaiming the merits of a "healthy lifestyle."

Of course, in Lawson's view, a healthy lifestyle was not simply meritorious but was also a matter of compliance with the dictates of Natural Law. Concerning humanity's moral duties under the Natural Law, Lawson had an expert's comprehensive knowledge, which he felt God had tapped him to share with others. Smoking, overeating, and failing to exercise, he declared, offended Natural Law, but so did a long list of other things denounced by Lawson, such as going to movies, dancing, drinking cocktails, wearing cosmetics, growing whiskers, reading trashy novels, and kissing. (In *Children*, Lawson asked whether anything "filthier" could be imagined than "a picture of a man and woman with their faces stuck together and spitting disease microbes into each other's mouths"?) For Lawson, it is plain, the world was a moral gymnasium, in which the fate of humanity was to submit to unending, exhausting workouts under the guidance of the proper calisthenics instructor. Nor does Lawson's fondness for sumptuary laws seem surprising; well-policed conduct obviously reduced the opportunities for the disorgs to get at the old Adam.

"Many years ago this writer realized that he was born to improve mankind," Lawson wrote in 1943. His intense yen to improve his fellows in every particular made him a prime example of that subcategory of humanity which H. L. Mencken aptly labeled the "virtuosi of virtue." According to Mencken, the virtuosi of virtue had found their most congenial home in the United States and, in fact, constituted that country's dominant character type, thanks to the twin American heritages of democracy and Puritanism. Whether or not Mencken was right about these matters, he certainly had put his finger on something real in the United States. From the glory years of Anthony Comstock's anti-smut crusades, through the heyday of the Prohibition movement, to these exquisite latter days of Ralph Nader, the Moral Majority, decriers of satanic rock lyrics, organizers of Washington prayer breakfasts, and zealous zoophilists dedicated to the liberation of laboratory rats, the virtuosi of virtue have been a very familiar American phenomenon. More so than most other national populations, Americans seem always to have had a pronounced taste for being "born again," scotching evils, enlisting in vice crusades, exhorting one another to improved conduct, enacting laws for this purpose, and submitting to verbal pummelings by self-anointed moralists; they have also had considerable talent for producing shining knights to lead the virtuous hosts in the endless series of great moral combats of which they suppose life to consist. To the list of such gifted leaders certainly should be added the name of Alfred Lawson. Here was one more respect in which Lawson actually turns out to have been a highly representative American.

Anyone sharing Mencken's values and outlook will not warm up to the virtuosi of virtue, of course, and is likely to conclude that Lawson particularly would have been unpleasant to be around. Self-deprecating good humor, a sense of irony, lightheartedness, and tolerance for the foibles of humanity—not these, but rather an insufferable egotism, self-righteousness, propensity to moralistic declamations, and an unattractive habit of hurling the Law of Maneuverability at all who opposed him were the prominent Lawson characteristics.

When viewed from the distance created by the passage of time, however, Lawson's life also yields up some other, more attractive, even admirable characteristics. In particular, even before the buzzwords of "human growth potential" and "self-actualization" were introduced into popular usage via humanistic psychology, Lawson already grasped the meaning of these concepts and governed his life accordingly, at least after his "born again" episode in his twenty-eighth year. From that time forward, he arranged never again to be anybody's employee, and he also kept clearly in mind how truncated and demeaning was a life spent chasing the dollar. So modest and easily met were his economic needs that he could devote his efforts almost entirely to the fulfillment of self-actualizing needs—that is, to building things, to exerting his powers toward the accomplishment of ends of his own choosing, to investing all of his time and effort in purposeful activity lying beyond that which was needed merely to sustain life. Nor was Lawson ever held back by careerist or family concerns, or by the present-day twaddle about the need to "prepare for retirement," or by the celebrated "mid-life crisis." Possessing an uncanny knack for spotting opportunities (a "positive genius" for "latching onto a new trend"), supremely confident of his ability to face new challenges, and indifferent to calculations of risk, Lawson exuberantly sailed into many career changes throughout his long life, always had many self-chosen projects in progress, and stayed active in creative pursuits right up to the end. Certainly few other persons ever crammed as much interesting and varied fare into a lifetime as did Alfred Lawson. In these respects, at least, his can serve as an admirable model of a life lived to the fullest.

But even in its most remarkable feature—that is, in its near-incredible breadth and variety—Lawson's remained a recognizably American life; it was, in fact, a splendid match of time, place, and man, intersecting many fields of activity—baseball, aviation, financial protest, utopian reform, educational experimentation—prominent in America between the Civil War and the mid-twentieth century. The opportunities, social conditions, and incentives existing in the United States in his day were both a license and a whet to his exalted ambitions; to grasp their significance, one has only to imagine how much more circumscribed Lawson's life would have been had his parents never immigrated to the New World. One can think of no other setting or age in which a sixth-grade dropout could have aspired to do so much or to

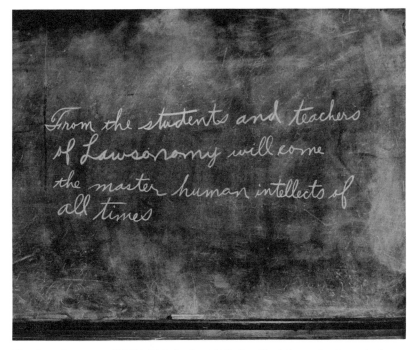

When the wrecking crew razed DMUL in 1955, they found this blackboard inscription, a poignant memento of palmier days of the Lawsonomy movement. Photo courtesy of the *Des Moines Register.*

be so many things—baseball player, manager, and promoter, magazine editor and publisher, industrialist, novelist, inventor, financial theorist and reformer, prolific writer of scientific and theological treatises, founder of a new religion, crusader for the reform of human nature, communitarian architect, aviator and avatar.

Does it still seem inconceivable that circumstances would have allowed Lawson or anyone else the opportunities to try his hand at so many things? Then one need only recall how permeable to entrepreneurship most fields have been in the United States—not only business but also politics, reform, education, professional sports, show biz, science, the arts, and religion—and also how relatively easy it has always been to move laterally among fields of enterprise. Even today, the United States, far more so than other countries, remains substantially open to entrepreneurial adventurism within and across many fields of endeavor; after all, this is the country in which recent aspirants to the top political office have included persons seeking to cash in blue chips earned as a Hollywood film star, the owner-manager of a large peanut farm, an army general, a TV preacher, an astronaut, and a pro football quarterback.

Still, it must be conceded that, even in a land in which opportunistic entrepreneurial hustle has long been authorized and esteemed, Lawson's life stands way out. With respect to persistence and variety of effort, imaginativeness, and daring, the records of virtually all other American self-starters pale by comparison with Lawson's. On these scores, surely his record of aspirations, enshrined in his many colorful titles, will never be excelled.

Lawson believed, of course, that his titles recorded solid achievements, not simply aspirations. To his mind, he never failed; success, he thought, steadily followed success in an upward progression of his life. Alas, he was wrong about that. Yet his well-lived years did yield for his life a fetching grandeur and even an important kind of success. Indeed, his life was a singular work of art and, as such, stands as Lawson's major legacy. The greatness he claimed may always have eluded him, but could anyone doubt that the astonishing zig-zag-and-swirl of the life of Alfred Lawson revealed greatness nonetheless?

Notes and Sources

The titles and dates of Lawson's books are as follows: *Born Again* (1904), *Manlife* (1923), *Creation* (1931), *Direct Credits for Everybody* (1931), *Lawsonomy* (1935), *Know Business* (1937), *Mentality* (1938), *Children* (1938), *The Almighty* (1939), *Penetrability* (1939), *Short Speeches* (1942), *Gardening* (1943), *A New Species* (1944), *Lawson's Proverbs* (1945), *100 Great Speeches* (1946), *Lawson's Mighty Sermons* (1948), *Lawsonian Religion* (1949), and *Aircraft History* (1952). Except for the first three titles, all were first published in Detroit by Humanity Publishing Co. or its successor Humanity Benefactor Foundation, and except for *Know Business*, all are currently in print and available from the Humanity Benefactor Foundation, whose address, as of publication date, is P.O. Box 3243, Melvindale, Michigan 48122.

Lawson also wrote some shorter works elucidating the Direct Credits doctrine, as follows: *Questions and Answers in Up-to-the-Minute Economics* (1933), *Elucidation of the Fourteen Points* (1934), *Watch the Slickers* (1934), *Help the Merchants* (1935), *Great Speeches* (1939), *Know the Game, Manufacturers* (1935), *Hey Farmers* (1935), *Police* (1935), and *Powerful Editorials* (1935). All were published in soft covers in Detroit by Humanity Publishing Co.; none is any longer in print. However, reprints of many issues of *Benefactor*, Lawson's one-man Direct Credits newspaper, are available from the Humanity Benefactor Foundation.

Although they don't bear his name, Lawson also wrote or claimed authorship of two plays and three books centering on his life. The plays are *Truth at Last* (1939), "A Four Act Drama by Genesee County, Michigan, Direct Credits Officers" published in Detroit by Humanity Publishing Co., and *Childhood Days of Alfred Lawson* (1943), a four-act play "compiled from his book *Children*" and published in Detroit by Humanity Benefactor Foundation. The books of an autobiographical nature are Cy Q. Faunce [Lawson pseudonym], *The Airliner and Its Inventor: Alfred W. Lawson* (1921), published in Columbus, Ohio, by Rockcastel Publishing Co.; *Lawson: From Bootblack to Emancipator* (1934), "compiled by V. L. A. Farrell" and published in Detroit by Humanity Publishing Co.; and *Lawson, Aircraft Industry Builder* (1937), published in Detroit by Humanity Benefactor Foundation with no indication of author. Of these five publications, only the last is in print and available from the Humanity Benefactor Foundation.

Although the secondary literature includes no books or monographs treating Lawson's life, several short articles have been published. The best of these is Martin Gardner, "Zig-Zag-and-Swirl," chapter 6 in *Fads and Fallacies in the Name of Science* (New York: Dover Publications, 1957), pp. 69–79. Less useful than Gardner is the entry on Lawson in Carl Sifakis, *American Eccentrics: 140 of the Greatest Human Interest Stories Ever Told* (New York: Facts on File, 1984), pp. 223–226. For the sake of completeness, I also note Peter Jonas, "Alfred William Lawson: Aviator, Inventor, and Depression Radical," *The Old Northwest: A Journal of Regional Life and Letters* 9, no. 2 (Summer, 1983): 157–173. Jonas' article offers a bizarre interpretation of Lawson's life, however, and is also full of factual errors, some astounding.

1. Childhood Days

NOTES

1. Irwin Wyllie, *The Self-made Man in America* (New York: Free Press, 1954), p. 29.

2. Wyllie, p. 30.

SOURCES

The meager sources on Lawson's childhood and adolescent years were all written by Lawson late in his life. In addition to his play, *Childhood Days of Alfred Lawson*, they include "The Start of Lawson's Career," in *Lawson: From Bootblack to Emancipator*, pp. 6–7; "Boyhood Days of Alfred Lawson" and "Early Environs of Alfred Lawson," in *100 Great Speeches*, pp. 4–7; "Memories of One in His 75th Year," *Benefactor* 3, no. 11 (1943), reprinted in *100 Great Speeches*, pp. 99–100; and Lawson's last speech, May 30, 1954, published in a souvenir program for the 1954 Lawsonomy reunion. Also, a "Publisher's

Affix" to *Children*, pp. 105–147, contains brief narratives and drawings covering aspects of Lawson's first three decades. An August 14, 1990, letter from the archivist of Oxford University reported no evidence in University records that Robert Henry Lawson had ever received a diploma or studied there.

2. The Magic Man of Baseball

NOTES

1. Bill Wagner, letter to the author, March 6, 1987.

2. David Q. Voigt, *American Baseball*, vol. 1 (Norman: University of Oklahoma Press, 1966).

3. Robert Obojski, *Bush League: A History of Minor League Baseball* (New York: Macmillan, 1975), p. 10.

SOURCES

Lawson's major league statistics can be found in several baseball encyclopedias. The library of the Cooperstown, N.Y., National Baseball Hall of Fame and Museum yielded only three one-inch clippings on Lawson. Also dashing my hopes was a letter from the editor of *The Sporting News* informing me that that publication had no clipping files for the years in which Lawson was active in baseball. From old newspapers and other sources I was able to piece together a bare-bones chronology of Lawson's baseball activities. Writings by Lawson helpful for this purpose included *Bootblack to Emancipator*, pp. 6–7; *100 Great Speeches*, p. 8; and "Athletics for Health, Wisdom, and Success," *Benefactor* 4, no. 22 (1951): 1–2. Of great help, too, were three items supplied by a Lawsonomist contact—a Union League letterhead bearing an inscription by Lawson and two newspaper clippings. Although the clippings carried no indication of dates or places of publications, internal evidence established that they appeared in 1908 and 1915, respectively. The latter clipping was especially valuable because it revealed that Lawson returned to baseball management in 1915–1916, a fact which Lawson never disclosed elsewhere and which I was subsequently able to verify from other sources.

Supplying more information for my chronology or confirming many of the entries were seven 1979–1980 members of the Society for American Baseball Research (SABR)—Ed Brooks, Oscar B. Eddleton, Clayton R. Gum, Jerry Jackson, E. V. Luce, Jr., Robert Obojski, and John F. Pardon. Another SABR member, Bill Wagner, gave me information about Lawson's ill-fated 1907–1908 Union League, and L. Robert Davids, 1980 editor of SABR's *Baseball*

Research Journal, helped me get documentation for each of Lawson's three major league appearances. I thank all of these SABR members for their good help.

Lawson's off-season activities have continued to elude me. Although a colleague of Lawson claimed that he was a Chautauqua speaker, Lawson never made the claim himself; moreover, a check with three major repositories of Chautauqua materials turned up nothing. A check with two historical libraries in Buffalo also produced no confirmation of a Lawson "college of phonography," but Lawson's numerous references to it and the specificity of his claims caused me to decide to discuss it in my text.

John McGraw's early association with Lawson gets several pages of coverage in each of the biographies of McGraw—Frank Graham, *McGraw of the Giants* (New York: G. P. Putnam's Sons, 1944), pp. 5–9; Joseph Durso, *The Days of Mr. McGraw* (Englewood Cliffs, N.J.: Prentice-Hall, 1969), pp. 9–11; and Charles C. Alexander, *John McGraw* (New York: Viking, 1988), pp. 17–20, 27–28. I drew on all three for information about Lawson's first expedition to Cuba and his team's post-Cuba activities in Florida in 1891. Unfortunately, however, there is wide disagreement among the authors about games which the American All-Stars played in Cuba. Graham has Lawson's team winning fourteen of seventeen games, all played against American teams. Durso agrees with the win-loss record cited by Graham but says that at least some of the games were played against Cuban teams. Differing fundamentally from both Graham and Durso, however, Alexander holds that the American All-Stars played only six games, all of them against Cuban teams, and lost all but one game. I decided to go with Alexander's account, because he told me in a phone conversation that he based his claims on information reported in the *New York Clipper,* a sporting publication of that day; in contrast, Durso obviously relied heavily on Graham concerning these points, but Graham gave no citations of sources.

3. Born Again

NOTES

1. Martin Gardner, *Fads and Fallacies in the Name of Science* (New York: Dover Publications, 1957), p. 73.

2. Kenneth Roemer, *The Obsolete Necessity: America in Utopian Writings, 1888–1900* (Kent, Ohio: Kent State University Press, 1976).

3. Roemer, pp. 88, 89.

4. Roemer, p. 90.

5. Jean Pfaelzer, *The Utopian Novel in America, 1886–1896* (Pittsburgh: University of Pittsburgh Press, 1984), pp. 21–22.

6. Pfaelzer, p. 3.

SOURCES

For appraising the place of *Born Again* in the American tradition of utopian fiction, I found useful material in Kenneth Roemer, ed., *America as Utopia* (New York: Burt Franklin and Co., 1981), as well as in Roemer, *The Obsolete Necessity*, and Pfaelzer, *The Utopian Novel in America*. Lawson's antipathy to conventional religious views and practices was expressed much more stridently in the original edition of *Born Again* than in the current edition, which omits chapter 11 and part of chapter 12 of the first edition and makes many smaller changes throughout. Lawson's discussion of how he fell into the clutches of vices as a young man but finally was able to shuck them off is found in "Retrospection and Introspection," first published in *Children*, pp. 150–151, and subsequently reprinted in *100 Great Speeches*, p. 9. His discussion of his experience with a "radical party" is found in *Help the Merchants*, p. 32.

4. Aircraft Industry Builder

NOTES

1. Howard Segal, *Technological Utopianism in American Culture* (Chicago: University of Chicago Press, 1985).

2. Joseph J. Corn, *The Winged Gospel: America's Romance with Aviation, 1900–1950* (New York: Oxford University Press, 1981).

SOURCES

Lawson's two decades in aviation are his most amply documented years, but I have not attempted to track down all of the materials which may be available. Although Lawson is entitled to a thorough examination of his role in early American aviation, I readily leave that task to George A. Hardie, Jr., of Hales Corners, Wisconsin, who has at least a thirty-year head start on me in studying Lawson's aviation exploits and is preparing to write. I have benefited enormously from many discussions of Lawson with Mr. Hardie over the past twelve years.

Complete runs of Lawson's magazines during the years of his editorship (*Fly*, 1908–1909, and *Aircraft*, 1910–1914) are very difficult to find in libraries today. However, the first ten issues (November, 1908–August, 1909) of

Fly which Lawson edited have been reprinted in facsimile in a single volume; see *The National Aeronautic Magazine, Fly, Volume 1, No's 1 to 10, November, 1908 through August, 1909* (Seattle: Salisbury Press, 1971). Fortunately, too, in *Aircraft Industry Builder* Lawson reprinted in facsimile his *Aircraft* editorials and much other content from that magazine. I relied heavily on these two sources for my exhumation of Lawson's vision of the utopian fruits of aviation's development. Lawson's article, "Natural Prophecies," first published in the October, 1916, issue of *Aircraft*, is reprinted as an appendix, pp. 195–201, in *The Airliner and Its Inventor* and is discussed in Corn, *The Winged Gospel*, pp. 40–42. An exhaustive examination of the position of "technological utopianism" reflected in Lawson's views during this period can be found in Segal, *Technological Utopianism in American Culture*.

For all activities by Lawson during his aviation years, *Aircraft Industry Builder* is a treasure-trove of documentary materials. Other sources of information on Lawson's aviation activities are *The Airliner and Its Inventor, From Bootblack to Emancipator*, the back pages of every Lawson book issued since the early 1930s, and most issues of *Benefactor*. Lawson's sixteen messages to Congress in 1918 were republished in 1932 by Humanity Benefactor Foundation as *Historical Documents [in] Aircraft History*.

5. The Columbus of the Air

NOTE

1. This scrapbook still exists but has reached an advanced stage of deterioration. Recognizing its great potential value to historians and also its iconic value to the Lawsonomists, in 1980 I approached the head librarian of the University of Wisconsin in Milwaukee, who suggested the following plan: to prevent further deterioration of the scapbook, the library staff could encapsulate every page in plastic, in return for the right to microfilm the scrapbook for researchers' use. All of this would be done at no cost to the Lawsonomists. Claiming that he would need to "think about it," however, the Lawsonomist who had unofficial custody of the scrapbook never followed up on this offer. If other Lawsonomists read this, I hope they will be emboldened to act before this relic, valuable both to them and to scholars, has completely turned to dust.

SOURCES

All of Lawson's autobiographical books—*The Airliner and Its Inventor, From Bootblack to Emancipator*, and *Aircraft Industry Builder*—contain valuable materials on Lawson's aviation work after World War I. The first book reveals his plans for becoming the dominant figure in the manufacture of airplanes and in the development of passenger service. In addition to presenting photographs of his airliners, the last of these three books reprints in facsimile much of the press coverage of the sensational first flight. Both also contain Lawson's account of the flight, "A 2000 Mile Trip in the First Airliner."

I made heavy use of another account of the flight—Vincent Burnelli as told to Booton Herndon, "The Non-Sked Adventure of the First Airliner," *True* (June, 1962): 56–60, 103–107. Thanks to George Hardie, Jr., I also have a typescript copy of Burnelli's original statement, which contains material not used in the published article—for instance, on Lawson's attempt in New York to raise money from baseball players through the good offices of John McGraw. The characterization of baseball players as "good sports in all respects" who would "go for such a romantic venture" as a national airline is Lawson's view as depicted by Burnelli in this unpublished statement.

George Hardie, Jr., has published two articles in *Historical Messenger of the Milwaukee County Historical Society* on Lawson's aviation work in Milwaukee: "Milwaukee's First Airliner," 15, no. 4 (December, 1959): 2–4, and "The Airline That Might Have Been," 27, no. 1 (March, 1971): 13–21. I drew extensively on the latter article for details on the crash of the Midnight Liner and on Lawson's desperate financial condition leading up to the crash.

Information about the two-tiered superliner can be found in *Aircraft Industry Builder*, pp. 260–269, 272, 274–277, and in Jerrold P. Kuntz, "The Jersey Superplane That Almost Was," *New Jersey History* 99, nos. 3 and 4 (Fall–Winter, 1981): 162–166. Information about the two-tier concept's application to trains and buses is in *Aircraft Industry Builder*, pp. 278–290.

In recent years Lawson's aviation work has begun to get some notice. Articles include Frank J. Clifford, "Ham and Eggs Lawson," *FAA Aviation News* (July, 1970):12–13; Robert J. Schadewald, "A Forgotten Pioneer," *Air Line Pilot* (November, 1976):11–13; and Lyell D. Henry, Jr., "Alfred W. Lawson, the Forgotten 'Columbus of the Air,'" *Journal of American Culture* 7, nos. 1 and 2 (Spring and Summer, 1984): 93–99. Lawson has also finally made it into general histories of American aviation, including Carl Solberg, *Conquest of the Skies: A History of Commercial Aviation in America* (Boston: Little, Brown, 1979), pp. 102–103, and Richard P. Hallion, *Legacy of Flight: The Guggenheim Contribution to American Aviation* (Seattle: University of Washington Press, 1977), pp. 8–10. Hallion, whose treatment of Lawson is particularly appreciative and sympathetic, depicts Lawson as one of two persons (the other was Inglis Uppercu) whose work stands out in the otherwise dreary years of American commercial aviation immediately following World War I.

6. The Wizard of Reason and the Origin of Lawsonomy

SOURCES

Here I must acknowledge that credit for being the first to bring together the words "aviator" and "avatar" in application to Lawson goes to Peter Spielmann, "Alfred W. Lawson—Aviator and Avatar," *Bugle American* 7, no. 28 (September 17, 1976): 14–19.

Lawsonpoise and How to Grow Young was published in 1923 by Cosmopower Co. of Detroit and reissued under the title *Manlife* in that same year by Cosmopower. The current edition contains the original's preface, "The Wizard of Reason," written by Lawson under the pseudonym of Cy Q. Faunce. The original edition of *Creation* was published in 1931 by Arnold and Co. of Philadelphia.

An account of Lawson's September 19, 1922, press conference in Washington, D.C., is found in James L. Wright, "This Milwaukee Man Puts It All Over Prof. Einstein," *Milwaukee Journal* (September 20, 1922). Lawson's "The Key to Perpetual Movement" is included as an appendix in the current edition of *Manlife*. Lawson's interview with an unnamed *New York Times* reporter resulted in a long article, "Keep Your Balance and Live 200 Years," appearing in that publication on September 23, 1922.

For other discussions of Lawson's scientific ideas, see Martin Gardner, *Fads and Fallacies in the Name of Science* (New York: Dover Publications, 1957 revised edition), pp. 69–79, and John Grant, *A Directory of Discarded Ideas* (Kent, Eng.: Ashgrove Press, 1981), pp. 84, 93–94.

7. The New Emancipator and His Perfect Economic Plan

NOTE

1. Although James Webb, *The Occult Establishment* (La Salle, Ill.: Open Court, 1976), claims that Lawson's Direct Credits doctrine "resembled the theories of Major Douglas" (p. 430), the similarities actually seem thinner than the differences. Both Douglas and Lawson called for a removal of the "credit power" from the financiers and bankers to the community and advocated an increased money supply and "birthright" credits for all citizens. However, the main concerns of Douglas and the Social Credits movement in England and Canada were the problems of underconsumption, maldistribution, and the "just price." In contrast, Lawson's unique advocacy of the abolition of interest revealed that his emphasis was on stimulating entrepreneurship, investments,

and production—a combination of means and objectives setting his program apart from more than one prominent panacea of the 1930s. Certainly, too, Lawson could not have been influenced by the Social Credits movement of Alberta, Canada, inasmuch as the movement came to prominence several years after publication of Lawson's treatise in 1931.

SOURCES

Although my basic source in this chapter was Lawson's *Direct Credits for Everybody*, I also drew material from various issues of Lawson's Direct Credits newspaper *Benefactor*, as reprinted in *100 Great Speeches*, and from Lawson's *Short Speeches, Know Business*, and DCS booklets from the 1930s. A useful book for supplying a context for Lawson's Direct Credits program is Joseph Reeve, *Monetary Reform Movements: A Survey of Recent Plans and Panaceas* (Washington, D.C.: American Council on Public Affairs, 1943). Another context is provided by Webb, *The Occult Establishment*. There Lawson is described as a practitioner of "illuminated politics," which Webb defines as follows: "When occult ideas are found tangled up with political and social projects, they indicate a sort of thinking which it is convenient to call 'illuminated,' a definition of reality that transcends the materialist point of view, and the emergence of the rejected—both in terms of ideas and of men—into unaccustomed positions of prominence" (p. 13). The "rejected ideas" Webb has in view here are Lawson's alternative physics and his Direct Credits ideas, but it was the fully developed doctrine of Lawsonomy, coming at the end of the 1930s, which more clearly revealed Lawson as an "illuminate." Webb also observes that the "illuminates . . . have a special relationship with the imagination in their pursuit of other realities" and accomplish "an extraordinary amount of creative work" (p. 512). Among the evidence Webb cites is Lawson's airliner.

8. The Man of Destiny and the Direct Credits Crusade

NOTES

1. Max Weber, *Economy and Society: An Outline of Interpretative Sociology*, ed. Guenther Roth and Claus Wittich (New York: Bedminster Press, 1968), vol. 1, pp. 241–246.

2. Albert Bandura, "Self-Efficacy Mechanism in Human Agency," *American Psychologist* 37 (1982): 187.

3. David H. Bennett, *Demogogues in the Depression* (New Brunswick, N.J.: Rutgers University Press, 1969), pp. 71–72.

SOURCES

My sources for this chapter included all of the DCS publications cited as
sources for the preceding chapter. Especially valuable, too, were Lawson's se-
rial publications, including the reprints in *100 Great Speeches* of *Benefactor*, the
DCS newspaper which Lawson began to publish in 1936, and the six issues of
Benefactor's predecessor, a magazine successively entitled *Humanity* 1, no. 1
(June, 1932), *Direct Credits for Humanity* 1, no. 2 (September, 1932), and *Direct
Credits* nos. 3–6 (1933–1936). I also consulted an earlier compendium of
Benefactor reprints entitled *The Benefactor with Pictures and Ten Speeches*, not
dated but probably published by the Humanity Benefactor Foundation in
1936 or 1937.

Other essential DCS publications included *General Orders of the Direct Credits
Society* (1934), six published "bulletins" to DCS members from Lawson (no. 1,
"Review-November, 1940"; no. 2, no title, no date; no. 3, "From God to Man,"
no date; no. 4, "The Commander's Advice to His Leaders," no date; no. 5,
"Referring to Personal Inclinations," no date; no. 6, "Safeguard the Organization," no date); *Songs That Will Be Sung Forever* (1940); and a four-page promotional flyer, "Advance with Lawson, the Man of Destiny," no date. For this
last item, I am indebted to the Michigan Historical Collections, Bentley Historical Library, University of Michigan.

Photographs of DCS members and activities are scattered through Lawson's
serial publications and books, but a particularly good source is *100 Great
Speeches*. The collection of tickets to Lawson's speeches I was able to examine
when the Lawsonomist curator of the Alfred W. Lawson Living Museum of
Murrieta, California, brought the museum holdings by van to the 1979 Lawsonomy reunion in Sturtevant, Wisconsin. Unfortunately, the Museum's holdings were far stronger in artifacts, photographs, and celebratory Lawson mis-
cellanea than in organization records and other archival materials. I am
indebted to Richard G. Young, Washington, D.C., patent attorney, for ascer-
taining Lawson's 1931 assignment of his U.S. patent.

As I note in my text, newspaper coverage of DCS in the 1930s seems to
have been mysteriously sparse. Librarians at the *Detroit Free Press*, *Detroit News*,
Detroit Public Library, and other historical collections in Michigan came up
with only a few newspaper clippings. Like these clippings, two clippings I
have from the *Milwaukee Journal* are not very useful. In contrast, extremely
informative, especially about DCS members' financial contributions and their
relations to Lawson, was a long investigative article by George Mills, "Lawsonomy's Ranks Falter As Chief Weds," *Des Moines Register* (June 3, 1945): 1L,
6L. In September, 1978, I also talked by phone with Mr. Mills about his recollections of Lawson.

In developing the contrast between Lawson and other agitators of the
1930s, especially Father Coughlin, I found useful David H. Bennett, *Dema-
gogues in the Depression* (New Brunswick, N.J.: Rutgers University Press, 1969).
My analysis of Lawson as an organizational entrepreneur, of the incentives he
offered to DCS members, of the costs and benefits of DCS membership, and
of the "free rider" problem as it applied to DCS was greatly guided by the
work of two interest group theorists: Mancur Olson, Jr., *The Logic of Collective
Action* (New York: Schocken Books, 1968), and Robert H. Salisbury, "An Exchange Theory of Interest Groups," *Midwest Journal of Political Science* 8, no. 1
(February, 1969): 3–11. I am indebted to Peter Snow for directing me to the
work of Albert Bandura on "proxy control" (as cited in note 2 of this chapter).

10. Toward the Self-perpetuating Social Body

SOURCES

The *Des Moines Register* has a large file of clippings from both the *Register* and
the *Tribune* covering Lawson's years in Des Moines, 1943–1954. I am grateful
to Vernon Brown, newsroom administrator of the *Register* in 1978, for granting me access to this file, an indispensable source for all three chapters in
this part.

From Andrew S. Regis, the Des Moines City Assessor in 1978, I obtained
some important legal documents, as follows: DMUL's Articles of Incorporation, Bylaws, and Operation Agreement; two opinions by the Des Moines City
Solicitor concerning DMUL's eligibility for a tax exemption; and the May 28,
1948, letter sent to the Board of Assessment and Review by the City Assessor,
Bert L. Zuver, reporting the findings of an on-site inspection of DMUL made
by Zuver and two associates on May 27, 1948. For these essential materials, I
offer profuse thanks to Mr. Regis, who also sent many newspaper clippings,
including some from a Des Moines neighborhood paper, the *Highland Park
News*, to which I would otherwise not have had access.

An important initial statement by Lawson about his plans for DMUL can be
found in "State of Iowa May Become the World's Center of Advanced Educational Methods," *Benefactor* 3, no. 14 (June, 1944), reprinted in *100 Great
Speeches*, pp. 79–81. Lawson's views on marriage are taken from *A New Species*,
pp. 109–111.

For background on Des Moines University prior to Lawson's purchase of
it, I used Robert H. Spiegel, "The Story of a Once-Proud College Here—
Fame . . . Strife . . . Lawson . . . And Now Wrecker," *Des Moines Tribune* (December 21, 1954): 1, 4. The history of Des Moines University has recently also

been recounted in David Wiggins, *An Iowa Tragedy: The Fall of Old Des Moines U.* (Mount Horeb, Wis.: Historical-Midwest Books, 1988).

I found several useful items in the Greater Des Moines Chamber of Commerce historical files, including the exchange of letters which I cite in the Prologue. These files are deposited in Special Collections in the University of Iowa Libraries.

11. Alma Mater of the New Species

SOURCES

Only a small minority of Lawson's followers were ever residents at Des Moines University of Lawsonomy. Before my contacts with Lawsonomists were abruptly ended, I had identified five in this select group, of whom I was able to interview four. I have relied heavily on them for much of the information presented in this chapter. Additional insider information was obtained from Des Moines reporters' accounts of interviews with the two twelve-year-old girls, Margaret Baker and Lois Hans, upon their exit from DMUL. For Margaret's statements, see John Zug, "Freed by Court, Girl Tells of Life in Lawson's 'College,'" *Des Moines Register* (July 4, 1945): 1, 5, and for Lois' statements, see George Mills, "Lawsonomy's Ranks Falter As Chief Weds," *Des Moines Register* (June 3, 1945): 1L, 6L. Further information on life at DMUL came from testimony of two residents at a U.S. Senate subcommittee hearing on March 19, 1952. Lawson also spoke at this hearing and at an earlier one on March 10, 1952. See U.S., Congress, Senate, Select Committee on Small Business, *Machine-Tool Shortages, Hearings* before the Subcommittee on Mobilization and Procurement, Senate, 82d Cong., 2nd Sess., 1952, pp. 161–181 and 375–420. Also of very great value for this chapter was Bert Zuver's May 28, 1948, report to the Board of Assessment and Review of his on-site inspection of DMUL.

Lawson's views about the activities and purposes of DMUL can be found in the 1952 U.S. Senate hearing record cited above, in a four-page promotional brochure for DMUL issued sometime in the second half of the 1940s, and in other DMUL promotional materials published in the back pages of some of his books. For my discussion of Lawsonian Religion, I consulted *Lawsonian Religion, Lawson's Mighty Sermons, Songs of Lawsonomy* (a hymnal and book of responsive readings compiled by several Lawsonomists and published by Humanity Benefactor Foundation in 1961), and several articles by Lawson published in *Benefactor*, as follows: "Lawsonian Religion," 4, no. 17 (1948),

"Free Religion Must Be Enjoyed by All Classes," 4, no. 18 (1949), "Thousand Churches to Be Built by Alfred Lawson," 4, no. 20 (1950), and "Churches for Everybody," 4, no. 26 (1953). The last two contain photographs of six of the Lawsonian churches in operation while Lawson was still alive.

12. Collapsing Equaeverpoise

SOURCES

The citation for the hearing record of Senator Blair Moody's investigation of DMUL's purchase and resale of government surplus machines is given in the sources for chapter 11. In preparing my account of DMUL's troubles with the federal government, I consulted many articles in the two Des Moines papers, the *Register* and the *Tribune*. Lawson responded to DMUL's mounting difficulties in "Trying to Prove White Is Black!" *Benefactor* 4, no. 25 (1952).

Lloyd Seaver of Des Moines, Iowa, who in 1952 was the surplus property supervisor for the Iowa State Department of Public Instruction, was involved in the 1952 investigation of Lawson's sale of war surplus machines. I am grateful to Mr. Seaver for allowing me to interview him in September, 1978.

Lawson's final interview in Des Moines was reported in Robert H. Spiegel, "Lawson Tells His Story of Des Moines Venture," *Des Moines Tribune* (November 16, 1954): 1, 3. In the following month (date not ascertained), another article in the *Tribune* reported Lawson's death on November 29 and gave information from the death certificate.

Lawson's discussions of his inventions are found in various issues of *Benefactor*, as follows: "Magnitudinous Improvements," 3, no. 23 (1945); "Solar Vehicles Will Run Non-Stop between Planets," 3, no. 25 (1945); "Atomic Action," 4, no. 6 (1946); "Magnified Knowledge," 4, no. 13 (1948); and "Planning Ahead for All Mankind," 4, no. 19 (1953). His fullest discussion of the smoke evaporator is in "Presto-Chango, Smoke Is Gone," *Benefactor* 3, no. 24 (1945), reprinted in *100 Great Speeches*, pp. 231–232. DMUL's letter to the federal government requesting "atomic machinery" is described in "Lawsonomy Tried to Get Atomic Tools," *Des Moines Register* (March 8, 1952).

In this chapter, I am on sound ground, I believe, in arguing that the circumstances leading to DMUL's decline can be traced ultimately to Lawson's letting the university aspect of DMUL take priority over the communitarian aspect. However, I must acknowledge that on a related issue the facts are uncertain. One Lawsonomist, present at DMUL at the time, recalls that Lawson and family did reside for a while at DMUL. This recollection is contradicted, however, by that of another Lawsonomist, who also was there and who claims that Lawson never brought his family to DMUL. In the absence of any other information bearing on the question, I decided to go with the first informant on grounds that this person not only conveyed very vivid recollections of Lawson and his family at DMUL but also lived there continuously for nearly two years. In contrast, the latter informant was usually away from DMUL, doing organizing and recruiting work for the Direct Credits Society.

Their disagreement on this matter of fact may also be linked to the two Lawsonomists' different perceptions of what Lawson was trying to do at the inception of DMUL. The first Lawsonomist cited above is convinced that *Mentality* and *The Almighty* establish that Lawson's purpose was to found an ideal community (and hence it would have made sense for him to install himself and family at DMUL, even if he remained often on the road). My second informant claims, however, never to have had any understanding that DMUL was intended to be a community; unaware of any shift in Lawson's thinking, this informant continued to give personal support to the Direct Credits doctrine and viewed DMUL as a launching station for continuing promotion of that doctrine. These starkly different understandings of DMUL illustrate beautifully what I describe in my text—that is, the division in doctrinal allegiances and emphases which came to the fore after 1940 and was present even among the residents of DMUL. Also exposed are Lawson's failure to clarify for his followers the relation between Lawsonomy and the Direct Credits doctrine and the consequent persistence of different ideological tendencies in his movement up to the present day.

13. The Last Knowledgians

NOTE

1. Martin Gardner, *Fads and Fallacies in the Name of Science*, p. 78.

SOURCES

This chapter of ruminations on the present and future of the Lawsonomy movement draws almost entirely on things which I saw or heard while attending the 1979 and 1980 Lawsonomy reunions at the Wisconsin University of Lawsonomy in Sturtevant, Wisconsin. I was privileged to observe at these reunions the awarding of the first Knowledgian degrees since Lawson's. It was at the 1979 reunion that a Lawsonomist, standing before the large portrait of Lawson, told me "when he looked at you with those eyes, he could see right through to your soul," a statement that I cited in passing in chapter 8. Lawson's plans to relocate his followers in California and his survey of generals' opinions about who should succeed him (and the results of that survey) were things I heard about at these reunions from more than one Lawsonomist. I also learned there that the Lawsonomy mailing list included about three hundred names. Ten years later, however, I would guess that that number has gone down.

At both reunions I found that most members wanted to talk with me mainly about Lawson's ideas on interest, money, and the evils of "financialism." The Direct Credits doctrine had brought most of them into the movement and clearly continued to be at the center of their involvement. Only a few members seemed to recognize that Lawson's ideas had changed drastically by the time he came to Des Moines and that his final ideas and ideals conflicted with the Direct Credits doctrine. For this handful, Lawsonomy and Lawsonian Religion lay at the heart of their involvement. To depict this difference of emphasis among the Lawsonomists, I fashioned the labels "economists" and "utopians"; they are not terms used by the Lawsonomists themselves, however. On the basis of my observations at the reunions, I concluded that the economists far outnumber the utopians, even though I believe the utopians more accurately express Lawson's final ideological position.

14. Lawson and America

NOTES

1. American Psychiatric Association, *Diagnostic and Statistical Manual of Mental Disorders (Third Edition-Revised)* (Washington, D.C.: American Psychiatric Association, 1987), pp. 349–351.

2. That examination is forthcoming from George A. Hardie, Jr., who is presently writing up the results of his more than forty years' study of Lawson's aviation involvements.

SOURCES

The Freedom of Information Act made it possible to obtain Lawson's FBI file. I am indebted to Jerrold Kuntz for undertaking to get this file for me and only wish the approximately five hundred pages of documents therein had contained more usable information. I am indebted to my wife, Gretchen B. Holt, for calling to my attention the discussion of the Narcissistic Personality Disorder in the American Psychiatric Association's diagnostic manual.

Lawson's tale, "The Death of Liberty," can be found in *100 Great Speeches*, pp. 208–209. He first published this tale in the October, 1916, issue of a short-lived magazine Lawson edited called *The Devil*. Because I know nothing about this magazine and have never seen issues, I say nothing about it in my text. Lawson never said anything about it or cited it in his list of publications; it is also not in the Library of Congress' list of holdings. Although I was told that there was at least one issue at the Lawsonomy farm in Sturtevant, Wisconsin, my request to see it was denied.

Lawson's moralistic denunciations of behavior he found offensive and in violation of Natural Law are scattered abundantly throughout his writings. The Lawson quotation on smoking is taken from "Disease Is the Lack of Right Action," *Benefactor* 2, no. 11 (1940), reprinted in *100 Great Speeches*, pp. 191–192. The Lawson quotation on kissing is found in *Children*, p. 8.

Index

no